AIDS: Legal and Regulatory Policy

William Curran
Larry Gostin
Mary Clark

University Publishing Group

KF
3803
.A54
C87

Copyright © 1988 University Publishing Group
107 East Church Street
Frederick, MD 21701

ISBN: 1-55572-009-9

Printed in the United States of America

TABLE OF CONTENTS

EXECUTIVE SUMMARY i

CHAPTER 1: Existing Public Health Law: Review of Twelve Jurisdictions

    Introduction 1
    I. New York 7
    II. California 31
    III. Florida 57
    IV. New Jersey 79
    V. Texas 94
    VI. Illinois 113
    VII. Massachusetts 128
    VIII. Pennsylvania 143
    IX. Georgia 158
    X. Colorado 167
    XI. Connecticut 180
    XII. Federal Law 191
    XIII. Summary Findings 204

CHAPTER 2: Proposed Legislation 209

CHAPTER 3: Regulatory Efforts on AIDS: Scientific Foundations 221

CHAPTER 4: Regulatory Efforts on AIDS: Legal and Constitutional Foundations 242

    A. The Public Health Cases 243

        1. True purpose
        2. Public health necessity
        3. The requirement of a safe environment for quarantine
        4. Substantial relationship between control measures and public health objectives

    B. Modern Equal Protection Analysis Applied in the Public Health Context 253

        1. Minimum rationality
        2. Strict scrutiny
        3. Intermediate standard of scrutiny
        4. The rigidity of traditional equal protection analysis: Toward a more flexible equal protection

    C. Conclusion 266

CHAPTER 5:	Testing and Screening Programs	274
	A. Introduction	274
	1. Operational definitions of "testing" and "screening"	
	2. Reliability of the ELISA and supplementary tests	
	B. Screening in the Aggregate	276
	1. Screening of tissue donors	
	2. Screening within a research protocol	
	3. Informing persons of the results of HTLV-III antibody testing	
	C. Voluntary Testing	279
	1. Personal choice for testing: Alternative test sites	
	2. Testing for diagnostic or other clinical purposes	
	D. Population Screening Standards	281
	1. Proposed criteria for assessing population screening	
	2. Legal and policy implications of screening programs	
	E. Screening of Selected Populations	294
	1. Screening of military personnel	
	2. Screening in schools	
	3. Screening of food handlers	
	4. General screening in high risk populations	
	5. Screening of prostitutes	
	6. Screening at STD and drug dependence treatment centers	
	7. Premarital screening	
	8. Prenatal screening	
	9. Screening of health care patients and staff	
	10. Screening in custodial institutions	
	F. Conclusion	322
CHAPTER 6:	Public Health Legal Control Programs	329
	A. Reporting Requirements	329
	B. Medical Surveillance Requirements	333
	C. Voluntary Means of Behavior Change	334

D. Compulsory Public Health Measures 336

    1. General quarantine
    2. Limited quarantine
    3. Procedural due process
    4. Less restrictive alternatives to quarantine
    5. Community health orders
    6. Criminal law deterrence of behavior leading to the transmission of HTLV-III

E. Control Over the Behavior of Incompetent Persons 348

    1. Civil commitment of the mentally ill
    2. Guardianship of mentally ill people

F. Civil Confinement of Drug Dependent Persons 357

G. Regulation of Public Meeting Places 359

SUMMARY AND POLICY OPTIONS 366

Legal and Regulatory Issues Connected with AIDS

Executive Summary

1. Methods

We surveyed public health statutes and regulations for the control of infectious diseases in twelve jurisdictions selected to provide a representative overview of the existing public health powers. Data were collected through an intensive library search, correspondence and personal communications. This review was not limited to AIDS-related activity, but covered the entire public health statutory and regulatory framework. We also surveyed all fifty states by correspondence and, when necessary, by telegram and telephone. We received responses from all fifty states and the District of Columbia. This survey concentrated on legislation, regulations and proposals specifically relating to AIDS or HTLV-III infection.

2. Classification of AIDS in State Public Health Statutes

State public health statutes tend to adopt classifications which distinguish between communicable or venereal diseases. Different legal consequences flow from each classification. Venereal disease classifications usually authorize personal control measures such as compulsory medical examination, sexual contact tracing and isolation or quarantine, and also provide more rigorous protection of confidentiality. Communicable disease classifications usually do not automatically authorize the use of compulsory personal control measures, but would require a specific regulatory amendment to accomplish this goal.

None of the twelve jurisdictions reviewed in Chapter 1 has explicitly classified AIDS as a venereal disease. Those jurisdictions which classify AIDS as a communicable disease have not amended their regulatory structure to empower public health officials to exercise compulsory powers involving restriction of liberty. Our impression is that the reason for this reluctance to amend the regulations is that any AIDS activity is subject to intense public scrutiny, and might be construed as an intention actually to exercise those compulsory powers against vulnerable risk groups.

We attribute the artificial boundaries between communicable and venereal diseases to historical circumstance, and find no substantial justification for their continuance in public health laws. It is anomalous, for example, that an airborne disease might not be subject to restrictive measures, while a venereal disease is automatically subject to those measures. Similarly, we see no clear justification for providing less confidentiality protection for AIDS than for venereal diseases. We recommend specific statutory protection for the confidentiality of information concerning AIDS patients, including immunity from judicially ordered disclosure of the information.

Many jurisdictions have not classified AIDS as either a communicable or venereal disease. Rather, AIDS is simply designated as a reportable, notifiable, special or unusual condition or disease. This usually means that most compulsory powers would not apply to the disease, but the state requires the disease to be reported to public health officials for epidemiologic purposes.

3. Reporting of People with AIDS and HTLV-III Infection

We found that in most jurisdictions in the country CDC-defined AIDS is reportable. We consider this requirement fully justified and suggest that it would be held constitutional provided that adequate confidentiality protections were in place.

There are several jurisdictions which now require HTLV-III infection to be reported, either as a result of a specific legislative or regulatory requirement or by implication because the law requires reporting of disease "carrier" states. We note several disadvantages to reporting of positive HTLV-III antibody tests. However, we suggest that such a requirement is likely to be held constitutional provided the true legislative intent is for the protection of the public health, and not a disguised response to ill-informed prejudice. The state must also have adequate confidentiality protections in place.

4. Screening

We propose a four point test for helping to determine whether particular screening proposals are justified. Our fifty state survey identifies several areas where screening or segregation of HTLV-III infected people has been adopted or is being actively considered around the country. We reviewed ten actual or potential screening programs, together with justifications for and against each program: military personnel, schools, food handlers, high risk populations, prostitutes, STD and drug dependence treatment centers, pre-natal, health care patients and staff, and custodial institutions.

The justification for legally authorized selective screening must be based upon the undisputed achievement of the protection of the public health which clearly outweighs the invasion of individual privacy and loss of occupation or profession which could result to individuals. At this time, legally authorized screening programs would be unlikely to achieve any clear public health benefit. Since there is currently no treatment or vaccine for prevention, knowledge of carriers of the virus could not be utilized to alleviate a person's infectious condition or to suggest precautions in personal conduct that are not already well known among risk groups.

5. Public Health Legal Control Measures

a. A broad range of public health options

Public health laws seldom contain a graded series of flexible less restrictive measures. In most states the options for public health officials are limited to voluntary programs or severe restrictions on personal liberty. The choice is either to exercise no statutory power or to reach for provisions which are too restrictive of individual liberty to be acceptable in a modern democratic society. In essence, public health legal control measures currently provide a stick that is too big to wield.

b. General quarantine

Given the impact on liberty and freedom of movement entailed in quarantine, it is likely to trigger the strictest level of judicial scrutiny. The courts would be likely to regard a general quarantine based upon positive antibody or disease status as unconstitutionally overbroad. Not all those who test positive or have AIDS would be likely to engage in behavior leading to viral transmission. There are, moreover, numerous public policy objections to a quarantine: the sheer number of people affected; the indefinite period of infectiousness, making the duration of quarantine exceedingly long; the absence of prevention or treatment; and the mode of transmission making segregation from society overly restrictive.

c. Limited quarantine

The limited quarantine of an individual, if it could be based upon a reliable prediction of imminent dangerous behavior, is more likely to be constitutionally acceptable. Public health officials have a duty to exercise effective disease control measures if there is a clear and imminent danger to the public health which could not be avoided by less restrictive means. There are, however, strong public policy reasons for reluctance in use of even strictly limited quarantines: coercive measures could discourage voluntary cooperation of risk groups; the absence of objective criteria to determine who will be a danger to the public health; and the potential intrusiveness of monitoring and enforcement.

d. Community health orders

A comprehensive public health program should be able to utilize a variety of less restrictive powers, more varied in scope than are currently contained in most public health statutes. We recommend that state legislations should consider the idea of community health orders which give public health departments flexibility in fashioning a remedy to a public health risk. The community health order could require the infected person to attend at specified places and times for the purpose of education, counseling, testing, medical examination or treatment, to submit to periodic inspections of the person's place of business or profession to assure that precautions to prevent transmission are observed when necessary, or to require the person to notify the department of any change of address. Methods of enforcement of community health orders could range from a small fine to some restrictions on liberty of movement. The statutory provision could specify various restrictive measures such as compulsory attendance at a hospital or clinic or at an alcohol or drug treatment facility on an outpatient or day patient basis.

The issuance of this order should be based upon a clear and imminent danger to health, the principle of the least restrictive alternative and respect of the rights of persons, and full procedural due process protections.

e. <u>Criminal law deterrence</u>

States could consider the adoption of public health provisions of a corrective nature. Such statutes would lay down criminal sanctions for knowingly or recklessly engaging in behavior which is likely to transmit the virus without consent. We found, however, strong reasons for reluctance in the use of criminal sanctions.

f. Control over the behavior of incompetent persons

We examine the applicability and desirability of various methods of confining incompetent patients with AIDS dementia: civil commitment under mental health or drug dependency laws and guardianship. We caution against misuse of the mental health or drug treatment system unless the person clearly fits within the respective statutory criteria and can benefit from services offered.

6. Regulation of Meeting Places

Regulation of meeting places where anonymous sexual contact takes place is likely to be found constitutionally justified. States have two options. First, states can close such meeting places. This would effectively meet a highly limited public health objective but would be the most intrusive course of action. Second, states can proscribe sexual encounters in such places entirely, and set up a system of strict enforcement. Consequently those establishments whose true purpose was to facilitate anonymous sex would effectively be required to close; but other establishments with more genuine social purposes could continue.

7. Conclusion

AIDS is a very serious disease which is spreading rapidly in the population. Control measures should be supported if based upon strong scientific and epidemiologic evidence that the measure will interrupt the spread of the disease, and will not cause wholly disproportionate restrictions of liberty, autonomy and privacy.

Our discussions with representatives of public health departments, epidemiologists, the medical profession, the bar, vulnerable risk groups and civil liberties groups indicate a strong interest in participation in some kind of consensus forum dealing with legal and policy issues connected to AIDS. There is an inherent tension between public health measures for the common good and the civil liberties of individuals. Public health policies should, whenever possible, proceed on the basis of consensus. A second phase of study in this area should involve the formulation of clear statements of principle and model regulatory policies. These should be reviewed by a group of individuals representing a spectrum of views in relation to AIDS, seeking to arrive at a consensus statement to form the basis of future regulatory policy.

William Curran

Larry Gostin

Mary E. Clark

CHAPTER 1

EXISTING PUBLIC HEALTH LAW: REVIEW OF TWELVE JURISDICTIONS

Introduction

Each state, through the exercise of its police powers, has the inherent authority to intervene in the private sphere when necessary to protect the public health, safety, and welfare.[1] The reach of the police power to preserve and promote the public health extends to encompass reasonably necessary measures for the control of communicable diseases. Typical public health disease control measures include, inter alia, immunization; public education; identification, reporting and investigation of communicable diseases; compulsory medical examinations; screening of identified populations (e.g. prenatal screening); isolation of cases or carriers of disease; and quarantine of healthy individuals who have been exposed to communicable disease.[2] The availability of and criteria for exercising disease control measures varies from jurisdiction to jurisdiction.

The epidemic of acquired immunodeficiency syndrome (AIDS) has refocused attention on public health issues, raising anew questions about the application, effectiveness, and legality of the various disease control measures. In determining how best to combat the spread of this new disease, it is necessary to first learn what tools are available for the job.

The Survey

For the purposes of this report, we have surveyed the public health statutes and regulations for the control of communicable diseases and venereal diseases[3] in twelve jurisdictions: New York, California, Florida, New Jersey, Texas, Illinois, Massachusetts, Pennsylvania, Georgia, Connecticut, Colorado, and the federal government. These jurisdictions were selected to provide a representative overview of existing public health powers. The first nine states (New York through Georgia) were included because they had reported the greatest number of AIDS cases at the beginning of the study. Five out of the top six states have also enacted AIDS-specific legislation. Connecticut and Colorado were included on the basis of specific legislative or regulatory actions taken--Connecticut because of recent revisions in its quarantine law to allow the detention of individuals with communicable disease who refuse or fail to conduct themselves in a way to prevent the transmission of disease, and Colorado because it was the first state to explicitly require reporting of positive HTLV-III/LAV antibody tests. The federal communicable disease control provisions were included because of their national application.

To gain insight into local jurisdictions' response to AIDS, the health departments in San Francisco, Los Angeles, New York City, and Houston were contacted concerning AIDS-related laws or regulations.[4] Chapter 1 includes an in-depth review of the New York City Health Code, as well as a description of the AIDS-related ordinances enacted in Los Angeles and San Francisco, and the recent proposal in Houston to require health certification of foodworkers.

In addition to a review of existing public health law, Chapter 1 also presents a description of proposed legislation and/or regulations relevant to AIDS in the selected jurisdictions. The review of proposed legislation is not exhaustive, but does provide a cogent overview of the variety of legislative responses to AIDS as a public health issue. Proposals from the remaining states are briefly discussed in Chapter 2.

Finally, the review also indicates, where information is available, the CDC or other guidelines or recommendations which have been adopted by the jurisdiction.

Methodology

The review of the relevant laws was achieved through a combination of library research and contact with appropriate state and local public health officials. Extensive library research was undertaken to obtain and review existing statutes and regulations from each of the twelve targeted jurisdictions. Concurrent with this research, written requests were sent out to health officials in all fifty states, the District of Columbia, and selected metropolitan areas, asking for copies of current statutes and regulations, AIDS-specific enactments, and proposed legislation. Information about any pending AIDS-related litigation was also requested. Where the initial written request or subsequent correspondence did not elicit a response, appropriate health officials were contacted by telephone.

Results of the Survey

Chapter 1 presents the results of the in-depth survey. Within each section, material is divided as follows: Part A--Public Health Powers; Part B--Public Health Laws and AIDS; Part C--Proposed AIDS-related Legislation; and Part D--Guidelines. In Part A, after a brief introduction, the general public health authority in the jurisdiction, as established by statute and regulation, is described.[5] Requirements for disease reporting and investigation are reviewed, including where they exist, specific provisions for contact tracing, communicable disease registries, or the reporting of specific lab tests. Finally, specific personal control measures are addressed, focusing on provisions for compulsory examinations for communicable and/or venereal diseases, premarital and prenatal screening, restrictions on foodhandlers, exclusion of ill school children, medical supervision or observation of individuals, and quarantine or isolation of cases, contacts, and carriers. Any hearing requirements which attach to the imposition of any of the personal control measures are described.

Part B examines the interface between these general public health measures and AIDS to determine which, if any, personal control measures, are applicable under the existing law. Reporting requirements for AIDS and for positive HTLV-III/LAV antibody tests are described, and the applicability of compulsory examination provisions, screening requirements, occupational and/or school exclusions, and quarantine or isolation measures are analyzed. Where AIDS control efforts have relied on public nuisance statutes (e.g., bathhouse closings), these provisions are included. AIDS-specific legislation and regulations which have been enacted are also included under Part B.

Findings

The final section of Chapter 1 presents a brief summary describing the applicability of public health measures to AIDS within the targeted jurisdictions.

References

1. See Jacobson v. Massachusetts, 197 U.S. 11 (1905).

2. Although "isolation" usually applies to infected individuals, and "quarantine" applies to healthy contacts, some states, such as Texas, use the term "quarantine" to cover any compulsory segregation of individuals for health purposes.

3. We have included a review of statutes relating specifically to venereal or sexually transmitted diseases because they might potentially be applied to AIDS. Other disease-specific control measures, such as those applicable to active tuberculosis, have not been included.

4. These cities represent four of the six metropolitan areas reporting the highest incidence of AIDS at the time this report was prepared.

5. Citations to the pertinent statutes, regulations, and ordinances are included at the beginning of each state's material. For brevity, citations to the laws in the text are abbreviated as follows: "S." for statutes, "R." for regulations, "HC." for health code (New York City); and "C." for charter (New York City).

I. New York

Statutes:
 N.Y. Pub. Health Law 201 (Department of Health)
 N.Y. Pub. Health Law 2100 et seq. (Communicable Diseases General Provisions)
 N.Y. Pub. Health Law 2120 et seq. (Control of Patients)
 N.Y. Pub. health Law 3381--3381a (Hypodermic Syringes and Needles)

Regulations:
 10 N.Y. Admin. Code 2.1 et seq. (Communicable Disease Control)
 10 N.Y. Admin. Code 24-1.1 et seq. (AIDS)
 10 N.Y. Admin. Code 24.2 (Prohibited Facilities)
 10 N.Y. Admin. Code 80.131--133 (Hypodermic Syringes and Needles)

New York City:
 N.Y. City Health Code, Article 11 (Reportable Diseases and Conditions)

Introduction

New York state public health law sets out comprehensive provisions governing the reporting of communicable diseases, the control of patients with communicable diseases, and the control of specific diseases such as the venereal diseases and tuberculosis. Separate statutes for the examination and quarantine of individuals who have or are suspected of having venereal disease have been retained, although state sanitary code provisions treat traditional "communicable" diseases and venereal diseases on the same basis.

The State public health laws, other than the provisions of the Sanitary Code, are expressly inapplicable to New York City, which has enacted its own comprehensive Health Code providing for the reporting of specific diseases and conditions and the control of communicable diseases. To review the parallel public health structures which thus exist at the state and local level, this section will describe relevant provisions of the state Public Health Law, the state Sanitary Code, and the New York City Health Code.

New York has reported the highest number of AIDS cases in the United States, the majority of which have been reported from metropolitan New York area. In response, specific AIDS reporting laws have been enacted at the state and local level. The state Sanitary Code has also been amended to apply the nuisance abatement powers of the state to facilities where high risk several activities take place. Legislation providing for the coordination of state AIDS activities, and regulations providing for the licensing of AIDS care hospitals, have also been enacted.

A. Public Health Powers

1. Generally

The commissioner of health ("commissioner"), who serves as the head of the state department of health ("department"), is directed to "take cognizance of the interests of health and life of the people of the state...." (S. 201) Pursuant to this authority, the commissioner supervises the work of the local boards of health and health officers, including New York City, except as provided by law; investigates the causes of disease and epidemics; obtains, collects, and preserves information on disease and health as may be useful in the discharge of his or her duties or may contribute to the promotion of health; and enforces the public health law and the Sanitary Code.

The public health council within the department is authorized to establish, amend, and repeal provisions of the state Sanitary Code. (S. 225) The code deals with matters affecting the security of life and health or the preservation and improvement of public health in the state, including identifying diseases for which specimens must be submitted for laboratory examination; designating the communicable diseases which are dangerous to the public health; and prescribing the information to be included in physicians' reports of communicable disease.

Every local board of health and every health officer is directed to guard against the introduction of communicable diseases designated in the sanitary code "by the exercise of proper and vigilant medical inspection and control of all persons and things infected with or exposed to such diseases." (S. 2100)

New York City

The city charter of New York City gives the city department of health and its commissioner the authority to regulate all matters affecting health in the city and to perform all those functions and operations performed by the city that relate to health. (C. 556) Under section 3.01 of the New York City Health Code, the commissioner may take necessary actions to assure maintenance of public health, the prevention of disease, or the safety of the city's residents.

2. Reporting Requirements

The New York Public Health Law defines "communicable disease" as an infectious, contagious or communicable disease. (S. 2) Section 2.1 of the state Sanitary Code enumerates those diseases which fall within this category. The list of communicable diseases encompasses venereal diseases, including chancroid, gonorrhea, granuloma inguinale, lymphogranuloma venereum, and syphilis.

Physicians are required to report to the local health officer the full name, address, and age of every person "apparently affected" with a communicable disease; cases of gonorrhea or syphilis may be reported by the patient's initials unless the health official specifically requests the name and address. (S. 2101(1); R. 2.10) If there is no physician in attendance, the head of a private household, or the person in charge of any institution, school, hotel, boardinghouse, camp, or vessel, or any public health nurse, or any other person having knowledge of an individual affected with what is presumably a commmunicable disease must report the name and address to the local health officer. S. 2101(2); R.212)

Laboratory Results

Laboratory test results which indicate the presence of a communicable disease must be reported to the local health officer, along with all pertinent facts, by the person in charge of the laboratory or the person making the test. (S. 2102) The statute requires that the laboratory maintain a record of all facts in connection with the test, including the identity of patient and the name of the physician who submitted the specimen.

Contacts

Upon receiving a report of a case of a communicable disease, the health officer is required to investigate as required to discover contacts and unreported cases. (R. 2.6)

Confidentiality

Reports of disease received by the commissioner, or his or her authorized representatives, are to be confidential, and may be used solely for the purposes of medical or scientific research, or the improvement of medical care through the performance of medical audits. (S. 206) Such information is not admissible as evidence in any action of any kind in any court, or before any tribunal, board, agency, or person.

Records of state or local health departments or local health officers, or of laboratories, clinics, or other institutions relating to cases of gonorrhea or syphilis are confidential. (R. 2.32) Access may be granted to official public agencies concerned with the control of these diseases.

Reports or information obtained by a board of health or a health officer relating to sexually transmitted diseases are, by statute, confidential except as necessary to carry out the purposes of the law regarding the control of sexually transmissible diseases. (S. 2306) As defined by the regulations, "sexually transmissible disease" does not include AIDS. (R. 23.1)

New York City

The Health Code specifies diseases and conditions which are reportable to the city health department. (HC. 11.03) The list includes communicable diseases as well as conditions such as narcotics addiction and drug abuse, but does not include AIDS. Cases and carriers of these diseases or conditions must be reported by physicians, and by any person in charge of a hospital, dispensary, clinic, other institution providing care or treatment, clinical laboratory, vessel, or aircraft. (HC. 11.05) The Code defines a "case" as a person who has a reportable disease or condition, or who shows evidence of such a disease or condition; a "carrier" is a person who harbors the pathogenic organisms of a communicable disease without any clinical manifestations, or who may be the source of one or more cases but refuses to submit specimens for examination. (HC. 11.02)

Confidentiality

Confidentiality protections afforded to venereal diseases and narcotics abuse were extended in 1983 to encompass AIDS. (HC. 11.07) Reports and records of cases of AIDS, venereal disease, and non-gonococcal urethritis are not subject to subpoena, or to inspection by persons other than authorized health department personnel without written consent of the patient, or his or her legal representative. Epidemiological information relating to the control of reportable diseases is not deemed to be a report or record under this provision.

But Authorized health department personnel may disclose information to a physician or institution providing examination or treatment to an individual suspected of or affected with the disease or condition, to an agency approved for prevention, treatment, or social care, or to any person when necessary for the protection of health. A person, institution, or agency receiving such information may not divulge the identity of the individual to whom it relates except when it is necessary for the treatment of a case or carrier, or for the protection of contacts.

3. Personal Control Measures

Compulsory Examination

There is no statute explicitly authorizing compulsory examination for the purpose of ascertaining whether an individual suspected of being affected with a communicable disease actually has the disease.

There is explicit authority for compulsory examination for venereal disease. A health officer who has reasonable ground to believe that any person within his or her jurisdiction is infected with a venereal disease "may cause a medical examination to be made for the purpose of ascertaining whether such person is in fact infected with such disease in a stage which is or may become communicable." (S. 2300) The person is required to submit to the examination, and to provide specimens as necessary for laboratory evaluation.

If the person refuses to submit to the examination, or to provide specimens, the health officer may petition a court of competent jurisdiction for an order compelling compliance. (S. 2301) The court may order compliance if, after hearing, it determines that the suspected person may constitute a source of infection to others. All papers pertaining to such a proceeding are to be sealed, and open to inspection only upon court order.

Every person arrested in connection with a prostitution offense, or for failure to comply with a court ordered venereal disease examination, or for frequenting a disorderly house or house of prostitution, shall be reported to the local health officer and examined for venereal disease. (S. 2302) The person may be detained until the results of the exam are known; if convicted, the individual may not be released until he or she has been examined.

A person found to be infected with a reportable venereal disease in a stage which is or which may become communicable may be ordered to submit to treatment and/or isolation as necessary to terminate the communicable stage. (S. 2303)

Premarital Examinations

The statute requiring premarital syphilis testing for marriage license applicants was repealed, effective August 1, 1985.

Prenatal Screening

Every person permitted by law to attend a pregnant woman must obtain a blood sample to be submitted for a standard serological test for syphilis.

Employee Screening

The commissioner is authorized to make rules and regulations as necessary to require pre-employment physical examinations and subsequent annual examinations of all hospital employees for discovery of tuberculosis and other communicable diseases as he or she deems necessary for the safety and well being of the people of the state. (S. 206)

Exclusion from School

Section 906 of the state Education Law requires the exclusion of pupils who have an "infectious or contagious disease reportable under the Public Health Law." The list of diseases defined as "infectious, contagious or communicable" is found at section 2.1 of the state Sanitary Code.

Placarding

Quarantine of premises includes the posting of a placard at the entrance of the premises where a case of communicable disease exists to warn of the danger. (R. 2.25)

Isolation, Quarantine, and Restriction

The state Sanitary Code establishes three separate methods of preventing contact between individuals affected with or exposed to communicable diseases; isolation and personal quarantine measures restrict the individual, and quarantine of premises limits access to places where a communicable disease exists.

Section 2.25 of the Sanitary Code defines these terms. "Isolation" is:

(1) the care of the patient in a hospital approved by the local health officer for the care of such patients, or the continuous separation of the patient, in a room used for no purpose other than the person's care, from all persons except the physician and nurse or other persons in attendance; and

(2) disinfection of articles likely to spread the disease before removal from the hospital or room.

"Personal quarantine" entails the restriction of household contacts and/or incidental contacts to premises designated by the health officer.

"Quarantine of premises" consists of:

(1) prohibiting entrance into or exit from any premises where a case of communicable disease exists;

(2) prohibiting the removal of contaminated articles from the premises unless they have been disinfected;

(3) posting a placard warning of the presence of a communicable disease.

In New York, isolation or quarantine of individuals is based either upon the communicability of the disease, or upon the conduct of the individual affected with or suspected of being infected with a communicable disease. The Public Health Law provides for isolation of individuals with communicable disease who fail or refuse to cooperate with health officials, while the Sanitary Code prescribes isolation requirements applicable to certain highly communicable diseases.

Every local board of health or health officer may provide for the care and isolation of cases of communicable disease in a hospital or elsewhere when necessary for the protection of the public health. (S. 2100) An individual afflicted with a communicable disease, or a carrier of any communicable disease, who is "unable or unwilling to conduct himself or live in such a manner as not to expose members of his family or household or other person with whom he may be associated to danger of infection," may be subject to isolation. (S. 2120 et seq.) If a health officer determines after investigation that the individual is a "menace" to others, the officer shall file a complaint with a magistrate seeking the individual's commitment; after notice and a hearing, the magistrate, if satisfied that the individual is a source of danger to others, may order commitment to an appropriate hospital or institution which offers care for persons with the communicable disease.

The Sanitary Code requires the local health officer to isolate only cases of measles, diphtheria, and typhoid. (R. 2.28, 2.30) Patients with other "highly communicable diseases," defined by regulation as cholera, diphtheria, plague, poliomyelitis, and smallpox, may be isolated as deemed necessary by the health officer. (R. 2.1, 2.29) A physician who discovers a case of highly communicable disease must cause the patient to be isolated pending action by the health officer. (R. 2.27)

Separate statutes authorize the isolation of individuals affected with or suspected of having venereal disease. An individual found to be infected with venereal disease in a stage which is or may become communicable may be required by the health officer to submit to treatment or isolation as necessary. (S. 2303) The health officer is authorized to designate the place and area of isolation, and the conditions under which treatment or isolation may be terminated.

An individual who is suspected of having a venereal disease but who refuses to submit to a medical examination, or to provide necessary specimens, shall be isolated. (S. 2300) If the individual refuses to submit to the isolation restrictions, the health officer may petition a court of competent jurisdiction for an order compelling compliance, which may be issued after a show cause hearing. (S. 2301)

New York City

Compulsory Examination

There is no express authorization for compulsory medical examination for non-venereal communicable diseases other than tuberculosis. An individual required under state law to submit to an examination for venereal disease shall be examined by the city health department or by a licensed physician approved by the department. (HC. 11.51)

Prenatal Screening

A physician who gives prenatal care to a pregnant woman shall take a blood sample at the first examination for the purpose of syphilis testing; an attendant other than a physician must refer the woman to a physician for testing. (HC. 11.51)

Exclusion from Employment

An owner or person in charge of a (1) food establishment; (2) vessel or aircraft; (3) barber shop or beauty parlor; (4) maternity or newborn service; or (5) day care service, school, or children's institution, is prohibited from knowingly or negligently allowing a case, contact, or carrier of communicable disease to work in the place when required to be isolated or excluded. (HC. 11.63)

Exclusion from School

Section 49.15(d) of the Health Code requires exclusion from elementary or junior high schools, and public or private high schools, of any child who is a case, contact, or carrier of a communicable disease when required to be isolated or excluded under Article II of the Code.

Isolation

The Health Code establishes the requirements for isolation or other special precautions on a disease-specific basis. (HC. 11.15-11.53) Section 11.57 of the Code prescribes the conditions of isolation for specific diseases in hospitals and other institutions.

In addition to the isolation authorized by these disease-specific provisions, the local health commissioner may order the removal and detention of a case, contact, or carrier, or suspected case, contact, or carrier of a communicable disease who is endangering the health of others. (HC. 11.55) The legality of the removal and detention may be tested by a writ of habeas corpus or by a mandamus action under the Civil Practice Act.

4. Hypodermic Syringes and Needles

It is unlawful in New York state for an individual to obtain or possess a hypodermic syringe or needle unless the individual has a written prescription issued by a practitioner, or has been authorized by the commissioner to obtain and possess such instruments. (S. 3381; R. 80.131--133) Syringes, needles and disposable hypodermic units which are no longer usable must be crushed, broken, or otherwise rendered inoperable in the process of disposal. (S. 3381a) A 1985 amendment to section 3381a removed a requirement that needles be detached from syringes before disposal.

5. Public Health Crimes

It is a misdemeanor, for an individual who knows that he or she has an infectious venereal disease to have sexual intercourse with another. (S. 2307) It is also a misdemeanor to violate any provision of sections 2300 through 2307 relating to the examination, treatment, or isolation of an individual with a venereal disease, or any rule, regulation, or order regarding the treatment or isolation of venereal disease patients. (S. 2309)

There is no public health statute which makes it unlawful to knowingly expose another person to a communicable disease other than a venereal disease.

6. Penalties

Civil penalties may be assessed under the Public Health Law. Any person who violates, disobeys, or disregards any provision of the law, or any lawful notice, order, or regulation issued pursuant to the law, may be subject to a civil penalty of up to one thousand dollars ($1000) for each violation. (S. 12) The penalty may be assessed by the commissioner, after a hearing or an opportunity to be heard. (S. 206) It is the duty of the state attorney general, upon request of the commmmissioner, to seek an injunction against any such person.

B. Public Health Laws and AIDS

The state Sanitary Code requires that all cases and suspected cases of AIDS be reported to the commissioner by city, county, and district health officers, physicians, hospital administrators, laboratories, and persons in charge of state institutions. (R. 24-1.1) Reports are also required from pathologists, coroners, medical examiners, or other persons determining that an individual apparently had AIDS at the time of death. All reports and additional information are to be kept strictly confidential as required by section 206 of the Public Health Law, which permits such information to be used solely for medical or scientific research purposes, or for the improvement of the quality of medical care through medical audits.

AIDS is also reportable under the New York City Health Code. The syndrome was not included on the general list of reportable diseases and conditions, but was made reportable in 1983 by amendment to a special section which requires strict confidentiality of reported information. (H.C. 11.07) The amendment extended to AIDS case records the confidentiality protections applicable to documents in cases of narcotics abuse and venereal diseases.

Although it is reportable, AIDS is not defined as a "communicable" disease under either the state Sanitary Code or the New York City Health Code. The state Public Health Council, while taking emergency measures to make AIDS reportable, chose not to include it on the list of diseases designated as "infectious, contagious or communicable."[1] Since it is not defined by the state as communicable, AIDS is not subject to the specific regulations relating to isolation, exclusion, and other restrictions which may be imposed upon cases, carriers, or contacts of the enumerated communicable diseases, or other measures required under the Sanitary Code to protect the public against "communicable" diseases.[2]

Similarly, New York City Health Code does not define the term "communicable disease," and the fact that AIDS is reportable does not indicate that it is considered communicable. The Health Code identifies separately each disease for which special precautions must be taken. (HC. 11.11--.53) The Board of Health did not choose to specify any restrictions applicable to AIDS when it made the disease reportable in 1983, and none have been enacted since that time. Thus, AIDS is not treated as a communicable disease under the Health Code, and is not subject to the control measures applicable to such diseases.

Restrictions applicable in the AIDS context have been added to the state Sanitary Code, grounded in the state's authority to control public nuisances. Subpart 24-2 (Prohibited Facilities) was adopted by the Public Health Council on an emergency basis on October 25, 1985, as a means of regulating establishments such as bars, clubs, and bathhouses, which have been used as places for engaging in high risk sexual activities associated with the transmission of the AIDS virus.[3] Section 24-2.2 of the subpart declares that any establishment which makes facilities available where anal intercourse and fellatio take place constitutes a public nuisance dangerous to the public health. The commissioner, local health officers, and local boards of health may close any such facilities or establishments. (R. 24-2.3)

New York City has obtained court orders closing three establishments, the Mine Shaft Club,[4] the New St. Mark's Bath's,[5] and Plato's Retreat,[6] relying on the provisions of subpart 24-2 and the general nuisance provisions of the state sanitary code. While these orders are subject to appeal, there is existing precedent for such closures. In Grossman v. Baumgartner,[7] the Court of Appeals upheld a New York City Health Code provision forbidding tatooing for nonmedical purposes even though the provision resulted in the closure of existing businesses. Applying a rational basis standard, the court found that a demonstrated connection between tatooing and hepatitis, along with proof that rigorous regulation would be ineffective, demonstrated the "compelling medical necessity" for the provision.[8] The court expressly declined to substitute its judgment of a public health problem for that of public health physicians.

Additional AIDS-related legislation and regulations have been enacted by the state. The legislature in 1983 established the acquired immune deficiency syndrome institute within the department of health to coordinate state AIDS policies. (S. 2775 et seq.)

A research council and advisory council have been established within the institute. The research council will be comprised of representatives of recognized centers engaged in scientific study of acquired immune diseases, and will advise the institute on scientific investigations and professional education. (S. 2777) Advisory council members are to be appointed as prescribed by the governor and the legislative officers, and will be responsible for advising the commissioner and making recommendations to the institute for carrying out its duties. (S. 2778)

Finally, the State Hospital Review and Planning Council has adopted regulations establishing minimum standards for AIDS centers. (R. 405.40 et seq.) As defined by the regulations, an AIDS center is a hospital approved by the commissioner as a provider of designated, comprehensive, and coordinated services for AIDS patients. Services must include inpatient, outpatient, community, and support services for the screening, diagnosis, treatment, care, and follow-up of patients with AIDS. The regulations establish minimum requirements for administration of services; patient referral, admission, and discharge; patient management plans; medical staff; utilization review and quality assurance; and patient care units.

Disability Law

In addition to the public health laws which may apply to AIDS, the department's legal staff indicates that the state's general anti-discrimination would apply to AIDS as a disability.[9] New York law prohibits discrimination because of disability in employment, public accommodations, housing. (S. 296) "Disability" is defined as a physical, mental, or medical impairment resulting from anatomical, physiological, or neurological conditions which prevents the exercise of a normal bodily function or is demonstrable by medically accepted clinical or laboratory diagnostic technique. A New York State trial court has determined that AIDS is a disability under section 292 of the Executive Law, and that discrimination because of AIDS may state a cause of action under the Executive and Civil Rights Laws.[10]

C. Proposed AIDS-Related Legislation and Regulations
Legislation

Several legislative proposals addressing AIDS issues have been filed in the New York legislature; two of the bills would limit the use of HTLV-III/LAV antibody test results by insurance companies. Program bill 173, filed by Governor Mario Cuomo on February 24, 1986, would prohibit the use of antibody testing for insurance purposes. The bill would require written consent to administration of the test, and would prohibit disclosure other than to the individual and his or her physician, or to the department for scientific research. A.O. 8529, filed in the Assembly in January, 1986, would prohibit insurers from requiring applicants to submit to an antibody test, or to disclose whether they had been previously tested.

Two other proposals focus on premarital screening requirements. A.O. 8436 would require marriage license applicants to provide certification that they were HTLV-III/LAV antibody negative. Similar legislation, S.O. 7006, was filed in January of this year.

The final two proposals, filed in early 1985, each address separate topics. A.O. 7881 would require that all blood be tested for AIDS [sic] before its distribution to hospitals, clinics, or other facilities. A.O. 6695, filed by Assemblymember Weprin, would require that needles used in connection with oncology drugs or AIDS patients be disposed of intact, in leakproof and puncture resistant containers.

D. Guidelines and Recommendations

The department of health has issued the following guidelines, recommendations, and memoranda related to AIDS.

(1) Acquired Immune Deficiency Syndrome (AIDS) (3/30/83), which includes general descriptive information and specifies precautions for clinical and laboratory staffs. The memo indicates that case registries are being developed at the New York City Health Department, and, for upstate cases, at the department's Bureau of Communicable Disease Control.

(2) Acquired Immune Deficiency Syndrome (AIDS) (6/29/83) which establishes precautions for funeral directors, undertakers, embalmers, and all funeral service personnel.

(3) Precautions to be used by EMT's, AEMT's and other EMS providers when handling a patient with acquired immune deficiency syndrome (AIDS) (8/22/84)

(4) Confidential and Identifying Patient Information (11/29/84) which recommends procedures to be followed by health officials to help prevent the publication of the names of AIDS patients in the news media; such publication "represents a violation of patient privacy and a potential precedent for future breaches of privacy in AIDS cases and other reportable diseases."

(5) Surveillance of pediatric AIDS in New York State (2/26/85) which declares the public health need to better define the population of children who acquire AIDS and to conduct studies to determine the risk of transmission from mothers to infants.

(6) Hospital care of Acquired Immune Deficiency Syndrome (AIDS) patients (8/21/85) declares that patients with AIDS or AIDS Related Complex (ARC) who require inpatient care must:

-Receive the same consideration as any other patient for admission purposes

-Be accorded proper nursing care and treatment

-Be afforded a safe environment, including linen and nourishment. The memo includes Hospital Code Requirements which bear directly on the care of AIDS patients (medical staff, nursing department, dietary department, emergency service or department, personnel, admissions and discharges, patient's rights, and housekeeping).

(7) Guidelines for the education and day-care of children infected with human T-lymphotropic virus Type-III lymphadenopathy-associated virus (HTLV-III/LAV) (9/4/85).

(8) Employment of persons with AIDS, ARC, or HTLV-III antibody (11/2/85) which declares the position of the department that "based on the best available scientific evidence, that no restriction be placed

on the employment of a person with AIDS, ARC or positive HTLV-III Antibody blood test, if that individual's health status enables him or her to perform the duties required by their employment."

The memorandum further declares that there is no scientific or medical justification for testing existing or prospective workers for presence of HTLV-III antibody for the purpose of assessing employability.

(9) Infection control guidelines for EMS personnel (11/8/85) were issued to re-emphasize to EMS providers appropriate methods of limiting exposure of their personnel to infectious disease.

References

1. District 27 Community School Board v. Board of Education of the City of New York, No. 14940/85, Memorandum op. at 35 (N.Y. Sup. Ct. Feb. 11, 1986).

2. Memorandum of Law for Respondents at 70, District 27 Community School Board v. Board of Education of the City of New York, No. 14940/85 (N.Y. Sup. Ct. 1986).

3. N.Y. Public Health Council Resolution (October 25, 1985).

4. City of New York v. Mine Shaft, Inc., No. (N.Y. Sup. Ct. 1985)

5. City of New York v. New St. Mark's, No. 43640/85 (N.Y. Sup. Ct. 1986).

6. Telephone interview with Frederick P. Schaffer, Associate Corporation Counsel for New York City (Feb. 1986).

7. 271 N.Y.S. 2d 195, 17 N.Y. 345 (1966).

8. Id. at 199.

9. Correspondence from Jeffrey Kimmer, Senior Attorney, to William Curran (dated January 27, 1986) (regarding statutes, regulations, and guidelines with a bearing on the AIDS issue).

10. People v. 49 West 12 Tenants Corporation, No. 43604/83 (N.Y. Sup. Ct. Dec. 20, 1983).

II. California

Statutes:
- Cal. Gov't. Code 202 (Authority to Confine for Health Purposes)
- Cal. Health & Safety Code 195 et seq. (AIDS Grants)
- Cal. Health & Safety Code 199.7 et seq. (California AIDS Program)
- Cal. Health & Safety Code 199.20 et seq. (Mandated Blood Testing and Confidentiality)
- Cal. Health & Safety Code 199.30 et seq. (Confidentiality)
- Cal. Health & Safety Code 1603.1 et seq. (Human Blood)
- Cal. Health & Safety Code 1630 (Antibody Testing)
- Cal. Health & Safety Code 3000-3002 (General Provisions and Definitions)
- Cal. Health & Safety Code 3050-3053 (Functions of State Department)
- Cal. Health & Safety Code 3110-3125 (Functions of Health Officers)
- Cal. Health & Safety Code. 3180 et seq. (Venereal Disease Control)
- Cal. Health & Safety Code. 3350-3355 (Violations)
- Cal. Health & Safety Code 27605 (Employees in Food Service)
- Cal. Bus. & Professions Code 4143 et seq. (Hypodermic Syringes and Needles)

Regulations: 17 Cal. Admin. Code 2500 et seq. (Communicable Disease Control)

Ordinances: San Francisco: Police Code, Art. 38 (1985) (Anti-Discrimination)
Los Angeles: Ord. No. 160289 (1985) (Anti-Discrimination)

Introduction

The California public health statutes vest state and local health officers with broad authority to take the actions necessary to prevent and control the spread of disease. As in many states, California statutes contain provisions for the control of communicable diseases, while retaining separate provisions identifying control measures applicable to venereal diseases and to tuberculosis. The general public health statutes--those establishing the powers and duties of state and local officials regarding communicable diseases as well as those providing for the control of venereal diseases--were made part of the current Health and Safety Code in 1957; there have been no extensive statutory revisions since that time.

This broad statutory grant of authority is implemented through the regulations promulgated by the state department of health services ("department"); local health authorities may also enact consistent health regulations. The department's regulations establish the list

of reportable diseases as well as prescribe requirements for isolation
or quarantine where appropriate. In addition to its regulations for
the control of communicable diseases, the department has also
published a handbook for public health and other personnel, Control of
Communicable Diseases in California, which identifies specific
California regulations for each communicable disease, describing the
disease and the methods of control appropriate. The handbook also
provides technical definitions of terms, such as communicable disease,
not specifically defined by statute or regulation.

California is one of four states reviewed in this chapter that has
taken legislative or regulatory action beyond declaring AIDS to be a
reportable disease. In addition, AIDS-related anti-discrimination
ordinances have been enacted at the local level in Los Angeles and San
Francisco.

A. Public Health Powers

1. Generally

Public health powers are exercised at both state and local levels.
The department is authorized by statute to "quarantine, isolate,
inspect, and disinfect persons, animals, houses, rooms, other
property, places, cities, or localities, whenever, in its judgment,
such action is necessary to protect or preserve the public health."
(S. 3051) When informed by a health officer of any "contagious,
infectious, or communicable disease," the department may take measures
necessary to ascertain the nature of the disease and prevent its
spread. (S. 3053) Neither the statutes nor the regulations define the

phrase "contagious, infectious, or communicable disease"; a "communicable disease" is defined by the department as an illness due to a specific infectious agent or its toxic products which arises through transmission from an infected person or animal or a reservoir to a susceptible host--either directly or indirectly.[1]

At the local level, health officers, defined by statute as county, city, and district health officers as well as city and district health boards, may take necessary measures to prevent the spread of disease or the occurrence of additional cases if they know or have reason to believe that a reportable disease, or any other contagious, infectious, or communicable disease, exists within their jurisdiction. (S. 3110)

Specific duties relating to venereal disease control are established. Local health officers have a duty to use all available means at their disposal to ascertain the existence of cases of infectious venereal disease within their jurisdictions, to investigate cases which are not or probably are not subject to proper control measures, to ascertain all sources of infection, and to take measures reasonably necessary to prevent the transmission of infection. (S. 3194) Venereal disease is defined by statute to include syphilis, gonorrhea, chancroid, lymphogranuloma venereum, and granuloma inguinale. (S. 3001)

2. Reporting Requirements

As authorized under section 3123 of the Health and Safety Code, the department has established a list of reportable diseases and conditions; every physician, practitioner, dentist, coroner, superintendent or manager of a dispensary, hospital, clinic, and any other person who knows of or attends a case or suspected case must report to the local health officer. (R. 2500) If there is no physician in attendance, any individual having knowledge of a person suffering form a disease presumably communicable or suspected of being communicable must report the facts, together with the person's name and address, to the local health officer. (R. 2504) Anyone in charge of a public or private school, kindergarten, boarding school, or day nursery must report the presence or suspected presence of any communicable disease. (R. 2508)

Diseases not specifically included on the list may also be reportable. Any person who has knowledge of an outbreak or undue prevalence of infectious or parasitic disease or infestation must report to the local health officer whether or not the disease is listed. (R. 2502) In addition, any person having knowledge of a case of "unusual disease" not included on the list must report the facts to the local health officer. (R. 2503)

Additional persons who must report instances of infectious, contagious, or communicable diseases are identified by statute. These include any clergy person, attendant, owner, proprietor, manager, employee, and person living or visiting, any sick person in a hotel, lodging house, house, building, office, structure, or other place where there is a person ill with an infectious, contagious, or communicable disease. (S. 3125) Case reports should provide the minimal identifying data of names, address, diagnosis, age, sex, and if possible, date of onset.[2]

Laboratory Results

A person in charge of a clinical laboratory must report any microscopical, cultural, immunological, serological, or other evidence suggestive of diphtheria, gonorrhea, syphilis, tuberculosis, or typhoid. (R. 2505)

Contact Tracing

Contact tracing is a fundamental feature of a program for control of venereal diseases.[3] Health officers have a statutorily imposed duty to ascertain the existence of cases of infectious venereal disease and to determine as far as possible all sources of infection. (S. 3194) Persons infected with venereal disease are required to name any person from whom the disease may have been contracted or to whom it may have been transmitted. (S. 3190)

There is no explicit statutory duty to investigate contacts of non-venereal communicable diseases.

Confidentiality

Records of interviews, written reports, and statements obtained by the department, or by persons, agencies, or organizations acting jointly with the department, in connection with special morbidity and mortality studies are confidential insofar as the identity of the individual patient is concerned. (S. 2115) Such information may be used solely for the purpose of the study. Any person, hospital, sanitarium, rest home, nursing home, or other organization furnishing such information is not liable in any action for damages.

3. Personal Control Measures

Compulsory Examination and Treatment

There is no explicit authority for compulsory examination of individuals infected with, or suspected of being infected with, a contagious, infectious, or communicable disease other than a venereal disease.

California law does provide for compulsory examination and treatment of individuals infected with or suspected of being infected with venereal disease. Every "diseased person" is required "from time to time" to submit to approved examinations to determine the condition of the disease. (S. 3191)

Premarital Examinations

Every marriage license applicant must file a physician's certificate stating that the applicant has been examined for syphilis and does not have the disease, or, if infected, is not in a stage which is or will become communicable. The health certificate of a female applicant must indicate whether she has rubella virus antibodies, unless the applicant is 50 or older, has undergone surgical sterilization, or presents earlier laboratory evidence of rubella immunity.

Prenatal Screening

A physician or other person who attends a pregnant woman must obtain a blood sample to be tested for syphilis unless the woman refuses to submit a sample. (S. 3222--3223) Violation of this requirement by the physician or other person is a misdemeanor. (S. 3229)

Exclusion from School

California law prohibits any superintendent, principal, or teacher of a college, seminary, or public or private school from permitting attendance of an instructor, teacher, pupil, or child who resides where there is any contagious, infectious, or communicable disease which is subject to strict isolation or quarantine of contacts, unless the health officer gives written permission. (S. 3118) The child or other person shall be excluded until the expiration of the required isolation period for the particular disease. (R. 2526)

Regulation of Foodhandlers

If there is evidence that the possibility of disease transmission exists within a food handling facility, an enforcement officer shall investigate conditions and may, after investigation and for reasonable cause:

(1) exclude any employee of the facility;

(2) close the facility; or

(3) require a medical examination of any employee, including lab workups as indicated. An employee who refuses to be examined may be immediately excluded until an acceptable lab or medical exam shows that he or she does not have a disease in a communicable form. (S. 27605)

Observation

As used in the department's regulations, observation refers to a "frequent check" of the individual being observed to determine whether the individual is free of the disease he or she is being observed for, or has contracted the disease. (R. 2522) Observation does not entail the restrictions common to isolation or quarantine, unless otherwise specified; it should be compared, however, with "personal surveillance," discussed under "Quarantine and Isolation" infra at p. 41.

Quarantine and Isolation

The state may imprison or confine an individual "for the protection of the public peace or health or individual life or safety." (S. 202) Power to establish a quarantine resides with the department of health services, which is authorized to identify those "contagious, infectious, or communicable diseases" for which strict isolation or quarantine is required. (S. 3115) The department may establish and maintain places of quarantine or isolation, (S. 3050) and may quarantine or isolate individuals whenever, in its judgment, such action is necessary to protect or preserve the public health.

(S. 3051) The department may, if it considers it proper, take possession or control of the body of any living person or the corpse of a deceased person, to prevent the spread of any contagious, infectious, or communicable disease. (S. 3053)

The department's regulations provide the necessary definitions of isolation (strict or modified) and quarantine. As in most other states reviewed in this chapter, isolation is defined as separation of infected persons from other persons for the period of communicability so as to prevent transmission of the infectious agent. (R. 2515) If the disease is one requiring strict isolation, such as smallpox or pneumonic plague, all persons except those caring for the patient must be excluded from the sick room. (R. 2516) When only modified isolation is required, the health officer will prescribe the isolation technique depending on the disease; an individual with tuberculosis, for example, fulfills the requirements of modified isolation as long as he or she is under adequate medical supervision and observes the local health officer's instructions.[4]

Quarantine, in contrast, is the restriction of freedom of movement of healthy persons who have been exposed to a communicable disease, for a period of time equal to the longest usual incubation period for the disease in order to prevent effective contact with persons not exposed. (R. 2520) Although the regulations do not explicitly provide for such a measure, a modified quarantine, which entails a selective, partial limitation of freedom of movement commonly based on known or presumed differences in susceptibility and related to the danger of disease transmission, may be applied to situations such as exclusion of school children from classes or restriction of military personnel to base.[5] Modified quarantine includes "personal surveillance," which involves close medical or other supervision of contacts in order to permit timely recognition of illness without restriction of movement, and "segregation," which entails the separation of part of a group for special consideration, control, or supervision.

Health officers are required to enforce all quarantine or isolation orders, rules, or regulations prescribed by the department. (S. 3111) The department may require each health officer to establish and maintain places of quarantine or isolation which are subject to the special directions of the department, and to quarantine or isolate individuals in accordance with the department's instructions. (S. 3112 and 3114) It is the health officer's responsibility to assure adequate isolation of the case and quarantine of any contacts and premises when there is a contagious, infectious, or communicable disease for which the department has declared the need for strict isolation or quarantine. (S. 3050)

The health officer may require isolation (strict or modified) or quarantine for any case of contagious, infectious, or communicable disease when the action is necessary for the protection of the public health. (S. 3123) Local health officers may also inspect and quarantine any place or person if the action is necessary to enforce the rules or regulations of the state advisory health board or the department pertaining to the control of venereal diseases. (S. 3195)

4. Public Health Crimes

California law makes it a misdemeanor for any person afflicted with any contagious, infectious, or communicable disease to willfully expose himself, and for any person to willfully expose another person afflicted with such disease.

5. Penalties

All persons are required to obey the rules, orders, and regulations of a health officer who establishes a quarantine or isolation (strict or modified). (S. 3116) Any person who knowingly violates, or refuses or neglects to conform to a rule, order, or regulation of the department respecting a quarantine or disinfection of persons, animals, things, or places is guilty of a misdemeanor. S. 3350) It is also a misdemeanor to refuse to comply with a proper venereal disease control measure. (S. 3198)

6. Hypodermic Syringes and Needles

California law prohibits the retail sale of hypodermic syringes or needles except upon written prescription of a physician and surgeon, dentist, veterinarian, or podiatrist. (S. 4143) Exceptions are provided for certain wholesale sales, industrial uses, and specific personal uses. No needle or syringe may be furnished without a prescription to a person unknown to the furnisher who is unable to properly establish his or her identity. (S. 4146) A hypodermic needle or syringe to be disposed of must be rendered unfit for reuse in any manner. (S. 4148)

It is a misdemeanor to obtain possession of a syringe or needle by a false or fraudulent representation or design, or by a forged or fictitious name, or contrary to or in violation of these provisions. (S. 4150) A person who uses a legally obtained hypodermic needle or syringe for a purpose other than that for which it was purchased is guilty of a misdemeanor punishable by a fine of up to $1,000 and/or imprisonment in the county jail.

B. Public Health Law and AIDS

AIDS is reportable in California under section 2503 of the California Administrative Code, Title 17, which pertains to the reporting of unusual diseases. It has not been added to the list of reportable diseases established under section 2500.[6] In addition, all confirmed AIDS cases are reportable by hospitals under section 1603.1(d) of the Health and Safety Code.

California by statute requires blood banks and plasma centers to test all human whole blood for the antibodies to the probable causative agent of AIDS. (S. 1603.1) Prospective donors must acknowledge the requirement in writing prior to donation. (S. 1603.3) Blood banks and plasma centers must also provide voluntary means for self-deferral of donors. Blood or blood components which have not been tested may not be used in vivo. (S. 1603.1)

Although blood may not be tested for antibodies without the written consent of the subject of the test, this prohibition does not apply to blood tests performed at an alternative site. Test results may not be used to determine insurability or suitability for employment. (S. 199.22)

A donor who tests positively must be retested and will be notified of positive test results only if a further test confirms the earlier test conclusion. All confirmed cases of AIDS antibody carriers must be reported to the appropriate health officer by name, date of birth, address, and social security number. Persons who are reactive for the antibody will be included on the Donor Deferral Register without any identification of the reason for the deferral status.

Designated counties are required to establish alternative test sites. Testing procedures must provide for confidentiality through use of a coded system which does not link individual identity with test results. Individuals who seek testing at the alternative sites must be informed about test validity and accuracy prior to testing.

There are specific confidentiality protections pertaining to screening tests for the causative agent of AIDS. No person may be compelled in any state, county, city, or other local civil, criminal, administrative, legislative or other proceeding to identify any individual who is the subject of a test to detect antibodies to "the probable causative agent of the acquired immune deficiency syndrome." (S. 1603).

The legislation specifies penalties for wilful or negligent disclosure of the results of such a test to a third party without a written authorization, which is required for each separate disclosure, and must specify to whom the disclosure would be made.

Additional AIDS-specific confidentiality protections are found in the AIDS Confidentiality Act, enacted in 1985. (S. 199.30 et seq.) The act makes all research records in a personally identifiable form confidential, and prohibits disclosure or discovery of such records, except under narrowly drawn circumstances. A person may not be compelled to disclose confidential research records in legal proceedings unless the court finds that there is a "reasonable likelihood" that the records will disclose material information as evidence of "substantial value" in connection with a criminal charge or investigation. (S. 199.35) A showing of good cause--a balancing by the court of the public interest and need for disclosure against the injury to the individual and potential harm to the research--must be made before a confidential research record may be disclosed, discoverable, or compelled to be produced.

Wilful or malicious disclosure to a third party is subject to a civil penalty of between $1,000 to $5,000; such disclosure which results in economic, bodily, or psychological harm to the research subject is a misdemeanor, punishable by imprisonment in the county jail for up to one year and/or a fine of up to $10,000. Negligent disclosure constitutes an infraction, punishable by a fine of $25. (S. 199.7)

The California legislature in 1983 established the AIDS Advisory Committee in the department to "advise and assist the state in addressing the public health issues associated with Acquired Immune Deficiency Syndrome, and ... work with the [department] in statewide efforts to promote primary prevention, public education, and the advancement of knowledge regarding [AIDS]." (S. 197) The committee is authorized to review and recommend approval by the director of grants on AIDS-related educational activities. In 1985, the legislature enacted Chapter 767 (codified as S. 199.7--199.77), establishing the California AIDS Program (CAP), with the declared intent to fund specified pilot projects and educational programs.

San Francisco Ordinance

San Francisco in 1985 enacted an ordinance prohibiting discrimination on the basis of AIDS, and associated conditions. The ordinance, Article 38 of the Police Code, was drafted collaboratively by City Supervisor Harry Britt, City Attorney George Agnost, and the local department of public health.[7]

In brief, the law prohibits discrimination in employment, housing, business establishments and public accommodations, educational institutions, and city facilities and services, based on the fact or belief that a person has AIDS or associated conditions. As defined under the ordinance, "AIDS" means the condition which occurs as a

result of infection with HTLV-III/LAV/ARV, including but not limited
to AIDS, ARC, progressive generalized lymphadenopathy, lymphadenopathy
syndrome, and asymptomatic infection; it also includes any perception,
whether real or imaginary, that a person is suffering from AIDS or an
associated condition, or is at risk for any of the covered conditions.

The ordinance also prohibits any person from requiring another to
be tested in order to show or help show that the person has AIDS or an
associated condition. Testing may be required by an employer if the
absence of AIDS is a bona fide occupational qualification. The
ordinance does not prohibit any act specifically authorized by state
law, or any actions taken by or under the director of the San
Francisco department of public health in order to protect the public
health.

Any person who violates or aids in violating Article 30 is liable
for actual damages and an amount as determined by a jury of up to a
maximum of three times the actual damages, but in no case less than
$1,000, plus costs and attorney fees as awarded by the court.
Punitive damages may be awarded.

A person may seek enforcement through the city's Human Rights
Commission or by civil action. Any person who commits or proposes to
commit a violation may be enjoined; an action for equitable relief may
be filed by any aggrieved person, the district attorney, the city
attorney, or any other person.

Guidelines

The Perinatal and Pediatric Advisory Committee of the department of public health has issued interim guidelines for the control of perinatally transmitted HTLV-III/LAV infection and care of infected mothers, infants, and pre-school age children.[8] The guidelines are intended for use by medical providers, and will be submitted to the Health Commission for approval.

The guidelines include general recommendations for risk-reduction and provider education; confirmatory antibody testing for high risk women; confidential or anonymous voluntary testing of high risk women; identification of infected pregnant women; and prenatal, intrapartum, and postpartum care of women known to be infected. Specific recommendations include the presumption that high-risk women who are not screened during pregnancy be presumed positive for intrapartum infection control purposes; targeting of IV drug using mothers for substance abuse treatment and risk reduction education.

The committee recommends identification of HTLV-III/LAV exposed infants in utero through confidential testing done with the voluntary consent of the child's parent or guardian. Separate recommendations address testing of infants of seropositive mothers, infants and pre-school children of high risk mothers with unknown serologic status, and infants and pre-school-aged children at risk for parenterally acquired infection. Testing of children of non-high-risk mothers is not recommended.

Finally, the recommendations address the care of exposed and infected infants and children. Particular emphasis is placed on issues arising in the foster care context, including the importance of assessing the risk of infection for the child. Although it encourages voluntary prenatal testing, where such information is unavailable, the committee supports court-ordered testing of high-risk children who are to be placed in foster care, after review by the committee to determine if testing is indicated.

Legal Action

A modified preliminary injunction was issued by Superior Court Judge Roy L. Wonder in 1984, imposing restrictions on the operation of commercial establishments, such as book stores and bathhouses, where "unsafe sexual activities" occurred.[9] The injunction was issued after the department of public health had closed the bathhouses because of the owners' "lack of voluntary compliance" with departmental efforts to prohibit high risk sexual activities as defined by the department.[10] Under the injunction, the establishments were allowed to remain open as long as prescribed structural changes were made and monitors were employed to periodically survey the premises; the establishments are required to expel persons engaging in high risk sexual activities.

Los Angeles Ordinance

In 1985, Los Angeles also enacted an AIDS anti-discrimination ordinance. Ordinance No. 160289 added Article 5.8 to Chapter III of the Municipal Code.

Similar to Article 38 of the San Francisco Police Code, Article 5.8 outlaws discrimination based on a person suffering from AIDS, or any signs or symptoms related to the disease, or any perception--real or imaginary--that a person has AIDS. AIDS-related discrimination in employment, housing, medical and dental services, business establishments, city facilities, city services, educational institutions and other public accommodations is prohibited. A party who asserts that an otherwise unlawful practice is justified bears the burden of proving (1) that the discrimination is a necessary result of a necessary course of conduct pursued to protect the public health or safety; and (2) that no less discriminatory alternative exists.

The liability and enforcement provisions of the Los Angeles ordinance differ from those of the San Francisco law. A person who violates or aids in violating Article 5.8 is liable for actual damages, costs, and attorney fees; punitive damages may be awarded by the court. Any aggrieved person may file a civil action to enforce the article. Violation may be enjoined by an action brought by the aggrieved person, the city attorney, or any person or entity who will fairly and adequately represent the interests of the protected class.

C. Proposed Legislation

The department of mental health has proposed legislation which would give health officers the authority to require HTLV-III/LAV testing of mental patients.[11]

An initiative measure concerning AIDS has been filed with the attorney general's office in California. The initiative, to be submitted to the voters, would define AIDS as an infectious, contagious, and communicable disease; the condition of being a carrier of the HTLV-III virus would be defined as an infectious, contagious, and communicable condition. Both would be added to the list of reportable diseases and conditions, and would be subject to quarantine and isolation statutes and regulations.

There is disagreement about the possible legal consequences which would follow if the initiative was passed. Although the department of health services believes that the measure would have little impact,[12] the American Civil Liberties Union of Orange County has released a tentative list of expected legal consequences,[13] which could include (1) reporting of individuals suspected of having AIDS or being HTLV-III/LAV positive; (2) regulation of food handlers suspected of having AIDS or being HTLV-III/LAV positive; (3) exclusion from school of staff or students who are HTLV-III/LAV carriers, have AIDS, or who reside with such persons; (4) the imposition of travel restrictions against carriers or persons with AIDS; and (5) more ready use of quarantine and isolation powers.

According to the March 10, 1986, legislative update provided by the state senate, a number of AIDS-related measures have been introduced in the California legislature, including the following.

S.B. 1478 would require marriage license applicants to submit to AIDS antibody testing.

S.B. 1513 would require AIDS antibody testing of any individual jailed for more than 3 days in a county jail, and of indivduals in state prisons.

S.B. 1518 would require a treating health facility to notify EMTs, paramedics, nurses, lifeguards, firefighters, peace officers, etc. who have come in contact with a person with a contagious disease.

S.B. 1542 would allow parents to donate blood to be used for transfusion of their child.

S.B. 1545 would allow a judge to order AIDS antibody testing of an individual convicted of engaging in lewd conduct, prostitution, engaging in lascivious or unlawful acts, or molesting a child under 18 years of age.

S.B. 1928 would provide funding for AIDS education for hospital workers; would require the state department of health services to define severe ARC; and require aggregate reporting of individuals with ARC, without identifying information.

S.B. 2192 would require school districts to provide annual training on students with AIDS or related conditions.

S.B. 2245 would create an AIDS institute to coordinate AIDS resources and services.

S.B. 2246 would create an AIDS reinsurance pool.

s.b. 2384 would make it a felony for an individual with AIDS or a positive HTLV-III antibody test to give blood.

S.B. 2447 would add 3 years to the sentence of an individual with AIDS or HTLV-III antibodies who is convicted of a sex crime.

S.B. 2449 would clarify existing confidentiality laws applicable To health care workers treating individuals with AIDS.

S.B. 2453 would recognize presumptive Medi-Cal eligibility for individuals with severe, disabling ARC.

S.B. 2454 would strengthen confidentiality protections for public health records relating to HTLV-III antibody testing or AIDS virus exposure.

S.B. 2484 would provide that disclosure of the existence or alleged existence of former real property occupants with AIDS is not a relevant fact relating to the transfer of property.

A.B. 3137 would authorize the department of corrections to contract with public or private agencies to provide housing, care, and treatment for inmates with AIDS.

A.B. 3318 would allow medical officers in state prisons or youth authority facilities to order an inmate or ward to submit to AIDS antibody testing.

A.B. 3393 would require the department of health services and department of corrections to develop policies to identify, classify, place, and treat state prison inmates with AIDS by January 1, 1987.

A.B. 3407 would require a minimum of 4 antibody testing sites in counties with 5 million or more residents.

A.B. 3425 would prohibit hospitals from restricting the clothing or masks that health care personnel may wear to protect themselves from infectious disease.

A.B. 3551 would require AIDS antibody testing of every blood sample taken in a hospital.

A.B. 3616 would add 3 years to the sentence of an individual convicted of a felony sex crime if the individual knew he or she had AIDS or AIDS antibodies.

A.B. 3667 would apply state law against handicap discrimination to individuals with AIDS or related conditions; would clarify existing confidentiality statutes for health professionals responsible for the care and treatment of individuals who have taken the AIDS antibody testing. The measure has passed the assembly and is pending in the Senate.

A.B. 4048 would allow county health officers to require medical examinations for persons suspected of having AIDS or of being able to transmit AIDS, and would require health officers to use all means to identify and investigate all known or suspected AIDS cases and take all necessary steps to prevent the spread of AIDS.

A.B. 4250 would limit the liability of vaccine manufacturers to provide an incentive for development of an AIDS vaccine, and would establish a state claims fund for vaccine-related injuries.

Although no specific proposal has been filed, the director of health services has recommended the serious consideration of instituting contact tracing in specific instances.[14] While in most instances contact tracing would not be productive or cost effective, the director suggests that it might be an effective intervention strategy when there are only a limited number of sex partners, or when female contacts (especially if they are child bearing age) are involved.

D. Guidelines

The public health department for the city and county of San Francisco has adopted guidelines pertaining to perinatally transmitted AIDS which are more extensive than the CDC guidelines. No guidelines were forwarded from California in time for inclusion in this report.

References

1. Control of Communicable Diseases in California at 535, Department of Health Services (1983).

2. Id. at 5.

3. Id. See, e.g., at 454 (Syphilis).

4. Id. at 487.

5. Modified quarantine, including personal surveillance and segregation, are defined in Control of Communicable Diseases in California, supra, at 540, but do not appear to be defined by statute or regulation.

6. Conversation with Augustine Detres, Epidemiologist for the State DHS (March 17, 1986).

7. Correspondence from Dean F. Echenberg, Director of the Bureau of Communicable Disease Control, to Larry Gostin (dated February 5, 1985) (concerning AIDS-related court rulings, ordinances, and guidelines).

8. Control of Perinatally Transmitted Human T-Lymphotropic Virus-Type III/Lymphadenopathy-Associated Virus Infection and Care of Infected Mothers, Infants, and Pre-School-Aged Children. San Francisco Department of Public Health (Feb. 4, 1986).

9. People v. Ima Jean Owen, No. 830-321 (Modified preliminary injunction) (Sup. Ct. Dec. 21, 1984).

10. Correspondence from Dean F. Echenberg, supra at note 6.

11. Correspondence from Sharon Mosley, Staff Attorney of the Department of Health Services Office of Legal Services, to Robert E. Anderson, M.D. (dated January 22, 1986) (regarding legal materials requested by letter from William J. Curran).

12. Memorandum from Sharon Mosley, Staff Attorney of the Department of Health Services Office of Legal Services, to the AIDS Section (dated March 11, 1986) (regarding the legal impact of the proposed AIDS initiative).

13. ACLU, List of expected legal consequences of the LaRouche initiative (dated February 23, 1986).

14. California Department of Health Services, Acquired immune deficiency syndrome in California: a prescription for meeting the needs of 1990, March 1986.

III. Florida

Statutes: Fla. Stat. Ann. 154.01 (County Public Health Units)
Fla. Stat. Ann. 381.031 (Duties of Department of Health and Rehabilitative Services)
Fla. Stat. Ann. 381.061 (Additional Duties of DHRS)
Fla. Stat. Ann. 381.071 (Rules and Regulations Superceded)
Fla. Stat. Ann. 381.101 (Municipal Regulations and Ordinances)
Fla. Stat. Ann. 381.112 (Administrative Fines)
Fla. Stat. Ann. 381.231 (Communicable Disease Reports)
Fla. Stat. Ann. 381.241 (Quarantine Regulations Limitation)
Fla. Stat. Ann. 381.351 (Department Control of Certain Cases)
Fla. Stat. Ann. 381.411 (Penalties)
Fla. Stat. Ann. 384.01 et seq. (Venereal Diseases)
Fla. Stat. Ann. 509.221 (Foodhandlers)
Fla. Stat. Ann. 741.051 (Premarital Syphilis Exam)

Legislation: 1985 Fla. Sess. Law Serv. 85-52 (West) (Infectious Diseases)
1985 Fla. Sess. Law Serv. 85-157 (West) (Infectious Disease Notification)

Regulations: Fla. Admin. Code Ch. 7C-4 (Public Food Service Establishments)

Fla. Admin. Code 10D-3 (Control of Communicable Diseases and Conditions Which May Significantly Affect Public Health)

Fla. Admin. Code 10D-93 (HTLV-III Antibody Testing)

Introduction

The public health statutes in Florida are organized into separate disease-specific chapters including, among others, public health statutes relating to communicable diseases generally, tuberculosis, and venereal disease. Although venereal diseases have been defined as communicable and thus subject to general control under the communicable disease statutes, Florida has also retained its venereal disease control statutes dating from 1919. These statutes authorize quarantine and compulsory treatment for individuals with venereal diseases; they, like the communicable disease control measures, incorporate no explicit due process protections, such as pre- or post-detention hearings for individuals subject to personal control measures.

In addition to requiring the reporting of cases and suspected cases of AIDS, Florida has enacted AIDS-related legislation concerning serologic testing for infectious disease, and notification of personnel who come into contact with individuals diagnosed as having an infectious disease. Voluntary, alternative site blood testing has been authorized.

A. Public Health Powers

1. Generally

It is the duty of the department of health and rehabilitative services ("department") to formulate the general policies affecting public health in the state and to supervise the enforcement of the laws, rules, and regulations relating to the control of communicable diseases among humans, quarantine, and the general health of the state. (S. 381.031)

The department is authorized to promulgate rules for the control of communicable diseases and the prevention and control of public nuisances (S. 381.031), and for implementation of the laws for the control of venereal disease (S. 384.09). A municipality may also enact health regulations and ordinances which are not inconsistent with the state public health laws and the department's rules and regulations. (S. 381.101) Health rules and regulations adopted by the department, however, supersede all such regulations adopted by other state departments, boards, or commissions, or ordinances or regulations enacted by municipalities. (S. 381.071)

Florida law provides for the creation of county public health units which are to work cooperatively with the state in the control and eradication of preventable diseases, and the prevention of communicable diseases. (S. 154.01) These units provide public health services at the county level under contract with the department.

2. Reporting Requirements

The department is obligated to "provide for a thorough investigation and study of the frequency of occurrence, causes, and modes of propagation and means of prevention, control, and cure of diseases among humans..., especially communicable diseases, epidemic and otherwise." (S. 381.031) Periodically, the department is required to issue a list of diseases determined to be "communicable" for the purposes of the public health law. (S. 381.231) A "communicable" disease is defined, by regulation, as an illness due to a specific infectious agent or its toxic product which arise through direct or indirect transmission from a reservoir to a susceptible host. (R. 10D-3.61)

Pursuant to its statutory authority, the department has, by regulation, established a list of notifiable diseases and conditions which are declared dangerous to the public health. (R. 10D-3.62) A notifiable disease is a communicable disease or condition of public health significance which must be reported. (R. 10D-3.61) The occurrence or suspected occurrence of any of these diseases must be reported by the attending practitioner to the county health unit director. All notifiable disease case reports must contain the diagnosis, name, address, age, sex, and date of onset of each case. (R. 10D-3.68)

Any attending practitioner licensed to practice medicine, osteopathic medicine, chiropractic, naturopathy, or veterinary medicine, who diagnoses or suspects the existence of a communicable disease is required to report to the department. (S. 381.231) The chief administrative officer of each civilian hospital is also required to appoint a staff member responsible for reporting each case or suspected case of notifiable disease; this reporting is to supplement that required of physicians. (R. 10D-3.77)

Any person with knowledge of an outbreak of any notifiable disease or condition is requested to report the information to the county health unit. (R. 10D.3.64) Others requested to report notifiable disease include parents, guardians, householders; nurses and midwives; school superintendents, teachers, or counselors; administrators of institutions of higher learning; owners, operators, or teachers of child care facilities; laboratory owners or operators; owners or managers of a dairy, restaurant, or food storage or processing establishment; superintendents or managers of a public camp, home, or institution; directors or supervisors of a military institution, military installation, Veterans Administration Hospital, jail, or juvenile detention center. (R. 10D-3.76)

Although syphilis, gonorrhea, and chancroid are included on the list of notifiable diseases, additional reporting requirements are described by statute. A physician or other person who diagnoses or treats a case of venereal disease, or any superintendent or manager of a hospital, dispensary, or charitable or penal institution in which there is a case of venereal disease, must report the case to the appropriate local health authority. (S. 384.06) An individual who prematurely terminates treatment from the original reporting source must also be reported.

Laboratory Tests

All records of laboratories which provide evidence "suggestive" of any notifiable disease or condition are to be made available upon request to designated state or county health personnel. (R. 10D-3.66)

Contact Tracing

There is no statutory requirement for contact tracing. Health officials may approach potential contacts identified through laboratory reports only after consulting with the attending practitioner. (R. 10D-3.66)

Registries

The county health unit director is required to maintain such records on notifiable diseases as directed by the state health program office staff director. (R. 10D-3.72)

Confidentiality

Information contained in notifiable disease reports is confidential, and shall be made public only when necessary to protect the public health. (S. 381.231) Submission of disease reports is not a violation of the confidential relationship between the practitioner and patient. Regulations adopted by the department specify that information identifying persons or institutions included in required reports, and subsequent correspondence, memoranda, and summary reports emanating from these reports are confidential. (R. 10D-3.69) Laboratory information required to be reported is also considered confidential, and is not open to public inspection. (R.10D-3.66)

There is a separate confidentiality statute applicable to venereal disease reports. (S. 384.10) All reports of cases of venereal disease must "be filed in a safe or some place of safekeeping" at the department, and shall not be open to public inspection; a clerk may release personal information as to such reports only upon court order. Information in the reports may be used by the department to require reported individuals to submit to treatment.

3. Personal Control Measures
Compulsory Examination and Treatment

Upon being notified of a case or suspected case of a notifiable disease, or of an outbreak or an epidemic of a notifiable disease or other disease condition, the county health unit director shall require the examination of the patient to verify the diagnosis if the nature of the disease and the circumstances warrant such action. (R. 10D-3.73)

Separate statutes specify compulsory examination authority for suspected venereal disease. When in their judgment it is necessary to protect the public health, state or local health officials may examine persons infected with or suspected of being infected with a venereal disease; they may require infected persons to report for and continue treatment until cured. (S. 384.07) The suspected person may not be apprehended, examined, or inspected against his or her will, however, except upon the sworn testimony of the accuser and a duly issued warrant.

All prisoners in state, county or city prisons may be examined and treated for venereal disease. (S. 384.08) Infected individuals may be isolated and treated, or in lieu of isolation, they may be required by the department to report to a physician for treatment. Florida has retained provisions, enacted in 1943, requiring persons with a venereal disease who are rejected for military service to report for treatment at a department venereal disease clinic.
(R. 384.12)

Premarital Examination

Each marriage license applicant must file a certificate stating that he or she has submitted to a standard serological test for syphilis and found not to be infected, or, if infected, not to be in a stage which is or may become communicable. (S. 741.053)

Prenatal Screening

A physician attending a pregnant woman for conditions related to pregnancy during the period of gestation or at delivery shall obtain a venous blood sample for syphilis testing; if the woman is not seen before delivery, the sample shall be collected by the person making the delivery. (R. 10D-3.91) Each certificate of birth or stillbirth must indicate whether the test was taken, and if not, the reasons for not making the test.

Exclusion from School or Employment

Regulations dealing with control of communicable disease in schools focus on mandating and documenting immunization practices. (R. 10D-3.88) There is a provision for the recognition of a "sensitive situation," defined as a setting in which the presence of an individual infected or suspected of being infected with a "notifiable or other communicable disease which may significantly affect public health" would increase significantly the probability of spread of such disease, and would, therefore, constitute a public health hazard." (R. 10D-3.93) Sensitive situations may include, but are not limited to, schools, child care centers, hospitals and other patient care facilities, food processing establishments of food outlets, or places of employment. Once invoked, prohibitions would remain in effect until the situation no longer presents a public health hazard, as determined by the county or state health official.

Regulation of Foodhandlers

Florida law prohibits any person "suffering from a contagious or communicable disease" from being employed in any public lodging establishment or public food service establishment to prepare or handle food, drink, dishes, towels, or linens, or in any other capacity that might communicate disease to the guests or tenants. S. 509.221) Each employee must submit a health certificate whenever required by the department.

Regulations adopted by the department prohibit any person who is affected with, or is a carrier of, any disease in a communicable form, or while afflicted with boils, pimples, infected wounds, sores, or an acute respiratory infection, from working in a food service establishment in any capacity in which there is a likelihood of contaminating food or food contact surfaces with pathogenic organisms, or transmitting disease to other individuals. (R. 7C-4)

Quarantine

Under Florida's general public health provisions, the department has the duty to declare, enforce, modify, and abolish quarantines "as the circumstances indicate." (S. 381.031 and 384.061) No quarantine regulation which restricts travel or trade within the state shall be promulgated or enforced except by authority of the department. (S. 381.241)

Again, the power and authority of health officers to quarantine individuals who are infected with venereal disease are addressed by separate statutes. State, county, and municipal health officers may, when it is in their judgment necessary to protect the public health, commit individuals with venereal disease for quarantine and compulsory treatment in any hospital operated by the department for that purpose. (S. 384.14) Any person "charged with or convicted of any misdemeanor ...who is infected with any venereal disease" may be transferred to the authority of the department for quarantine and treatment. (S. 384.15) Infected individuals may be isolated, quarantined, and treated in a county or city jail if they cannot for any reason be received at a department hospital. (S. 384.17)

Regulations adopted by the department specify the notifiable diseases for which quarantine may be required. Quarantine is defined as an official order that limits the freedom of movement and actions of persons which is deemed necessary to prevent the spread of a notifiable disease or other disease condition; quarantine orders remain in effect for a time period "in accord with accepted public health practice." (R. 10D-3.81) Unlike most of the other states reviewed in this chapter, the regulations do not make a distinction between quarantine and isolation, nor do they explicitly recognize less restrictive measures such as modified quarantine or medical supervision orders.

When quarantine is required by the department for the control of any notifiable disease or other disease condition, the state health officials may, or the county health unit director shall initiate procedures to establish the quarantine. (R. 10D-3.78) The department has established procedures for the control of specific communicable diseases, which indicate the control measures applicable to cases and contacts exposed to shigella and salmonella infections, tuberculosis, typhoid fever and venereal diseases. (R. 10D-3.91) The county health unit director or the department's health program office staff director shall determine which individuals are subject to quarantine, and shall issue appropriate instructions. (R. 10D-3.81)

4. Public Health Crimes

It is a misdemeanor in the second degree to:

(1) violate a provision of the general public health law, any quarantine, or any rule or regulation promulgated by the department under the public health provisions;

(2) interfere with, hinder, or oppose any agent or officer of the department in the discharge of his or her duty; or

(3) maliciously disseminate any false rumor or report concerning the existence of any infectious or contagious disease. (S. 381.411)

It is also a misdemeanor in the second degree for any person infected with spyhilis, gonorrhea, or chancroid who knows that he or she has venereal disease to have sexual intercourse with a person of the opposite sex, or to expose another to infection. (S. 384.01 and 384.02)

5. Violations and Penalties

The department in addition to other administrative actions, is authorized to impose a fine not to exceed five hundred dollars ($500) for each violation of the sanitary code. (S. 381.120) The amount of the fine will be based on (1) the gravity of the violation, including the probability that death or serious physical or emotional harm will result or has resulted, the severity of the actual or potential harm, and the extent to which the statutes or rules were broken; (2) any actions taken to correct violations, and (3) any previous violations.

6. Hypodermic Syringes and Needles

Under Florida's drug paraphernalia law, it is a first degree misdemeanor to use or possess with the intent to use any hypodermic syringe or needle for the purpose of illegally injecting a controlled substance into the body; it is a third degree misdemeanor to deliver, possess with intent to deliver, or to manufacture with intent to deliver a hypodermic syringe or needle knowing, or under circumstances where one reasonably should know, that it will be used for such a purpose. (S. 893.147)

B. Public Health Laws and AIDS

AIDS was declared by the department to be reportable in a letter issued to county health directors on August 18, 1983.[1] Although the department has proposed an amendment to add AIDS to the list of notifiable diseases, the list has not yet been revised.[2]

Reporting of positive HTLV-III/LAV antibody tests is not currently required,[3] but there is language in the current regulations for the imposition of such a requirement. Section 10D-3.66(1) authorizes county or department health officials to require laboratories to report any evidence "suggestive" of a notifiable disease. While a positive antibody test alone is clearly insufficient to justify a diagnosis of AIDS, it might be considered "suggestive" for the purposes of the regulation.

Testing: Confidentiality

Recently enacted law in Florida addresses the confidentiality of serologic testing for "infectious diseases." Chapter 85-52 of the laws of 1985 authorizes the department to declare that a threat to the public health exists when there is the occurrence of an infectious disease that may be transmitted from human to human through serologic or other means. After issuing such a declaration, the department secretary "shall order such preventive, treatment, and ameliorative measures as shall be advisable from medical and public health perspectives, consistent with provisions of the law relating to the preservation of the public health..."

The secretary has declared AIDS to be a threat to the public health under Chapter 85-52 and has ordered the department to establish alternative test sites for "voluntary serologic testing of individuals to identify those persons who may have, or be at risk of developing," the disease.[4] As prescribed by the legislation, the specific test results will be reported to the individual tested; no person may be compelled to identify or provide identifying characteristics of any individual who receives a serologic test. Unauthorized disclosure constitutes a misdemeanor in the first degree. Disclosure is authorized only if the individual tested consents in writing; the information is disclosed pursuant to the standard practice of medicine, such as through physician consultations; or the information is disclosed without names or identifying characteristics during medical or epidemiologic research.

Chapter 85-52 specifically prohibits the use of results of a serologic test conducted under a declaration by the secretary to determine whether the individual may be insured for disability, health or life insurance, or to screen or determine suitability for, or to discharge a person from, employment. Violation of the prohibition is a first degree misdemeanor.

The department is to promulgate implementing rules which are to be governed by the rules and recommendations of the United States Department of Health and Human Services and other recognized public health authorities. Procedures are to be established for follow-up, referral for psychological and social services, and similar measures for persons who receive a positive test result.

Regulations governing testing for HTLV-III antibody are found at chapter 10D-93 of the Florida Administrative Code. The rules require that the strictest confidentiality be maintained in administering the test and all associated record keeping; anonymity is to be ensured by collecting or releasing identifying information only with the consent of the individual and assigning a unique number to identify individuals and their records. (R. 10D-93.64)

Infectious Disease Notification

Additional legislation enacted in 1985 requires that an emergency medical technician, paramedic, or other person who comes into direct contact with a patient subsequently diagnosed as having an infectious disease must be notified as to the exposure and appropriate treatment, if any. (Chapter 85-157, Laws of 1985) The notification shall not include any patient's name.

Control Measures

Although AIDS has been declared reportable in Florida, it has not been added to the list of notifiable diseases which are deemed communicable and dangerous to the public health. It does, however, fall within the definition of "communicable disease" found at section 10D-3.61 of the regulations and so may be subject to control measures authorized for such diseases. (See supra at p .63) AIDS does not fall within the current statutory definition of venereal diseases, and thus is not subject to measures specifically applicable to venereal diseases.

The existing measures which might be applicable in the AIDS context are compulsory examination (R. 10D-3.73), and exclusion of individuals with AIDS in certain "sensitive situations" (R. 10D-3.93). It is possible that the law regulating the employment of foodhandlers might also come into play under limited circumstances, such as when a communicable infection or illness such as Pneumocystis carinii pneumonia is present. Quarantine of individuals with AIDS or those suspected of having the disease or of being carriers is not authorized under the existing law.

Under section 10D-3.73 of the department's regulations, a county health unit director who is notified of a "disease condition," which could include a case or a suspected case of AIDS, might require an examination of the individual "[i]f the nature of the disease and the circumstances warrant." Clearly, the regulation would not authorize widescale screening or random testing of high risk groups. Instead, it would offer only limited authority to require compulsory examination, to be exercised on an individual, case-by-case basis. The authority to compel an examination could be exercised only after the director had received notice of a particular individual who has AIDS or is suspected of having the illness.

An individual diagnosed with AIDS would not be automatically excluded from working in a public lodging or food establishment under the existing law and regulations. HTLV-III/LAV is not food-borne, nor is it spread by casual contact, so it is unlikely that an individual in such an establishment would be employed in any "capacity whereby such disease might be communicated to guests or tenants." (S. 509.221) It is possible that an individual with AIDS might develop an infected sore or wound, or an acute respiratory infection, that would preclude employment as a foodhandler. (R. 7C-4) In such a circumstance, however, it would be the secondary illness and not AIDS, which would serve as the basis for exclusion.

Section 10D-3.93 of the regulations recognizes that certain "sensitive situations" may warrant greater precautions because they present a greater risk of disease transmission; specific environments identified include, among others, schools, day care centers, and hospitals. (R. 10D-3.93) If it were demonstrated that a particular individual represented a special hazard within one of these settings--for example a young child with AIDS who exhibits biting behavior when at day care--restrictions on attendance might be imposed under this regulation. It would not seem, however, to support any across the board exclusion for school or other settings where the risk of transmission has not been demonstrated to be greater.

As currently drafted, the laws and regulations of Florida do not authorize quarantine of AIDS patients or carriers. Only the state department of health and rehabilitative services has authority to declare, enforce, modify, and abolish quarantines. (S. 381.031 and 381.061) Although municipalities may enact health regulations and ordinances, only the state may promulgate a health regulation, such as quarantine, which restricts travel and trade within the state. (S. 381.241)

Regulations issued by the department authorize state or county health officials to issue orders to establish a quarantine when it "is required for the control of any notifiable disease or other disease or condition." (R. 10D-3.78) The department has specified the isolation and other control procedures required for the control of specific communicable diseases. Isolation is called for with three (3) of the diseases: rabies in humans, tuberculosis, and typhoid fever. Individuals with shigella or salmonella infections are prohibited from being present in selected sensitive situations as determined by the director of the county public health unit or the health program office staff under section 10D-3.93. Quarantine is expressly authorized only for syphilis, gonorrhea, and other venereal diseases. There are no provisions expressly applicable to AIDS. Thus, patients who have or are suspected of having AIDS would not be subject to isolation or quarantine unless the department promulgates and adopts additional regulations, or specific authority is established by statute.

C. Proposed AIDS-Related Legislation

A variety of legislation relating to AIDS has been introduced in the Florida legislature.

H.B. 137, which is no longer under consideration, would have required
that district and private school teachers found to be infected with AIDS be separated from active duty with pay. It would have authorized the department of education to require a teacher or student to submit to screening tests when there is probable cause to suspect that the individual may be infected with AIDS. Students with AIDS would have

been separated from the rest of the school population, and these separated students with AIDS would have been taught by the teachers with AIDS removed from active duty.

H.B. 279 would require AIDS screening for any person convicted of prostitution, and would subject such individuals to follow up screening, medical examination, and inspection. Failure or refusal to submit is a second-degree misdemeanor.

H.B. 310 would require the department to develop a comprehensive program to disseminate designated information about the prevention, control, and treatment of AIDS. Literature would be distributed to health care personnel, members of the public, and health education instructors.

H.B. 344 would establish a 13-member Task Force on AIDS to prepare and submit policy recommendations for public health, public education, patient care, and research; the recommendations should include issues related to housing, employment, insurance, and education. The Task Force would also function as a clearinghouse for AIDS policy issues.

H.B. 482 would designate AIDS as a venereal disease and prohibit its being transmitted of others. The bill also prohibits unlawful AIDS-related discriminatory practices by schools, colleges, universities, insurers, employers, employment agencies, labor organizations, and persons offering rental housing.

H.B. 566 would require marriage license applicants to submit to "an approved serological test for acquired immune deficiency syndrome."

H.B. 736 would require the department of health and rehabilitative services to notify school superintendents of the identity of a student or employer who has a disease which threatens the health, safety, and welfare of other students or employees.

H.B. 853 would allow temporary detention of an individual reasonably believed to be engaging in prostitution based on a number of criteria which may be considered by law enforecement officials.

S.B. 576 includes an amendment permitting any individual arrested for prostitution to request an HTLV-III/LAV antibody test; such a test would be required for any individual convicted of prostitution. The amendment would make it a second degree misdemeaner for an individual who knows he or she has a sexually transmitted disease to have sexual intercourse.

H.B. 1055 has been prepared by the department which would replace the current venereal disease statutes with provisions applicable to sexually transmitted diseases, including HTLV-III infection.[5] The intent of the legislation is to provide a flexible program that can effectively reduce the incidence of STDs while assuring the confidentiality of information provided. Provisions under the proposal address reporting requirements, contact investigation, physical examination and treatment, quarantine and isolation, confidentiality, premarital examination, and examination of prisoners. Quarantine would be allowed only upon court order.

D. Guidelines

The department of health and rehabilitative services has issued pamphlet HRSP 150-3, AIDS: Information and procedural guidelines for providing health and social services to persons with AIDS (September 1, 1985). The pamphlet includes guidelines for (1) infection control for AIDS/ARC patients and people at risk for AIDS; (2) accidental exposure to AIDS/ARC; (3) personnel management; (4) employees with AIDS/ARC; (5) AIDS/ARC in children.

References

1. Correspondence from Stephen H. King, M.D., Staff Director of the Health Program Office, Department of Health and Rehabilitative Services, to county and district health personnel (dated August 18, 1983).

2. Telephone conversation with Dr. Carlton Prather, Epidemiologist for the Department of Health and Rehabilitative Services (February, 1986).

3. Telephone interview with Dr. Ronald Wright, Medical Examiner for Broward County, Florida (February, 1986).

4. Declaration of Threat to the Public Health, Department of Health and Rehabilitative Services (August 1, 1985).

5. Department of Health and Rehabilitative Services, Draft Legislation on Sexually Transmitted Diseases.

IV. New Jersey

Statutes: N. J. Stat. Ann. 24:21-51 (Regulation of Hypodermic syringes and Needles)

N. J. Stat. Ann. 26:4-1 et. seq. (Communicable Diseases)

N. J. Stat. Ann. 26:5C-1 et. seq. (AIDS Assistance Act)

N. J. Stat. Ann. 37:1-20 et. seq. (Premarital Syphilis Testing)

Regulations: N. J. Admin. Code 8:57-1.1 through 8:57-1.12 (Reportable Diseases)

Introduction

New Jersey has established by statute broad general powers for state and local health officers to act to prevent the spread of certain communicable diseases. The authority to implement these powers is vested in the department, and in the local boards of health within their respective jurisdictions and subject to state provisions. Regulations issued by the department provide the specific requirements for imposing control measures for communicable disease.

These statutes were enacted, for the most part, before 1960. The statute prescribing the basic powers of the state department of health ("department") and local boards of health to prevent the spread of disease, originally established in 1887, has not been amended since

1930. Current provisions governing the control and prevention of venereal diseases date from 1945; general reporting statutes were enacted in their present form in 1954 and have not been amended since that time.

New Jersey, in addition to making AIDS reportable, has enacted legislation to coordinate the development and dissemination of educational materials for health professionals and the public.

A. Public Health Powers

1. Generally

In order to prevent the spread of disease, the department, and the local boards of health within their respective jurisdictions and subject to the state sanitary code, have the power to define communicable diseases; require the reporting of such diseases; declare when a communicable disease has become epidemic; maintain and enforce quarantine, whenever necessary; remove infected individuals; disinfect premises when necessary; and remove and destroy infected property. (S. 26:4-2)

2. Reporting Requirements

Under New Jersey law, a "communicable" disease is defined as any infectious or contagious disease declared communicable by law or which has been or may be declared communicable by the department. (S. 26:4-1) The department, and local boards of health within their jurisdictions and subject to the state sanitary code, are authorized by statute to define and require the reporting of communicable diseases. (S. 26:4-2)

The department has promulgated a list of reportable diseases.
(R. 8:57-1.2) For purposes of research, surveillance, and in
response to technological advances in disease control, the state
commissioner of health ("commissioner") may amend the list of
reportable diseases and the manner of reporting as may be necessary to
control disease.

Every physician must report any individual who is diagnosed as ill
or infected with a reportable disease by name, age, sex, exact
location of the individual ill or infected with the disease, the home
address and telephone number of the individual, the date of onset of
the illness, and other information as required by the department.
(S. 26:4-15; R. 8:57-1.3) Physicians with knowledge of any outbreak
of any disease must immediately report the facts by telephone to the
local reporting officer. If there is no physician in attendance, a
house owner or householder must file a report if he or she has reason
to believe that an individual in a building under his or her control
is ill or infected with a reportable disease. (S. 26:4-16)

The superintendent or the person in control of or supervising any
hospital, sanitorium, nursing home, penal institution, or any other
institution in which an individual is ill or infected with a
reportable disease must report to the local reporting officer within
twenty-four (24) hours after the disease is diagnosed; cases of
venereal disease must be reported directly to the department.
(S. 26:4-19; R. 8:57-1.4) A report of the fact must also be filed
with the department.

The principal or other person in charge of a public, private, parochial, or other school, college, nursery school, or day care center must report the "suspected presence" of any reportable disease to the local reporting officer within twenty-four (24) hours. (R. 8:57-1.5) The report must include the name, age, sex, home address, and telephone number of the ill individual. Unusual absenteeism thought to be due to disease must also be reported.

Additional reporting requirements specific to venereal disease are prescribed by statute. A physician, nurse, or other person treating a venereal disease must report the case immediately to the department. (S. 26:4-38) The superintendent or other person having control or supervision of a hospital, sanitorium, or other public or private institution must immediately report the case of any person who enters the institution to receive treatment for venereal disease, and the case of a person who enters to receive care for another disease but is found to have a venereal disease. (S. 26:4-39) Reports must include the name, address, color, sex, nationality, and age of the infected individual, the character of the disease, the probable source of infection, and whether the case was previously reported. (S. 26:4-40)

Laboratory Findings

All laboratories must promptly report laboratory results indicating or suggesting the existence of a reportable disease or the outbreak of disease to the department and to the health professional submitting the specimen. (R. 8:57-1.10) The report must contain at least the name of the patient, the name and address of the submitting physician, veterinarian, or institution, and the date of examination.

Registries

Each reporting officer is required by statute to maintain a register of the information included in the reports of communicable disease he or she receives. (S. 26:4-23) The register is subject to inspection only by officers of the local board or the department.

Confidentiality

The New Jersey public health statutes do not include a confidentiality provision which is generally applicable to reportable disease reports or information.

There is limited statutory protection for venereal disease reports. No person shall disclose the name, address, or identity of any person known or suspected of having a venereal disease except to the individual's physician or to a health authority; in the event of a prosecution under the public health statutes or the criminal law, disclosure may be made to the prosecuting attorney or the court. (S. 26:4-41) The individual's physician or a health authority may disclose the name, address, or identity only if he or she deems the disclosure necessary to protect the health or welfare of the individual, his or her family, or the public. The statute does not in any way restrict disclosures to the department. Identifying documents, reports, or records are open to inspection only by the department, a prosecuting officer or the court, or a licensed physician or health officer. The custodian of any hospital record may permit any person authorized by law to inspect the record in connection with any claim for compensation or damages for personal injury or death.

3. Personal Control Measures

Compulsory Examination and Treatment

The department or a health officer may order a person suspected of being ill or infected with a <u>reportable or communicable disease</u> to submit to a physical examination and/or to submit specimens of blood, bodily discharges, or other specimens to determine whether the individual is infectious to others or is a carrier of disease. (R. 8:57-1.9) Any person ordered to submit to examination or to submit specimens shall comply with the order.

If a communicable disease is suspected, a health officer or the department may require that a person employed in an establishment where food is manufactured, processed, prepared, stored, or served for public consumption to submit to a physical examination and/or submit specimens of blood, bodily discharges, or other specimens for the purpose of ascertaining whether the individual is ill or infected with a communicable disease.

There are a number of older statues authorizing compulsory examination of individuals suspected of being infected with specific diseases, focusing primarily on venereal diseases. A local health board or health officer who receives a report on a person who is, or is suspected of being, infected with venereal disease may require the person to undergo a medical examination. (S. 26:4-30) Any person in the infectious stage of a venereal disease who fails to report for medical treatment may be examined, and if found to be infectious, may be isolated and treated. (S. 26:4-35)

Several statutes originating in the 1940's identify specific categories of individuals who may be required to undergo venereal disease exams. There is a presumption that a prostitute "or other lewd person" may reasonably be suspected of having venereal disease, and may be required to submit to examination at any time. (S. 26:4-32) A migrant laborer who does not have satisfactory proof of examination for venereal disease within ninety (90) days prior to entry into the state may be required to submit to an examination; employers of migrant laborers must notify the department whether their employees have been examined. (S. 26:4-49.6) If it appears that a person coming before the court on any charge may have venereal disease in an infectious stage, the court has a duty to order a medical examination. (S. 26:4-49.7) If the individual has infectious venereal disease, he or she may be ordered to submit to treatment. Finally, any person incarcerated for seven (7) days or longer and all persons admitted to a detention or contagious disease hospital or any public charitable institution must be examined for venereal disease. (S. 26:4-49.8)

Premarital Examination

Each applicant for a marriage license must submit a physician's certificate indicating that the individual has submitted to an approved serologicical test for syphilis and, in the physician's opinion, does not have syphilis or is not in a stage of the disease likely to become communicable. (S. 37:1-20) A license may be issued without the certificate if the physician submits a statement indicating that the female applicant is nearing the termination of her pregnancy or the death of one or both of the applicants is imminent.

Issuance of a license in violation of these provisions, or misrepresentation of any required facts is subject to a penalty or ten dollars ($10) to one hundred dollars ($100). (S. 37:1-25)

Prenatal Screening

A physician or other person authorized to attend a pregnant woman for conditions related to pregnancy during the period of gestation or at delivery must obtain a blood sample for syphilis testing. (S. 26:4-49.1) Every report of birth or stillbirth must state whether such a test was made. (S. 26:4-49.3)

Regulation of Foodhandlers

A health officer or the department may prohibit a person ill or infected with a communicable disease that may be transmitted through food from working in an occupation that manufacturers, processes, stores, prepares, or serves food for public consumption. (R. 8:57-1.11) A person living with an individual ill or infected with a foodborne disease may also be prohibited from working in such occupations.

An individual having venereal disease in an infectious stage may not engage in the preparation, manufacture, or handling of milk, milk products, or other foodstuffs, nor may he or she work in a dairy, creamery, milk depot, or other place where milk or its products are produced, manufactured, or sold, or in any establishment where foods are exposed or handled. (S. 26:4-42)

Exclusion from Schools

A local board of health may declare any epidemic or cause of ill health to be so injurious or hazardous that it necessitates the closure of any or all of the public or private schools within the jurisdiction. (S. 26:4-5) A public school may be closed only if the school board determines that closure is necessary.

Anybody having control of a school may, because of the prevalence of any communicable disease, or to prevent the spread of communicable disease, prohibit the attendance of any teacher or pupil under their control and specify the time during which the excluded individual must remain away from school. (S. 26:4-6)

Isolation and Quarantine

In order to prevent the spread of disease, the department, and local boards of health within their jurisdictions and subject to the state sanitary code, are empowered to maintain and enforce proper and sufficient quarantine, whenever deemed necessary; they may remove any person infected with a communicable disease to a suitable place, provided that it may be done without undue risk to the infected individual. (S. 26:4-2) A health officer or the department, upon receiving a report of communicable disease, may by written order establish isolation or other restrictive measures as required by law or regulation or as may be necessary to prevent or control disease, and may restrict the individuals allowed to come in contact with or visit the person hospitalized or isolated. (R. 8:57-1.8) Under the regulation, the department, or a health officer, if authorized by the department or local board of health regulations, may by written order restrict any person who has been exposed to a communicable disease. The period of restriction may not exceed the period of incubation of the disease.

There are statutes specifically authorizing the isolation or quarantine of individuals having or suspected of having venereal disease. The department has the authority to make and enforce any rule or regulation for the quarantine and treatment of venereal disease which it deems necessary for the protection of the public health; it is directed to define which stages of venereal disease will be regarded as infectious. (S. 26:4-48)

Quarantine for venereal disease is intended to prevent the transmission of the disease, and involves the restriction of the actions, behavior, and movements of an individual or confinement to a defined place and area. (S. 26:4-36) The statute empowers any licensed health officer or the state director of health, or their authorized representatives, to quarantine for venereal disease an individual who:

(1) Has or is believed on reasonable grounds to have a venereal disease in its infectious stage, and who is likely to spread the disease because of his or her failure or refusal to submit to treatment, or because of his or her habits, or for any other reason;

(2) Refuses or neglects to submit to a medical examination for venereal disease required by statute;

(3) Refuses or neglects to supply, or permit to be taken, specimens required or requested;

(4) Refuses or neglects to submit to treatment for venereal disease in an infectious stage.

A quarantine may extend until the individual is free of disease, or until the official imposing the restriction believes it is safe for the individual to be released.

The restriction of actions, behavior, and movement, or the place or limits of the area in which an individual is to be confined, must be established by written notice from the official imposing the measures. (S. 26:4-37) The official may also order the removal of an individual to the place or area in which he or she is to be confined; the quarantined individual must observe and obey the notice. Pursuant to the statute, a licensed health officer or the commissioner, or their authorized representatives, may file a complaint in county district court, municipal court, or county court against any individual who:

(1) While quarantined for venereal disease fails, refuses, or neglects to observe and obey the written notice of restriction or removal;

(2) Fails, neglects, or refuses to submit to, observe, or obey the conditions of commitment, or to comply with any court order issued pursuant to the statute; or

(3) Is included in section 26:4-26.

The court may commit the individual to a public hospital, or to any other institution or place which offers suitable detention, examination, care, and treatment facilities. The complaint, commitment, and all other papers relating to the case will be impounded, and are not open to public inspection; hearings are not open to the public.

4. Regulation of Hypodermic Syringes and Needles

A written prescription issued by a physician, dentist, or veterinarian is required before a hypodermic syringe or needle may be sold or furnished to any individual other than specified medical personnel or others who are authorized to use such equipment in the course of their business. (S. 24:21-51) It is unlawful for any other person to possess a hypodermic syringe or needle without a written prescription; violation constitutes a disorderly persons offense.

5. Violations

Upon due proof that an individual has been twice convicted within six months of violating the same provision of law governing quarantine for venereal disease, the individual, in addition to being fined, may be imprisoned, with or without hard labor, for any number of days not exceeding one for each dollar of the penalty. (S. 26:4-49)

Violation of order or judgment of the county court regarding examination of suspected typhoid carriers is subject to a fine of not more than one hundred dollars ($100). (S. 26:4-57)

B. Public Health Law and AIDS

AIDS has not been added to the list of reportable diseases. It is not defined as either a communicable or venereal disease, and would not be subject to the control measures for such diseases.

Laboratories could be required to report positive HTLV-III/LAV antibody tests under section 8:57-1.10 of the regulation.

The New Jersey Legislature in 1985 enacted the AIDS Assistance Act to establish a program within the department to educate the public and heath professionals about the diagnosis and treatment of the syndrome, and to promote efforts to combat AIDS. (S. 26:5C-1-4)

The statutes require the commissioner to establish:

(1) A public education program, including an information campaign encouraging individuals who suspect exposure to AIDS to seek medical testing and counseling, and a statewide telephone hotline to provide information and referral assistance.

(2) An education program for health care professionals who are required to have contact with AIDS patients about the diagnosis and treatment of AIDS; and

(3) Support programs to provide early detection, counseling, social services, and referral for those who suspect exposure to the disease. The University of Medicine and Dentistry of New Jersey, in coordination with the department, serves as a resource center and may offer diagnostic procedures, medical treatment, counseling, and other services to AIDS patients and their families.

C. Proposed Legislation and Regulations

A draft bill which would provide for the reporting of AIDS has been prepared for introduction; a final version has not yet been introduced. In its present form, the bill would require the reporting of AIDS cases and such other conditions related to AIDS as determined by the commissioner by regulation to be reportable. "Other conditions related to AIDS" are defined by the legislation to include ARC, pre-AIDS, AIDS prodrome, chronic generalized lymphadenopathy syndrome, wasting syndrome, and HTLV-III/LAV/infection.

The bill also establishes confidentiality provisions applicable to records of AIDS patients or those suspected of having AIDS or a related condition. The provisions are similar to those currently found in California statutes. Disclosure to qualified personnel without prior written consent is authorized for specifically enumerated purposes such as research, management audits, or treatment. Records would be subject to disclosure under court order issued upon a showing of good cause; disclosure could be made for the purpose of investigating or prosecuting a crime for which the patient is suspected only if it is a crime in the first degree and there is a reasonable likelihood that the records will provide material information or evidence of substantial value.

Disclosure to third-party payors would be permitted only with written consent of the patient or an authorized representative.

The legislation would also impose fines for negligent or wilful violation of its provisions.

D. Guidelines Adopted

The department issued recommendations on the admissibility of school age children with AIDS/ARC or HTLV/III antibody in August of 1985. Under these recommendations, a child could be excluded from school only under exceptional conditions. An expert medical advisory panel had been established to review proposed exclusions.

V. Texas

Statutes: Tex. Rev. Civ. Stat. Ann. art. 4414b (Board of Health)
Tex. Rev. Civ. Stat. Ann. art. 4419b-a (Communicable Disease Prevention and Control Act)
Tex. Rev. Civ. Stat. Ann. art. 4445d (Venereal Disease)

Regulations: Tex. Admin. Code tit. 25, Sec. 97.1--97.10 (Communicable Diseases)

Introduction

Of the jurisdictions surveyed for the purposes of this report, only Texas has recently undertaken a major overhaul of its basic disease control statutes. Recognizing that many of the state's laws pertaining to communicable diseases had been enacted under public health conditions no longer relevant to contemporary conditions, the legislature in 1983 enacted the Communicable Disease Prevention and Control Act ("Act") which governs the identification, reporting, prevention, and control of communicable diseases or conditions "that are injurious or threaten the health of the people of Texas." (S. 4419b-1)

The Texas public health statutes are quite comprehensive, including the type of specific detail often found only in the regulations developed by the board or agency charged with administering the health laws. The statutes give state public health officials broad powers for controlling disease. These statutes are, in turn supplemented by the regulations promulgated by the state board.

As in most jurisdictions, Texas has retained its specific venereal disease statutes.

A. Public Health Powers

1. Generally

The board has the general supervision and control of all matters pertaining to the health of the citizens of Texas. (S. 4414b) It is directed by statute to exercise its powers to prevent the introduction of disease into the state, and to impose control measures to prevent the spread of disease within the state. (S. 4419b-1) Other enumerated duties of the board include the employment and supervision of the commissioner; adoption of rules for the board, the commissioner, and the state department of health; and the investigation and inspection of public buildings or public places to discover and suppress disease and enforce state health and sanitation laws.

The commissioner administers and enforces the state health laws subject to the board's supervision. He or she functions as the executive head of the department, and must be a physician licensed to practice medicine in Texas. The board may delegate to the commissioner the authority to perform any duty or to exercise any power other than the power to adopt rules. (S. 4414b)

The governing body of each incorporated municipality, and each county commissioners court, is empowered to enforce any law "reasonably necessary to protect the public health." (S. 4436b) The city or county may establish a local health department which is authorized to perform all public health functions which the incorporated municipality or county is authorized by law to perform. Subject to the approval of the board, the municipality or county shall appoint a physician to serve as director of the local department.

An incorporated municipality or a county may appoint a qualified physician to serve as the health authority for its jurisdiction. The health authority must be a licensed physician of "reputable professional standing," who is a resident of the jurisdiction in which he or she is appointed.

The health authority performs all duties necessary to implement and enforce any law to protect the public health, and all duties prescribed by the board, including:

(1) establishing, maintaining, and enforcing quarantine within his or her jurisdiction;

(2) assisting the board in all matters of local quarantine, inspection, disease prevention and suppression, birth and death statistics, and general sanitation within the jurisdiction;

(3) reporting contagious, infectious, and dangerous epidemic diseases within the jurisdiction; and

(4) aiding the board in enforcing rules, regulations, requirements, and ordinances, and all sanitation laws, quarantine regulations, and vital statistics collections in the jurisdiction.

Unless specifically preempted by the board, the health authority exercises supervisory authority and control over the administration of communicable disease control measures within his or her jurisdiction. (S. 4419b-1) Control measures imposed by a health authority must be consistent with and equal to or more stringent than the control measure standards in the board's rules. The board may amend, revise, or revoke a control measure imposed by a health authority if it finds such action to be necessary or desirable for the administration of a regional or statewide health program or policy.

2. Reporting Requirements

The board has the authority to identify and classify each communicable disease and health condition that must be reported under the Act. (S. 4419b-1) The classification must be based upon the nature of the disease or condition and the severity of its impact upon the public health. Under the statute, the board is required to establish and update as necessary a list of reportable diseases.

The regulations of the board list forty (40) communicable diseases, which are reportable by name, address, age, sex, race/ethnicity, and date of onset. (R. 97.4) There are other diseases, such as cholera or plague, which must be reported immediately by telephone, and some, such as chickenpox, which must be reported by numerical total. In addition, epidemics or unusual outbreaks of illness which may be of public concern are also reportable, regardless of whether the disease involved is included on the board's list.

Texas law requires that every physician, dentist, and veterinarian report to the local health authority, after the first professional encounter, each patient or animal having or suspected of having a reportable disease (S. 4419b-1) These professionals are also required by regulation to report any recognized outbreak of illness of any kind whether or not the disease is known to be communicable or reportable. (R. 97.2) In addition, local school authorities are required under the Act to report to the local health authority any children attending school who are suspected of having a reportable disease.

If a case of reportable disease is not reported by those listed above, the following persons are required under the Act to notify the local health authority or the department:

(1) professional, registered nurses;

(2) medical laboratory directors;

(3) the administrator or director of a child-care facility or day-care center;

(4) the administrator or director of a nursing home, personal care home, maternity home, adult respite care center, or adult day-care center;

(5) the administrator of a home health agency;

(6) school superintendents (or their designees);

(7) the administrator or health official of a college or university;

(8) the owner or manager of a restaurant, dairy, or other food handling or processing establishment or outlet;

(9) the superintendent, manager, or health official of a camp, home, or institution;

(10) a parent, guardian, or householder;

(11) professional health care workers; and

(12) the chief executive officer of a hospital.

Rules adopted by the board also require reporting by any other person having knowledge of any person affected with any disease apparently or presumably communicable. (R. 97.2)

A physician must also report to the local health authority whenever the physician knows or suspects that an individual he or she has attended during the last illness has died of a reportable disease, or a communicable or possible epidemic disease which, in the physician's judgment, may present a threat to the public health.

Separate reporting requirements applicable to venereal disease are set out in Article 4445d. A physician who diagnoses or treats a case of syphilis or gonorrhea, and every administrator of a hospital, dispensary, or charitable or penal institution in which there is a case of syphilis or gonorrhea must report the case, within a reasonable time, to the appropriate health authority.

Laboratory Results

Any person in charge of a clinical or hospital laboratory, blood bank, mobile unit, or other facility which performs tests yielding microscopical, cultural, serological, or other evidence suggestive of syphilis or gonorrhea must notify the Department of the findings. (4445d)

Registries

Texas statutory law authorizes the compilation of information about cases of communicable disease and venereal disease. Each health authority is required to keep a record of every reported case of communicable disease or condition. (S. 4419b-1) The board is also authorized to establish and use appropriated funds to maintain registries of those venereal diseases which are not reportable, provided that the information in the registry is obtained on a voluntary basis. (S. 4445d)

Confidentiality

Under the Texas Open Records Act, information collected, assembled, or maintained by governmental bodies in the course of carrying out their duties is deemed public information. (S. 6252) There is an exception, however, for information which is deemed confidential either by law, by Constitution, or by judicial decision.

There are confidentiality statutes specifically applicable to reports of communicable diseases and of venereal disease. Reports of communicable diseases furnished to health authorities or the department are confidential, and may be used only for the purposes of the Act; such reports are not public information (S. 4419b-1) Information contained in the reports may be used for statistical and epidemiologic studies that are public information so long as individuals are not identifiable. Disclosure under subpoena is not expressly prohibited.

The Venereal Disease Act provides stronger confidentiality protection. All information and records held by the department or local health departments relating to known or suspected cases of venereal disease are declared strictly confidential, and may not be released or made public upon subpoena or otherwise. (S. 4445d) Exceptions are provided to allow release of medical or epidemiological data:

(1) for statistical purposes, if no individual is identifiable;

(2) with the consent of the identified individual;

(3) to medical personnel, appropriate state agencies, or county or district courts for use in controlling venereal disease;

(4) to medical personnel in a medical emergency as necessary to protect the health or life of the named party; or

(5) in the case of a minor twelve years of age or younger, only the name, address, age, and venereal disease treated shall be reported to appropriate agents are provided under the Family Code.

The statute prohibits examination of any state or local health department officer or employee in a civil, criminal, special, or other proceeding as to the existence of records of a person examined or treated for a venereal disease by a state or local health department, nor of records received form a private physician or private health facility without the consent of the person examined or treated.

3. Personal Control Measures

Compulsory Examination

Section 4.01 of the Act explicitly identifies nine control measures applicable in the communicable disease context. The list includes but is not limited to: (1) immunization; (2) detention; (3) restriction; (4) disinfection; (5) decontamination; (6) isolation; (7) quarantine; (8) disinfestation; and (9) chemoprophylaxis.

There is no explicit statutory authority for compulsory examination of individuals suspected of having a communicable disease, although the local health authority is required to:

(1) investigate as necessary to verify the diagnosis, ascertain the source of the causative agent, disclose unreported cases, and find contact;

(2) collect and submit laboratory specimens as necessary to confirm the diagnosis or ascertain the source of the infection;

(3) institute necessary control techniques, including designating the limits of the areas in which an individual is quarantined or isolated; and

(4) provide to the patient or a responsible member of the patient's household information on preventing further spread of the disease.

Premarital Examination

Texas repealed its requirement for a premarital syphilis examination, effective 1983.

Prenatal Screening

Every physician or other person permitted by law to attend a pregnant woman during gestation or at delivery shall obtain a blood sample for syphilis testing. A blood sample must also be obtained within 24 hours after delivery. Each birth or fetal death certificate must state whether such tests were performed. (S. 4445d, Sec 3.01)

Exclusion from School

The regulations require the exclusion from child-care centers or schools of any child "having or suspected of having a reportable disease" unless (1) the attending physician certifies that the child does not have a communicable disease or is noninfectious; or (2) a permit for readmission is issued by the local health authority; or (3) the period of communicability as determined by the commissioner has expired. (R. 97.6)

Isolation and Quarantine

The board has defined "quarantine" as "[t]he officially imposed application of measures to prevent contact between infected individuals, animals, objects, or places and individuals, animals, objects, or places not known or suspected of being or having been infected." (R. 97.1) "Isolation" is the voluntary separation for the period of communicability, of infected persons or animals from others, in such places and under such conditions as to prevent the direct or indirect transmission of the infectious agent from one individual to another.

The Act permits the quarantine of an individual if he or she is infected with, or suspected of being infected with, "a communicable disease that presents an immediate threat to the public health." (S. 4419b-1, Sec. 4.02) The board has defined by regulation those communicable diseases that represent a threat to the public health if not immediately controlled. These quarantinable diseases are cholera, diphtheria, gonorrhea, plague, syphilis, tuberculosis, viral hemorrhagic fever (any etiology), and yellow fever. (R. 97.10)

Section 4.02 of the Act establishes the procedures which must be followed in quarantining an individual. Before the department or a health authority may impose a quarantine, it must first issue written orders for the individual to "implement control measures that are reasonable and necessary to prevent the introduction, transmission, and spread of the disease in the state." These orders must be personally served on the individual, or his or her parent, legal guardian, or managing conservator if the individual is not of legal age.

An individual may then be quarantined only if he or she:
(1) fails or refuses to comply with the written orders of the department or health authority; and
(2) is infected with or "reasonably suspected" of being infected with a quarantinable disease.

Based on the affidavit of the department or the health authority that the individual is infected with or reasonably suspected of being infected with a quarantinable disease, a magistrate may issue a warrant of detention, ordering a peace officer to place the individual in a hospital or other facility deemed suitable by the commissioner; a jail or other detention facility may not be used unless it is staffed and equipped to provide disease control measures. If the individual to be detained is under age, the department or health authority must notify his or her parent, legal guardian, or managing conservator by registered or certified mail or by personal service.

The quarantine provisions under the Act require a post-detention appearance before a magistrate who will explain the basis for the detention; the individual, or, where appropriate, the parent, legal guardian, or managing conservator, must be taken before a magistrate of the county in which the individual is detained "without unnecessary delay." Counsel will be appointed if the individual cannot afford to retain private counsel. At the appearance, the magistrate:

> in clear language shall advise the individual or the parent, legal guardian, managing conservator of the order that is alleged to have been violated.... The magistrate shall advise the individual that the individual will be released when he no longer presents a threat to the public health as determined by the health authority or the commissioner or on the granting of a writ of habeas corpus by a court of competent jurisdiction. (S. Art. 4419b-1, Sec. 4.02)

The statute does not explicitly authorize the introduction of evidence to establish or refute the basis for the quarantine order, nor does it provide for the presentation of testimony or cross-examination of witnesses. It appears that the quarantined individual would be able to challenge the imposition of quarantine measures only through a habeas corpus proceeding.

There are separate quarantine statutes applicable only to venereal disease, which is defined as:

> an infection, with or without symptoms or clinical manifestations, that is or may be transmitted from one person to another during or as a result of sexual relations of whatever kind between two persons and that produces or might produce a disease in or otherwise impair the health of either person or might cause an infection or disease in a fetus in utero or a newborn. (S. 4445d)

Syphilis, gonorrhea, chancroid, granuloma inguinale, condyloma acuminata, genital herpes simplex infection, and genital and neonatal chlamydial infections, including lymphogranuloma venereum, are designated by statute as venereal diseases. (S. 4445d, Sec. 1.03) The board may add, delete, or modify the list by regulation.

Section 2.04 of Article 4445d prescribes venereal disease quarantine procedures. The department or a health authority may quarantine an individual known or reasonably suspected of being infected based upon laboratory evidence or exposure to a reported case with syphilis or gonorrhea. A series of orders must be issued before such a quarantine may be imposed, however. First, the department or health authority must instruct the individual to seek a medical examination and/or treatment. If the individual refuses or fails to comply with these instructions, the department or health authority may then issue written orders for the individual to submit to an examination and/or treatment; these orders must be served on the individual personally or by certified or registered mail, or, if the individual is a minor, sent to his or her parent, legal guardian, or managing conservator.

If the individual refuses or fails to comply with the written orders, and the department or health authority "knows that the person is infected with [syphilis or gonorrhea] or is reasonably suspected of being infected based upon laboratory evidence or exposure to a reported case of [syphilis or gonorrhea]", it may request a magistrate to issue a detention warrant. A warrant may be issued based upon the affidavit of the department or health authority declaring that the person is infected with syphilis or gonorrhea or is reasonably suspected of being infected based upon laboratory evidence or exposure to a reported case. If a warrant is issued, the individual will be taken to the nearest venereal disease center or other suitable facility for examination, and, if determined to be infected with syphilis or gonorrhea, the person may be detained for treatment. The Venereal Disease Act does not explicitly require a pre- or post-detention hearing or appearance before a magistrate.

4. Public Health Crimes

Under the Communicable Disease Prevention and Control Act:

(1) It is a Class C misdemeanor if a person attends or attempts to attend a public or private place or gathering when he or she will be brought into contact with others if the person knows he or she has a communicable disease that constitutes a threat to the public health. 9S. 4419b-1, Sec. 6.05)

(2) It is a felony in the third degree for a person to (a) knowingly conceal or attempt to conceal the fact that he or she has, has been exposed to, or is a carrier of a communicable disease that constitutes a threat to the public health, or (b) to knowingly refuse to perform or to allow the performance of control measures ordered by a health authority or the department, or (c) to knowingly fail or refuse to obey a rule, order, or instruction of the board or an order or instruction of a health authority issued pursuant to a rule of the board published during an area quarantine. (S. 4419b-1, Sec. 6.01, 6.04, 6.07)

Under the Venereal Disease Act, it is a Class B misdemeanor:

(1) To knowingly expose another person to infection with a reportable venereal disease. (S. 4445d, Sec. 6.01)

(2) For a physician or other person attending a woman during pregnancy to fail to perform required syphilis testing or prophylactic treatments. (S. 4445d, Sec. 6.02)

(3) For a person to fail or refuse to comply with a written order from the department or a health authority to be examined for a venereal disease. (S. 4445d, Sec. 6.03)

B. Public Health Laws and AIDS

AIDS has been added to the list of diseases which must be reported by name, address, age, sex, race/ethnicity, and date of onset. (R. 97.4) Currently, there is no requirement for the reporting of a positive HTLV-III/LAV antibody test.

Classified as a communicable rather than a venereal disease, AIDS is subject to the control measures available under the Communicable Disease Prevention and Control Act; no AIDS-specific control measures have been enacted. Measures identified under the Act which might potentially be applicable to AIDS include detention, restriction, isolation, and quarantine. In addition, department regulations would authorize exclusion from school of affected children. The authority to compel examination of an individual suspected of being a carrier, or of having AIDS, or having been exposed to the disease, might be inferred in the department's and local health authorities' power to "implement control measures that are reasonable and necessary to prevent the introduction, transmission, and spread of [communicable] disease in the state." (S. 4419b-1, Sec. 4.01)

Of the statutorily identified measures, only detention, restriction, and isolation could apply; AIDS has not been defined as a quarantinable disease, so quarantine measures are not authorized. (See S: 4419b-1, Sec. 4.01 (b); R. 97.10) Isolation of an AIDS patient would depend on the cooperation of the affected individual, since, as defined by the department's regulations, isolation involves the voluntary separation from others to prevent the spread of disease.

More coercive limitations might be justified under the rubric of "restriction," but neither the statute nor the regulations define the scope of this measure. Similarly, the law does not expressly define "detention," or specify when the measure would be warranted. It is unclear how detention, as a public health measure, differs from quarantine.

C. Proposed Legislation and Regulations

The Texas legislature will not meet in general session again until 1987.

The board in late 1985 proposed a rule adding AIDS to the list of quarantinable diseases so that public health officials would be authorized to quarantine AIDS patients whose conduct presented particular danger for spreading the disease. The proposal was withdrawn after the initial public hearing by the commissioner, who cited oppositon from gay leaders as an important factor in the decision.[1] The commissioner has indicated that some other mechanism, in rule form, will be developed to accomplish the same purpose.[2]

Houston

Although there have been no AIDS-specific ordinances, rulings, statutes, or guidelines enacted or developed at the local level, concerns about AIDS transmissibility have led some residents to call for the reinstitution of health certification for food and restaurant workers. In response, the Houston City Council in 1985 created the Committee on Communicable/Infectious Disease Control to consider a proposed ordinance which would require screening of foodhandlers for communicable diseases in order to prevent food-borne disease transmission.[3]

Testimony presented during five meetings of the committee covered:

(1) The history and purpose of screening foodhandlers and why the practice was discontinued;

(2) Current tracing for foodhandlers;

(3) Transmission mechanisms for AIDS;

(4) The most effective methods of AIDS prevention (e.g., education); and

(5) Limitations and interpretations of the HTLV/III/LAV antibody test.[4]

After considering the expert testimony, the Council "is leaning toward rejecting this proposal"; the final decision will be announced in late February or early March of 1986.[5]

D. Guidelines Adopted

The Texas Education Agency and the department have jointly issued recommended guidelines for providing education to students with AIDS/ARC or HTLV-III infection; these guidelines were adapted from "Information and Guidelines" published by the Connecticut Departments of Education and Health Service in March, 1985, and the CDC recommendations, "Education and Foster Care of Children Infected with Human T-lymphotropic Virus Type-III/Lymphadenopathy-Associated Virus," published August 30, 1985.

References

1. Austin American Statesman, January 17, 1986, at 1.

2. Letter from Robert Bernstein, Texas Commissioner of Health, to William J. Curran and Larry O. Gostin, dated January 22, 1986 (regarding legislation, regulations, guidelines, and court decisions relating to AIDS).

3. Houston Department of Health and Human Services, AIDS Information Update: January 1986.

4. *Id*.

5. Letter from Robert L. Falletti, AIDS Coordinator, Houston Bureau of Epidemiology, to William Curran, dated February 4, 1986 (Concerning AIDS-related ordinances or regulations in Houston, Texas).

VI. Illinois

Statutes: Ill. Rev. Stat. Ch. 34, Secs. 5001-5002 (Local boards of health)

Ill. Rev. Stat. Ch. 51, Secs. 101-102 (Confidentiality)

Ill. Rev. Stat. Ch. 89, Sec. 6a (Premarital examinations)

Ill. Rev. Stat. Ch. 91, Secs. 113a-113c (Prenatal screening)

Ill. Rev. Stat. Ch. 111 1/2, Secs. 22-24 (Department of public health)

Ill. Rev. Stat. Ch. 126, Sec. 21 (Confidentiality)

Regulations: Rules and Regulations for the Control of Communicable Disease, Department of Public Health. 10 Ill. Reg. (Emergency rules, effective, 1/3/86)

Introduction

The Illinois statutes provide the bare framework of the powers available to public health officials. The department of public health ("department") has broad discretion in promulgating the rules and regulations necessary to implement the statutory powers. These rules and regulations establish the scope and applicability of specific control measures.

The state's quarantine statutes date from the turn of the century, and have not been revised within the last decade. The statute empowering the department to impose a quarantine was enacted in 1877, and most recently amended in 1976; the statutory authorization for local boards of health to impose measures such as quarantine was enacted in 1901, and most recently amended in 1943. Neither of these statutes explicitly provide due process components such as pre- or post-detention hearings to safeguard the rights of those individuals who may be the subject of personal control measures.

Illinois, unlike the majority of states reviewed for this report, does not distinguish between communicable and venereal diseases in its statutes governing disease control. The rules and regulations of the department do treat communicable diseases and sexually transmitted diseases separately.

Illinois is one of the four jurisdictions reviewed in this chapter which has enacted AIDS-specific legislation.

A. Public Health Powers

    1. Generally

Section 22 of chapter 111 1/2 of the Illinois Revised Statutes contains the basic statement of the public health powers of the state, vesting the state department of public health with the "general supervision of the interests of the health and lives of the people of the State." It is empowered to investigate the causes of "dangerously contagious or infectious diseases, especially when existing in

epidemic form, and take means to restrict and suppress the same...."
The department may adopt, promulgate, repeal, or amend rules and
regulations for the preservation and improvement of the public health,
and enforce such measures as it deems necessary to protect the public
health whenever a "dangerously contagious or infectious disease"
becomes or threatens to become an epidemic and local health
authorities fail to take appropriate action as authorized under the
department's rules and regulations.

A separate statute sets out the general public health powers held
by the local boards of health throughout the state. Under section
5001 of chapter 34, local boards may, upon the outbreak of any
dangerously communicable diseases in their county, town, or immediate
vicinity, make and enforce rules and regulations "tending to check the
spread of the disease within the limits of the county or town...."

2. Reporting Requirements

Pursuant to its general authority under section 22, the department
has adopted rules identifying those diseases, including AIDS,
considered to be "contagious, infectious, communicable and dangerous
to the public health," and requiring that each suspected or diagnosed
case be reported to the department. (R. Chapter I) AIDS was added to
the list as of November 23, 1983.

Chapter II of the department's rules requires every physician,
dentist, other practitioner, attendant, nurse, laboratory, parent,
householder, school authority, or any other person having knowledge of

a known or suspected case or carrier of communicable disease or
communicable disease death to report to the local board of health. A
known or suspected case or carrier who is hospitalized or examined in
a hospital or long-term facility must be reported by the institution's
administrator. The report must include the name, age, sex, and
address of the case, as well as the name of the attending physician.

Separate rules of the department prescribe the reporting
requirements for sexually transmitted diseases, defined to include
syphilis, gonorrhea, chancroid, lymphogranuloma venereum and granuloma
inguinale. (R. Chapter VI) Every physician, medical practitioner,
clinic, hospital, or institution having knowledge of a case of
reportable sexually transmitted disease must report it within 24
hours. Disease reports must include the name, age, sex, race, marital
status, diagnosis, and laboratory findings. In addition, diagnostic
labs must file weekly reports on test results which are reactive for
specified sexually transmissible diseases; these reports must include
the name, age, sex, and race of the person examined; the name and
address of the person submitting the sample; the lab results; the
method employed; date test performed; total number of tests performed
for specified sexually transmitted diseases; and the number found
positive, reactive , or weakly reactive.

Registries

There is no explicit statutory authority supporting the creation
of communicable or venereal disease registries. To the extent that
such a registry was shown to be necessary, it could be justified under

the general authority of the department or local board to act to preserve the public health.

Confidentiality

Illinois provides strong statutory protection for the confidentiality of reported information. Section 21 of chapter 126 of the Illinois Revised Statutes declares that reports of communicable disease, including venereal disease, made by medical practitioners or other persons pursuant to any statute, municipal ordinance or resolution, or administrative agency rule are confidential. The identity of any individual contained in a report of a communicable disease, venereal disease, or foodborne illness, or an investigation into such a disease or illness, is confidential, and shall not be disclosed publicly or in any action of any kind in any court, or before any tribunal, board, or agency. Under the statute, medical practitioners or others making a report in good faith are immune from suit for libel or slander based upon statements contained in such a report.

Additional statutory language covers the confidentiality of information relating to sexually transmitted diseases. Under sections 101 and 102 of chapter 51 of the Revised Statutes, information identifying specific persons as infected or suspected of being infected with sexually transmitted diseases is confidential, and is not admissible as evidence in any legal action.

3. Personal Control Measures

The department's general power to impose and enforce control measures to prevent the spread of disease is enunciated in section 22, which gives the department "supreme authority in matters of quarantine," as well as the authority to take other measures to restrict and suppress dangerously contagious or infectious diseases. The scope and application of the types of control measures available is detailed in Chapter V of the Department's Rules and Regulations for the Control of Communicable Diseases.

Compulsory Examination and Treatment

Neither section 22 nor the department's rules and regulations explicitly authorize the imposition of compulsory examination measures to ascertain whether an individual is infected with a communicable disease other than a sexually transmitted disease. The department's rules and regulations do authorize any state, county, city, or other health officer to require the medical examination of a "suspected person" within his or her jurisdiction if there are reasonable grounds to believe that the person is infected with a reportable sexually transmitted disease and is likely to infect any other person. (R. Chapter VI (F)) A "suspected person" is one who has been in direct or indirect contact with a case of sexually transmitted disease. The person may be detained in a hospital or other suitable place until the results of the examination are known; persons who refuse to submit to the examination may be placed under quarantine until the necessary examinations may be completed.

A health official may also order the examination of any person apprehended and/or committed to or confined in any lockup jail, house of correction, or other penal or correctional institution, detection hospital, or any state, county, or city charitable institution to determine the presence of sexually transmitted disease. A person who is infected will be removed and held in quarantine until non-infectious. (R. Ch. VI (K))

Premarital Examinations

All marriage license applicants must submit a physician's certificate that they are free of venereal disease as determined by a physical examination and serologic test for syphilis. (S. Ch. 89, Sec. 6a) It is a Class B misdemeanor to obtain a license without complying with these requirements.

Prenatal Screening

Blood testing is required for all pregnant women to detect and prevent prenatal syphilis. Every physician or other person who attends a pregnant woman in a professional capacity shall take or cause to be taken a blood sample at the time of the first examination. (S. Ch. 91, sec. 113a) If the serologic test for syphilis shows a positive or a doubtful result, a second test will be made. Each birth certificate and stillbirth certificate must indicate whether such a test was performed, but may not indicate the results of the test. (CS. Ch. 91, Sec. 113b)

Contact Tracing

There is no contact tracing requirement generally applicable to reportable communicable diseases other than sexually transmissable diseases. Health officials are required to investigate each case of reportable sexually transmitted disease to obtain the names of contacts of infectious cases and to cause those contacts to be examined and treated if necessary. (R. Ch. VI, F.1)

Observation

The department defines "observation" as the practice of close medical or other supervision of contacts, without actually restricting their movement, in order to promote prompt recognition of infection or illness. The rules require observation of contacts only for cholera, plague, poliomyelitis, psitticosis, and whooping cough. (R. Ch. III)

Regulating School Attendance

Children who are suspected of having a reportable infectious disease for which isolation is required under the rules of the department will be excluded from school. (R. Ch. V (G)) A person having a communicable disease may be sent home immediately. (R. Ch. V (C.1))

Placarding

This control measure, seldom used by contemporary public health authorities, involves the posting of a public notice at the premises of an individual who is subject to isolation or quarantine to direct the public to keep out. The notice must also warn violators that they would be subject to a fine and/or imprisonment. Placarding would be considered appropriate only in "unusual and compelling circumstances when isolation, quarantine, examination or treatment of a case, carrier or suspect of a communicable disease is necessary and cannot otherwise be implemented." (R. Ch. V, Sec. D)

Isolation and Quarantine

The department has by rule defined isolation and quarantine restrictions applicable to cases, carriers, and contacts. "Isolation" is the separation of a person who has a communicable disease, or who is a carrier of the infecting organism, or who is suspected of having the disease or being a carrier, from other persons under conditions which prevent the direct or indirect transmission of the infectious agent; "modified isolation" involves a selective, partial limitation of freedom of movement that is applicable to certain specified diseases, most notably to typhoid fever carriers. (R. Ch. IV, Sec. 10a, 10b) "Quarantine" is the limitation of freedom of well persons who have been exposed to a communicable disease, for a period of time equal to the longest usual incubation period of the disease, in a manner which prevents effective contact with persons not exposed. (R. CH. IV, Sec. 14)

Isolation or quarantine measures may be imposed only as specified under the rules and regulations of the department establishing detailed procedures for the control of communicable diseases. The control measures are intended for use in the patient's home or in similar situations; isolation or quarantine within a hospital should comply with appropriate isolation techniques for use in hospitals.

It is the duty of local health authorities to invoke isolation or quarantine measures. When informed of the existence of a case or carrier, or of a suspected case or carrier, of a disease requiring isolation under the department's rules, the local heath authority must immediately establish isolation of the patient. (R. Ch. V (A)) The isolation will be maintained for the minimum period of time specified in the rules, and may be terminated only by the presiding local health authority.

The local health authority shall quarantine the contacts of a case or carrier, or of a suspected case or carrier of a disease requiring quarantine under the department's rules. The quarantine will continue for the time period specified in the rules (the longest usual incubation period for the disease), and may be terminated only by the presiding local health authority. (R. Ch. V, Sec. B)

4. Public Health Crimes

The rules of the department provide that no person who knows himself or herself to be infected with a sexually transmitted disease shall perform or commit any act which exposes any other person to infection with the disease. Violation is a Class A misdemeanor.

5. Penalties

Section 24 of chapter 111 1/2 of the Revised Statutes makes it a Class A misdemeanor to violate or refuse to obey any rule or regulation of the department. It is a Class B misdemeanor to violate or refuse to obey any rule or regulation of a local board of health. (S. Ch. 34, Sec. 5002)

Under the rules and regulations of the department, every person with a communicable disease who is ordered by the director of the department or the local health authority to be isolated must comply with the order, and remain isolated until no longer a danger to the public health. (R. Ch. V, Sec. I.3)

B. Public Health Law and AIDS

AIDS is a communicable disease under Illinois law, and all cases and suspected cases must be reported. (R. Ch. I) In addition, positive HTLV-III antibody tests may also be reportable under Chapter II of the rules and regulations which require physicians and laboratories to report suspected carriers of communicable disease. A "carrier" is defined as a person who, without current symptoms of a communicable disease, harbors and disseminates the specific micro-organism. (R. Ch. IV)

The department has not issued rules or regulations prescribing detailed requirements for the control of AIDS. Absent such provisions, there is currently no authority in Illinois for the isolation of AIDS patients or the quarantining of individuals exposed to the disease. Nor is there authority to require physical examinations or screening since such provisions are currently authorized only in the case of venereal diseases.

Recently enacted legislation requires the department to conduct an AIDS information campaign for physicians, hospitals, health facilities, public health departments, and the general public, and to "promote necessary measures to reduce the mortality from AIDS." (S.B. 325) The legislation requires the establishment of a statewide telephone hotline.

Emergency amendments to the rules governing clinical laboratories and blood banks took effect in January, 1986. (Ill. Register) The amendatory rules require ELISA testing of all donor blood for evidence of infection with the HTLV-III virus; units found to be positive will be subjected to a confirmatory test, such as the Western Blot. HTLV-III virus test results are confidential, and may not be disclosed except as authorized in writing by the donor.

Any prospective donor who tests positive must be rejected; prospective donors who request HTLV-III testing must be informed about the availability of alternative test centers.

Prospective donors must be informed that:
(1) All donated blood will be tested for evidence of HTLV-III;
(2) Persons at increased risk of HTLV-III infection must not donate blood; and

(3) HTLV-III virus test results, when confirmed, will be disclosed in a confidential manner to the donor's physician or the donor within 55 days after the donation. The donor must sign a consent to such disclosure before donating blood.

The emergency rules also prescribe procedures for notifying a donor of positive test results. A donor who tests positive will be advised to contact the blood bank for an appointment to discuss the test results. The results of the test may be presented and explained to the donor only in a person to person interview. If the donor does not attend a blood bank appointment, the confirmed test results will be sent to him or her by certified mail with restricted delivery, messenger, or personal visit, along with explanatory and referral information.

C. Proposed Legislation and Regulations

House Bill 2553, introduced in October, 1985, by Representatives Vinson and Shaw, would create the AIDS Contagion Control Board within the department. The Board would include seven (7) physicians appointed by the governor to research and recommend methods for the prevention and control of AIDS. It would recommend "prudent and effective" regulations, and any state or local officer who decided not to adopt a recommended regulation would be required to advise the General Assembly of the reasons for that decision.

The Board would be authorized to recommend mandatory or voluntary screening for AIDS for any population associated with disease contagion, including but not limited to public school students, significant workforce concentrations, and public institution populations; order creation of a central registry for AIDS victims or carriers, provided that it is approved by the director of health; conduct research into AIDS transmission mechanisms; recommend the quarantining or limited quarantining of AIDS victims where it would be an effective contagion control; and research and recommend screening procedures and tests.

House Bill 2565, introduced in November, 1985, would require that the premarital medical examination include a test "to determine existence of or freedom from...acquired immune deficiency syndrome (AIDS)." License issuance would be subject to the same requirement now applicable to premarital syphilis tests.

S.B. 16.50 would direct the department of public health to adopt rules to allow designated blood donations.

S.B. 1685 would prohibit health and accident insurers from denying coverage to applicants who have AIDS or who test positively for the HTLV-III/LAV virus.

S. 2073 would prohibit life and health insurers from requiring or requesting an HTLV-III/LAV antibody test as a condition for coverage.

The department has proposed AIDS-related amendments to its communicable disease rules and regulations. The proposed amendments would establish detailed procedures to be followed for the control of AIDS. Isolation of cases would be required only when the case is hospitalized, resides in a long-term care facility, or is receiving outpatient health care; isolation precautions must conform to the CDC Guidelines for Isolation Precautions in Hospitals."

Under the proposed rules, persons known or suspected of having AIDS would not be allowed to donate blood, plasma, body organs, other tissues, or sperm. All blood or serum from donors of blood, plasma, organs, tissues, or sperm must be tested for infection with the HTLV-III virus unless the delay would jeopardize the recipient's life. The body of a deceased AIDS patient or suspected AIDS patient must be labeled as an infectious hazard to inform the funeral director of precautions that must be taken during he embalming process.

D. CDC Guidelines Adopted

The department's interim policy on school children with AIDS recommends that schools use the CDC guidelines on the education and foster care of children infected with human T-lymphotropic virus type III/lymphadenopathy-associated virus.

VII. Massachusetts

Statutes: M.G.L. ch. 71, sec. 55-55B (Exclusion of School Children)

M.G.L. ch. 94C, sec. 27 (Regulation of Hypodermic Syringes and Needles)

M.G.L. ch. 111, sec. 6 (Power to Define Dangerous Diseases)

M.G.L. ch. 111, sec. 7 (Investigation of Disease)

M.G.L. ch. 111, sec. 31 (Local Health Regulations)

M.G.L. ch. 111, sec. 95-98 (Control Powers of Local Boards)

M.G.L. ch. 111, sec. 104 (Public Notice of Infection)

M.G.L. ch. 111, sec. 109-113 (Reporting)

M.G.L. ch. 111, sec. 119 (Confidentiality of Venereal Disease Reports)

M.G.L. ch. 207, sec. 28A (Premarital Syphilis Testing)

Regulations: 105 CMR 160.300 (Clinical Lab HTLV-III Testing)

105 CMR 300.000 et. seq. (Regulations Governing Reportable Diseases and Isolation and Quarantine Requirements)

105 CMR 340.000 et. seq. (Reporting and Control of Venereal Diseases)

Introduction

The basic statutes defining the public health powers concerning communicable disease control in Massachusetts are largely the products of the 1930's and 1940's. Although there have been some major additions, such as the provisions concerning the compulsory hospitalization of individuals with active tuberculosis (M.G.L. ch. 111. sec. 94C-94H) there has been no comprehensive revision of the statutory framework. The statutes establishing the powers of the Massachusetts department of public health ("department") to define, investigate, and prevent dangerous diseases, including venereal diseases, were enacted in their current form in the 1930's and 1940's. (S. Sec. 6-7) The current statute prescribing the powers of local boards of health to make reasonable health regulations was established in 1937, and has been subject to only minor amendments since; the statutory language authorizing local boards of health to impose quarantines dates most recently from 1907. (S. Sec. 31 and 95)

The regulations adopted by the department pursuant to its statutory authority expand upon the concise enunciation of the public health powers set out in the General Laws. It is through these regulations that the implementation of the public health powers is made possible. They clarify reporting requirements as well as delineate the scope and applicability of personal control measures.

A. Public Health Powers

1. Generally

Public health powers in the commonwealth may be exercised by state and local health officials. It is the state, operating through the department, which is empowered to define diseases dangerous to the public health, including venereal diseases, and to make rules and regulations for their control. (S. Sec. 6) It is also the obligation of the state whenever "smallpox or any other contagious or infectious disease declared by the department to be dangerous to the public health exists or is likely to exist . . . to make an investigation thereof and of the means of preventing the spread of the disease, and [to] consult thereon with local authorities." (S. Sec. 7) Under section 7, the department has coordinate powers with local boards of health.

Each local board of health may also make reasonable health regulations. (S. Sec. 31) Local boards are authorized by statute to isolate individuals when there is an outbreak of a disease dangerous to the public health in the town. (S. Sec. 95-98)

2. Reporting Requirements

The department of public health ("department") is empowered by statute to define which diseases are considered "dangerous to the public health," and to make rules and regulations for the control and prevention of these diseases. (S. Sec. 6) Under section 6, the department is also authorized to define what diseases are included within the term "venereal diseases."

Pursuant to this authority, the department has issued regulations identifying those diseases which must be reported to the appropriate health officials. The regulations are for use by local boards of health, hospitals, physicians, educational and recreational program health officials, and the public. (R. 300.001)

Forty-three (43) diseases are reportable to local boards of health by telephone or in writing; local boards must also be notified of epidemics of disease, including those not specifically identified as reportable. (R. 300.100) Other dangerous disease or syndromes must be reported directly to the department.

Individuals and institutions who may be required to make disease reports are specified by statute. Under section seven of chapter 111 of the General Laws, the department may require physicians, local boards of health, and the officers in charge of any city or state institution, charitable institution, public or private hospital, dispensary, or maternity hospital to report cases of any disease deemed dangerous to the public health. (S. Sec. 7) Failure to give notice when required by the department is subject to a fine of fifty dollars ($50) to two hundred dollars ($200).

Other statutes impose reporting responsibilities on designated individuals. A physician who knows or has cause to believe that a person he or she visits is infected with a disease dangerous to the public health must give immediate, written notice to the local board of health. (S. Sec. 111) A physician or house medical officer who refuses or neglects to give the notice required under this section is

subject to a fine of fifty dollars ($50) to two hundred dollars
($200). If there is no physician in attendance, a householder who
knows or has cause to believe that a person in his or her family or
house is infected with a disease dangerous to the public health must
notify the local board of health. (S. Sec. 109) Violation of this
section is subject to a fine of not more than one hundred dollars
($100).

Separate reporting requirements applicable to individuals who have
or are suspected of having a venereal disease have also been
established by regulation. (R. 340.100) A physician who has reason to
believe that a patient he or she is treating has a venereal disease
must report to the department the name, address, age, sex, race, and
marital status of the individual; the report must indicate the name
and stage of the disease, as well as whether the patient has received
treatment. A physician must also report the name, address, sex, age,
race, marital status, and other identifying data on any individual who
fails to return within one week after being notified of a positive
physical and/or laboratory finding strongly suggesting the probable
presence of venereal disease. A patient who fails or refuses to
return for observation or necessary treatment must be reported by
name, address, age, race, marital stauts, state of the disease, date
of last physician visit, and date of infection.

The department is authorized to forward to a local board of health
the name, address of place frequented by or place of employment, age,
sex, race, and marital status of a patient reported to the department.
(R. 340.200)

Contact Tracing

A contact is a person who has been in such association with an infected person as to have had the opportunity to acquire the infection. (R. 300.020) A patient with venereal disease who does not cooperate with the physician in identifying contacts, including members of the family, from whom the patient may have acquired the infection or to whom he or she may have transmitted it, must be reported to the department, indicating the name, address, age, race, sex, and marital status of the patient along with the reason for the report. (R. 340.100) The regulation requires the physician to report the name, address, age, sex, race, and marital status, or as complete an identification as can be obtained, of any person from whom the patient may have acquired gonorrhea, syphilis, chancroid, granuloma inguinale, or lymphogranuloma venereum, or to whom he or she may have transmitted such a disease.

Registries

Each board of health must keep a record of all disease reports containing the name and location of the person infected with a dangerous disease, the disease, the name of the person reporting the case, the date of the report, and other information as required by the department. (S. Sec. 113)

Confidentiality

There is no public health confidentiality statute generally applicable to reports or records of diseases deemed dangerous to the public health.

There is limited statutory protection for information collected regarding venereal disease. All hospital, dispensary, laboratory, and morbidity reports and records pertaining to venereal disease as defined by the department are not considered public records, and may not be divulged except upon proper judicial order. (S. Sec. 119)

3. Personal Control Measures
Compulsory Examination and Treatment

There is no explicit statutory or regulatory provision authorizing compulsory examination or treatment of a dangerous disease other than tuberculosis or venereal diseases.

The regulations relating to the control of venereal diseases identify several situations in which a local board of health may act to require examination or treatment. Local boards of health are empowered to advise venereal disease contacts to obtain medical care; individuals who do not obtain such care within two weeks after being advised shall be isolated by the board until it is satisfied that the individual is not infected with venereal disease. (R. 340.300) A local board that receives notice of a person who has prematurely discontinued treatment shall immediately request the person to return to medical care, and shall isolate a noncomplying individual until it is satisfied that the disease is no longer communicable or that the person will immediately return to medical care for his or her infection. (R. 340.400)

Premarital Examinations

Applicants for a marriage license are required to submit to approved serologic tests for syphilis before a premarital medical certificate may be issued. (S. Sec. 28A) If the test is positive, the medical certificate may be issued when, in the physician's opinion, the patient with communicable syphilis has received adequate treatment. (R. 375.200) Premarital rubella immunity testing is optional.

Placarding

Although there is no explicit provision for placarding under Massachusetts law, local boards of health are authorized by statute to "give notice of infected places by such means as in their judgment may be the most effectual for the common safety." (S. Sec. 104) A fine of ten dollars ($10) to one hundred dollars ($100) may be imposed for wilfully and without authority removing, obliterating, defacing, or handling posted notices.

Isolation and Quarantine

Authority to isolate or quarantine individuals is exercised at both the state and local levels. The state's power to impose personal control measures to prevent the spread of communicable disease is grounded in the general grant of authority to make rules and regulations for the control of diseases dangerous to the public health. (S. Sec. 6) Local boards of health are specifically authorized to cause the removal to a hospital of any sick or infected person, if it can be done without endangering the person's health. (S. Sec. 95) A magistrate may issue a warrant to the appropriate law enforcement officer requiring him or her, under the direction of the board, to remove any person who has a disease dangerous to the public health, or who is a carrier of the causative agent of such a disease. S. Sec. 96) This power of removal applies only to situations where, in the board's opinion, the patient cannot be properly isolated. (S. Sec. 97)

Regulations have been issued by the department which establish the minimum isolation and quarantine requirements for each disease reportable to the department or local boards of health. (R. 300.300) Separate regulations authorize the isolation of venereal disease patients or contacts based on their failure to obtain treatment or to cooperate with health officials. Neither set of regulations prescribes specific procedures to be followed in imposing control measures.

Individuals who have certain dangerous diseases or sexually transmissable diseases may be isolated as required under the general isolation and quarantine regulations. (R. 300.200) Isolation is defined as the separation, for the period of communicability, of an infected individual from other individuals in such places and under such conditions that will prevent the direct or indirect transmission of the infectious agent to susceptible persons or to those who may spread the disease. The regulations identify those diseases which require isolation, and specify the minimum period of isolation.

Healthy individuals who have been exposed to individuals with certain dangerous diseases may be quarantined as required under R.

300.200. As defined by the regulation, quarantine measures may involve varying degrees of restrictiveness. A complete quarantine restricts the freedom of movement of well persons who have been exposed to a communicable disease in order to prevent effective contact with those who have not been exposed; the restriction is applicable for the period of time equal to the longest usual incubation period of the disease. "Modified quarantine" is a selective, partial limitation of freedom of movement, reflecting known or presumed differences in susceptibility and the danger of disease transmission. The exclusion of children from school or contacts from working in food establishments are examples of modified quarantine measures. Finally, "personal surveillance," the least intrusive of the quarantine measures, involves close medical or other supervision of contacts without restricting their movements in order to promote prompt recognition of infection or illness. The department's general quarantine regulations indicate when contacts are subject to control measures.

In addition to the isolation and quarantine requirements set out under R. 300.200, there are specific instances in which local boards of health may isolate individuals who have or have been exposed to venereal diseases. As noted above in the discussion of compulsory examination and treatment, contacts who do not obtain medical care and patients who terminate care prematurely may be isolated by a local board of health. (R. 340.300-400) An individual with open syphilis lesions who refuses a board request to discontinue any occupation requiring contact with other persons, may be isolated by the board in his or her home or a hospital until the lesions are healed and the person agrees to remain under medical care. (R. 340.500) Finally, a local board may isolate a patient who refuses to cooperate in bringing to medical observation any contact from whom the venereal disease may have been acquired, or to whom it may have been transmitted; the patient is to remain isolated until he or she cooperates or until the infection is no longer communicable. (R. 340.600)

Exclusion from School

A child who is infected with a disease dangerous to the public health, or who resides in a household where a person is infected with a dangerous disease, shall not attend public school while infected or living in such a household if required by the regulations of the board of health. (S. Sec. 55) A child who shows signs of ill health or of being infected with a disease dangerous to the public health shall be sent home immediately, as soon as a safe and proper conveyance is available, or shall be referred to the school physician who may order the child sent home. (S. Sec. 55A) The superintendent of schools must notify the board of health of any children excluded from school under these provisions.

4. Regulation of Hypodermic Syringes and Needles

The availability of hypodermic syringes and needles is regulated under the Massachusetts controlled substances act. (S. Sec. 27) No syringe, needle, or instrument adapted for the administration of a controlled substance by injection may be obtained, received by, or purchased by any person who has not received a written prescription issued by a physician, or who is not otherwise authorized by statute to possess such equipment. The prescription must include the name and address of the patient, a description of the instrument prescribed, and the number of the instruments prescribed.

B. Public Health Law and AIDS

There has been no AIDS-specific legislation enacted in Massachusetts as of June, 1986.

In 1984, the department amended its communicable disease regulations to define AIDS as a dangerous disease, and to require that it be reported directly to the department. There is no requirement for HTLV-III antibody test reporting.

The department has also amended the clinical laboratories licensing regulations relating to the performance of HTLV-III antibody screening tests. (R. 180-300) Before they may be approved to conduct such tests, each laboratory must have documented arrangements for examination and confirmatory testing of positive specimens, and must maintain written procedures and policies to ensure confidentiality. Patient consent to testing must be based on written procedures, filed with the department, which include an explanation of:

(1) the voluntary nature of testing for non-blood donors;

(2) the purpose of the test;

(3) an interpretation of the significance of test results, including the limitations

(4) the availability of a second or confirmatory test; and

(5) the availability of additional information and counseling.

A clinical laboratory operated by a hospital or clinic which performs the test for purposes other than blood donor screening, must obtain approval by the internal review mechanism of the hospital or clinic.

In amending the regulations to include AIDS, the department also prescribed minimum requirements for control of the disease. The only restrictions specified for AIDS patients under the regulations are "appropriate exclusion from blood donation and appropriate modification of sexual activities through health education." (R. 300.200) For sexual contacts, no minimum period of quarantine is required; personal surveillance provisions would not be applicable, since that would constitute a form of quarantine. Health officials are directed to seek appropriate modification of sexual activities through health education, or, otherwise, to contact health authorities for the latest information. Restrictions applicable to children contacts are the same as those for adults.

Defined as a disease dangerous to public health, AIDS would also be subject to other control measures applicable generally to dangerous disease. Exclusion from school would be authorized if required by the regulations of the local school board. (S. Sec. 55) Compulsory examination would not be applicable since it is authorized by statute only for venereal diseases, not dangerous diseases in general.

C. Proposed Legislation and Regulations

Legislation has been introduced in the State Senate which would prohibit insurers from requiring HTLV-III/LAV antibody testing as a condition for obtaining medical and life insurance.[1]

D. Guidelines Adopted

The Massachusetts department of public health has adopted the following policies and recommendations concerning AIDS and HTLV-III infections:

(1) Recommendations for Caretakers of Children with Clinical AIDS or Evidence of Infection with the HTLV-III Virus Infection;

(2) School Attendance Policy;

(3) Residential Treatment Policy;

(4) Recommendations for Health Officials and Food Industry Personnel on AIDS and HTLV-III Antibody Screening; and

(5) Workplace Policy.[2]

References

1. Boston Globe, March 10, 1986, at p. 21.
2. Boston Globe, March 8, 1986, at p. 1.

VIII. Pennsylvania

Statutes: 35 P.S. Sec. 521.1 et seq. (Disease Prevention and Control Act of 1955)

35 P.S. 655.7 (Food Establishment Employees)

Regulations: 28 Pa. Code Sec. 27.1 et seq. (Communicable and Noncommunicable Diseases)

Introduction

The Disease Prevention and Control Act of 1955 ("Act") establishes provisions for the control of venereal disease, tuberculosis, and other communicable diseases in the commonwealth of Pennsylvania. The act provides a straightforward, concise statement of the public health powers available to state and local health officials. There have been no major revisions of its provisions since it was enacted in the mid-1950's.

The Act of 1955 is implemented by regulations issued by the Pennsylvania department of health ("department"). These regulations fill out the contours of the authority established by statute, establishing the list of reportable diseases, and prescribing the appropriate prevention or control measures applicable for each. Consistent regulation may also be promulgated at the local level.

A. Public Health Powers

1. Generally

The department, through its Advisory Health Board ("Board") is authorized to issue rules and regulations governing, among other things:

(1) the reporting of specified communicable and noncommunicable diseases;

(2) the communicable diseases which are subject to isolation, quarantine, or other control measures;

(3) the duration and enforcement of isolation, quarantine, and other control measures;

(4) disease prevention and control in schools;

(5) the regulation of carriers; and

(6) the prevention and control of noncommunicable disease.
(S. 521.16)

Municipalities which have established local boards or departments of health and county departments of health may enact ordinances and regulations relating to disease prevention and control which are not less strict than the Act and the rules and regulations of the department. Thus, local ordinances and regulations may be more stringent than the state provisions.

It is the local boards and departments of health that are primarily responsible for the prevention and control of communicable and noncommunicable disease, including disease prevention and control in schools, in accordance with the Board's regulations and subject to the department's supervision. (S. 521.3) The department may step in if it finds that the local efforts at prevention and control are so inadequate as to constitute a menace to the public health.

2. Reporting Requirements

A reportable disease, as defined in the regulations of the board, includes:

(1) any communicable disease declared reportable by regulation;

(2) any unusual or group expression of illness which, in the opinion of the department, may be a public health emergency; and

(3) noncommunicable diseases and conditions for which the department may authorize reporting to provide data and information which, in the board's opinion, are needed in order to protect the public health. (R. 27.1)

A communicable disease is an illness due to an infectious agent or its toxic products which is transmitted, directly or indirectly, to a well person from an infected person, animal or anthropod, or through the agency of an intermediate host, or a vector, or through the inanimate environment. (R. 27.1) The board has by regulation established a list of thirty-six (36) communicable diseases, unusual outbreaks of illness, noncommunicable diseases, and conditions to be reportable. (R. 27.2) In addition, the regulations require that any occurrence of unusual disease or group expression of disease which may be of public concern, whether or not it is known to be communicable, must be reported. (R. 27.28)

Every physician who treats or examines a person suffering from or suspected of having a communicable disease, or a person who is or is suspected of being a carrier, is required by statute to report the person to the local board or department of health, or to the state department as required by regulation. (S. 521.4) The report, which may be made on a standard form or by telephone, must include the name of the patient or carrier, his or her address, the date of onset of the disease, and the name, address, and telephone number of the attending physician. (R. 27.21)

In addition, the following individuals are required to report cases or suspected cases of reportable disease to local health authorities:

(1) school nurses; (R. 27.23)

(2) superintendents of hospitals or persons in charge of any institution for the treatment of disease, an institution maintaining dormitories, or an orphanage; (R. 27.24)

(3) any chiropractor, dentist, nurse, optometrist, podiatrist, or other licensed health practitioner; (R. 27.25)

(4) any householder, proprietor of a hotel, rooming house, lodging house, boarding house, or other person having knowledge or suspicion of a reportable disease; (R. 27.26) and

(5) any person who has knowledge of the occurrence of any unusual disease or group expression of illness which may be of public concern. (R. 27.28)

The regulations of the department also require any person in charge of a laboratory to report test results which indicate the presence of specified diseases or conditions, including viral infections. (R. 27.22) Reports must include the name, age, and address of the person from whom the specimen was obtained, and the name and address of the physician ordering the test.

Contact Tracing

If, pursuant to the department's regulations, a disease requires quarantine of contacts as well as isolation of the case, the local health authority shall identify the contacts who are subject to the requirement, specify the place of quarantine, and issue appropriate instructions. (R. 27.65) Provisions must be made to insure that medical observation of the contacts occurs as frequently as necessary during the quarantine.

Registries

Each local health official of a municipality is required to maintain records that will permit the efficient function of the local department for the prevention and control of communicable diseases. (R. 27.46)

Confidentiality

The confidentiality of information reported, collected, or created pursuant to the Act is protected by statute. State and local health authorities may not disclose reports of disease, records maintained as a result of any action taken because of such reports, or any other record kept pursuant to the Act or department regulations, except as necessary to carry out the purposes of the Act. (S. 521.15) State and local authorities may permit use of data for research purposes, subject to strict supervision to insure that such use is limited to specific research purposes.

3. Personal Control Measures

Compulsory Examination and Treatment

If there are reasonable grounds to suspect that an individual is infected with or is a carrier of venereal disease, tuberculosis, or "any other communicable disease," the secretary of health or a local medical health officer may require the individual to submit to a medical examination and diagnostic testing. (S. 521.7; R. 27.81, 27.82) If the individual refuses, the secretary or medical officer may:

(1) cause the individual to be quarantined until it can be determined whether he or she is infected or is a carrier; or

(2) petition a court of competent jurisdiction to order the individual to submit to an examination. The petition must be supported by an affidavit declaring that the individual is suspected of being infected or of being a carrier. If, after a hearing, the court determines that the individual has refused to submit to an examination and that there is no valid a reason for such a refusal, it will order the individual to submit to the examination. A person refusing to undergo examination may be committed to a suitable institution.

Pennsylvania law also specifically authorizes compulsory examination for venereal disease of any person:

(1) taken into custody and charged with a crime involving lewd conduct or a sex offense; or

(2) under the jurisdiction of the juvenile court; or

(3) convicted of a crime or pending trial, who is confined in a state or local penal institution, reformatory, or other house of correction or detention. (S. 521.8; R. 27.84) Individuals found to be infected will be given appropriate treatment.

An individual who is found to be infected with "venereal disease, tuberculosis, or any other communicable disease" in a communicable phase and who refuses to submit to approved treatment may be isolated by the secretary or local medical officer in an appropriate institution for "safekeeping and treatment until the disease has been rendered noncommunicable." (S. 521.11; R. 27.87) The secretary or health officer may petition a court of competent jurisdiction to commit the individual, and the court shall order the commitment if, after a hearing, it finds that the individual has refused to submit to treatment.

An individual isolated or quarantined because of venereal disease may be placed in a county jail or any other appropriate facility for safekeeping and treatment.

Premarital Examinations

Marriage license applicants must submit to a medical examination, including a standard serologic test, to determine whether they are infected with syphilis in a communicable stage. (S. 521.12; R. 27.89) A statement of the examining physician certifying that the applicant is free of syphilis, or, if not free, is not in a communicable stage, must be filed separately from the license application, and is regarded as confidential. An applicant who has been denied a physician's statement may appeal to the department, which may issue or refuse to issue a statement in lieu of the physician's statement. (R. 27.90)

Prenatal Screening

Every physician or other person who attends, treats, or examines a pregnant woman for a condition related to pregnancy during the period of gestation or at delivery shall obtain a blood sample for syphilis testing, unless the woman dissents. (S. 521.13; R. 27.94) If the woman dissents, it is the physician's duty to explain the desirability of the test. Birth certificates and fetal death certificates must indicate whether the required test was performed, and if it was not performed, whether it was because the test was not advisable or because the woman dissented. (R. 27.95)

Regulation of Food Handlers

No employee who is a carrier of typhoid fever or of other intestinal infections, or who has diphtheria, active tuberculosis, syphilis in a transmissible stage, or any infectious disease or open external lesion may be involved in any way with the handling, preparation, serving, or providing of food or drink to the public. (S. 655.7)

Regulation of School Attendance

A form of modified quarantine involves the exclusion from school of children with communicable diseases and conditions. The department's regulations require each teacher, principal, superintendent, or other person in charge of a public, private, parochial, Sunday, or other school to exclude children who have been diagnosed with or who are suspected of having any one of fifteen (15) specific diseases or conditions, not including AIDS; the regulations establish the period of exclusion required for each disease. (R. 27.71)

In addition, any person showing an unusual skin eruption, having soreness of the throat, or showing signs or symptoms of whooping cough or diseases of the eyes shall be excluded from attending school. (R. 27.71) No person who has been excluded will be readmitted unless the facility's nurse is convinced that the condition is not communicable or the child presents a physician's certificate of recovery or noninfectiousness. (R. 27.73) And no person who was excluded for having or living on the premises where there was a disease for which isolation is required may be readmitted without permission of the health authorities. (R. 27.74)

Placarding

Placarding involves the posting at a home or other building of a sign or notice warning of the presence of a communicable disease and the danger of infection. (R. 27.1) It may be used only when the local health authority is unable to enforce isolation or quarantine measures as required, and the specific use is approved by the department. (R. 27.66)

Isolation and Quarantine

Under Pennsylvania law, "isolation" is the separation for the period of communicability of infected persons from others in a manner that will prevent the direct or indirect transmission of the infectious agent from infected persons to others who are susceptible or who may spread the disease. (S. 521.2; R. 27.1) "Quarantine" is the limitation of freedom of movement of healthy persons who have been exposed to a communicable disease, for a period of time equal to the longest usual incubation period of the disease, in such a way as to prevent effective contact with persons not exposed. There are graduated levels of quarantine:

(1) "Segregation" is the separation for special control or observation of one or more persons from others to facilitate the control of a communicable disease.

(2) "Modified quarantine" entails a partial limitation of freedom of movement determined on the basis of differences in susceptibility or danger of disease transmission, and includes but is not limited to the exclusion of children from school and restrictions imposed on the employment of infected individuals in certain occupations. The isolation technique depends on the disease involved. (R. 27.63)

(3) "Surveillance" involves close supervision of persons exposed to a communicable disease without restricting their movements.

The requirements for isolation or quarantine of individuals are prescribed under the regulations of the department which specify particular procedures for the treatment of each reportable disease. (R. 27.101 et seq.) These regulations prescribe the general requirements for the control of the infected individual, his or her contacts, and his or her environment.

The imposition of isolation or quarantine measures may also be based on the conduct of an individual who has a communicable disease or is suspected of being a carrier but refuses to submit to treatment or examination. An individual who refuses to undergo a medical examination to determine whether he or she has or is a carrier of venereal disease, tuberculosis, or any other communicable disease may be quarantined until the disease status is determined; an infected individual who refuses to submit to approved treatment may be isolated until his or her disease is rendered noncommunicable. (See Compulsory Examination and Treatment, supra.)

The local board or department of health is responsible for applying the appropriate measure upon receiving a report of a disease subject to isolation, quarantine, or other control measure. (S. 521.5) If the disease is one requiring isolation, the local health authority must instruct the patient and members of his or her household on the measures to be taken to prevent the spread of the disease. (R. 27.62)

4. Penalties

Any person who violates any of the provisions of the disease prevention and control act or any regulation shall, upon conviction for each offense in summary proceedings, be fined not less than twenty-five dollars ($25) nor more than three hundred dollars ($300), plus costs; in default of the fine and costs, the person may be imprisoned in the county jail for up to thirty (30) days. (S. Sec. 521.20) Prosecutions may be instituted by the department, by a local board or department of health, or by any person having knowledge of a violation of any provision of the Act or any regulation.

The Act establishes separate penalties for individuals with active tuberculosis who violate quarantine requirements. (S. Sec. 521.19)

B. Public Health Powers and AIDS

There has been no AIDS-specific legislation enacted thus far in Pennsylvania.

By notice in the Pennsylvania Bulletin, dated August 6, 1983, the department declared AIDS to be an "unusual disease of public concern;" cases and suspected cases must be reported to the department's division of epidemiology. AIDS has not, as yet, been incorporated into the list of reportable communicable diseases, unusual outbreaks of illness, noncommunicable diseases, and other conditions found in section 27.2 of the regulations.

AIDS has not been specifically defined by statute or regulation as a communicable disease; it does however, fall within the definition of "communicable disease" set out in section 27.1 of the regulations (See Reporting Requirements, supra). Treated as a communicable disease, AIDS would fall within the compulsory examination provisions; if there were reasonable grounds to suspect that an individual was infected with or is a carrier of AIDS, the secretary or medical officer may require a medical examination and diagnostic testing. (See S. 521.7; R. 2781, 2782, supra). Refusal to submit could result in quarantine.

The department has identified by legislation those diseases which require isolation or quarantine; the list does not currently include either AIDS or HTLV-III/LAV antibody positivity. Similarly, the department's list of diseases for which children may be excluded from school does not include AIDS. Thus isolation or quarantine is not required generally or in the school setting.[1] It should again be noted that local regulations may be more strict than those of the state and could require quarantine or isolation in such situations. No such regulations are in place now, however.[2]

Statutes governing employment of food handlers prohibit employment of persons with any infectious disease or open external lesion from being involved in food handling, preparation, or serving. (See S. 655.7) To the extent that AIDS is defined as an infectious disease--a term not defined by the regulators--or that a person with AIDS has an open lesion, he or she might be excludable from employment as a food handler. The thrust of the statute, however, is to exclude persons with diseases which may be foodborne; since there is no evidence that AIDS or HTLV-III/LAV infection is foodborne, application of the statute seems wholly unwarranted. Guidelines issued by the department of public welfare recommend that employees known to be infected with HTLV-III/LAV need not be restricted unless they have evidence of other infections or illnesses for which any food service handler would be restricted.[3]

C. Proposed Legislation and Regulation

Legislation has been proposed in Pennsylvania that would establish criminal liability for knowingly transmitting AIDS by sexual contact. House Bill 1787 would make it a misdemeanor in the first degree for a person who, knowing that he is "infected by acquired immune deficiency syndrome," transmits the disease to another person through sexual contact. Second or subsequent offenses would constitute a felony in the second degree.

The department has recently rejected a draft proposal to create a confidential registry of persons who are HTLV-III/LAV antibody positive but who have not contracted AIDS.[4]

D. Guidelines

Advisory memoranda relating to AIDS have been issued by the department of public welfare (DPW), the department of corrections, and the commissioner for basic education.

The memorandum of the DPW sets out precautionary guidelines for work settings where transmission of HTLV-III/LAV could occur, particularly in settings where employees, patients, residents, or students could be exposed to blood or body fluids from infected individuals.[5] These settings are where health care and treatment, personal care, and laboratory services are provided.

In late 1985, the commissioner of corrections issued an advisory to "provide information regarding the risk of transmitting AIDS and the virus which causes it, symptoms, identify risk groups, define modes of transmission of the disease and outline medical care within a correctional environment."[6] The advisory specifies a number of recommended procedures, including the medical quarantining of inmates with a confirmed diagnosis of ARC/AIDS.

Also in October of 1985, the commissioner of basic education issued an advisory regarding issues which might arise regarding the educational opportunities for children with AIDS.[7] The advisory notes that automatic exclusion of children with AIDS is legally inappropriate, but suggests that a case by case review would determine when exclusion would be in the child's best interests.

References

1. Telephone interview with Robert D. Gens, M.D., Director of Division of Communicable Disease Control and Surveillance, Department of Health (March, 1986).

2. Id.

3. Administrative Bulletin, No. 7137-85-2, Department of Public Welfare (January 14, 1986).

4. AIDS Policy and Law 8, March 12, 1986.

5. Id.

6. Advisory Memorandum on AIDS, Department of Corrections (October 8, 1985).

7. AIDS Advisory Memorandum, Commissioner for Basic Education, (October 22, 1985).

IX. Georgia

Statutes:
    Ga. Code Ann. Sec. 16-13-32--32.1 (Drug-related Objects)

    Ga. Code Ann. Sec. 19-3-40 (Premarital Syphilis Exam)

    Ga. Code Ann. Sec. 31-2-1 et seq. (Department of Human Resources)

    Ga. Code Ann. Sec. 31-12-1 et seq. (Control of Hazardous Conditions, Preventable Diseases, and Metabolic Disorders)

    Ga. Code Ann. Sec. 31-17-1 et seq. (Control of Venereal Disease)

Regulations:
    Ga. Admin. Comp. ch. 290-5-3 (Notifiable Diseases)

Introduction

Georgia's basic public health statutes--those relating to the control of communicable diseases and venereal disease--have not been comprehensively updated since they were enacted in 1964. Some provisions, such as those related to screening for genetic disorders, were added later as scientific knowledge increased. The disease control statutes were enacted in 1964, and have not been subsequently amended.

Separate chapters have been established under the public health law to address control of specific types of disease. For the purposes of this report, we will focus on those chapters which establish the

overall authority of the state department of human resources
("department"); prescribe measures for the prevention and control of
"hazardous conditions, preventable diseases, and metabolic disorders;"
and specify provisions relating to the control of venereal disease.

A. Public Health Statutes

1. Generally

The department is established to "safeguard and promote the health of the people [of Georgia] and is empowered to employ all legal means appropriate to that end." (S.31-2-1) It may provide research, conduct investigations, and disseminate information concerning reduction in the incidence and proper control of disease, disorders, and conditions. The department has the general authority to isolate and treat persons afflicted with a communicable disease who are unable or unwilling to observe the department's rules and regulations. It is authorized to adopt and promulgate rules and regulations to prevent, abate, and correct situations which would "militate against the health of the people [of Georgia]." (S. 31-2-4)

2. Reporting Requirements

The department is authorized by statute to declare certain diseases and injuries to be "diseases requiring notice," and to require reporting of these diseases to the county board of health and the department. (S. 31-12-2) The department shall require submission of all data it deems "necessary and appropriate" for the prevention of certain diseases and accidents.

The official list of notifiable diseases has been established by regulation. (R. 290-5-3) The list identifies thirty-three (33) notifiable diseases or syndromes, including AIDS, which must be reported. Reports must include the patient's name, address, age, race, sex, and disease, as well as an identification of the source of the report.

There are separate reporting requirements relating to venereal diseases, defined by statute to include syphilis, gonorrhea, and chancroid. (S. 31-17-1) Any physician or other person who diagnoses or treats a case of venereal disease, or any superintendent or manager of a hospital, dispensary, or charitable or penal institution where there is a case of venereal disease must report as directed by the department. (S. 31-17-2) The statutorily defined venereal diseases, along with chlamydial infections, herpes II, and non-specific urethritis are grouped together as sexually transmissible diseases on the official list of notifiable diseases. (R. 290-5-3)

Confidentiality

The reporting statute includes a confidentiality provision, declaring that all reports and data regarding notifiable diseases are deemed confidential, and shall not be open to public inspection. (S. 31-12-2) The department may release reports and data in statistical form, or for "valid research purpose."

3. Personal Control Measures

The department is empowered to employ all legal means to safeguard and promote health. One of the "legal means" available to the department by statute is the power to "isolate and treat persons afflicted with a communicable disease who are either unable or unwilling to observe the department's rules and regulations for the suppression of such disease and to establish, to that end, complete or modified quarantine, surveillance, or isolation of persons...exposed to a disease communicable to man." (S. 31-2-1)

Compulsory Examination and Treatment

The department, pursuant to its general statutory authority, may "[i]solate and treat persons afflicted with a communicable disease who are either unable or unwilling to observe the department's rules and regulations for the suppression of such disease..." (S. 31-2-1) There is, however, no explicit statutory authority to compel examination of persons suspected of having a communicable disease.

Both the department and the county boards of health may, when necessary to protect the public health, examine persons infected or suspected of being infected with syphilis, gonorrhea, or chancroid, and may require that persons with such diseases submit to treatment until cured. (S. 31-17-3)

Premarital Examinations

Section 19-3-40 of the Georgia Code requires all marriage license applicants to submit to a standard serologic test for syphilis; a marriage license may be issued following a positive test if both applicants are made aware that a syphilitic infection is present and the applicant with syphilis has been treated so that the disease is non-communicable. The statute also requires female applicants capable of pregnancy to undergo a standard serologic test for rubella immunity, and to receive counseling concerning the possibilities of birth defects associated with rubella during pregnancy. Finally, the statute requires that standard serologic testing for sickle cell anemia and appropriate counseling be made available to license applicants.

Isolation and Quarantine

Georgia statutory law permits the isolation of persons with a communicable disease, as well as the quarantine of carriers or suspected carriers. The department and all county boards of health may require the isolation or segregation of persons with communicable diseases or conditions "likely to endanger the health of others"; in addition, the department may require quarantine or surveillance of carriers and of persons exposed to, or suspected of being infected with, infectious disease, until they are found to be free of the infectious agent or disease in question. (S. 31-12-4) The statute does not specify which communicable diseases and conditions are considered "likely to endanger the health of others," nor does it define "infectious disease," "isolation," "segregation," "surveillance", or "quarantine."

There is also express statutory authority for isolation or quarantine of individuals with venereal disease. The department and the county boards of health may, when it is in their judgment necessary to protect the public health, isolate individuals infected with or reasonably suspected of being infected with syphilis, gonorrhea, or chancroid. (S. 31-17-3)

4. Penalties for Public Health Violations

The Georgia statutory provisions for the control of hazardous conditions, preventable diseases, and metabolic disorders do not establish specific penalties for violation of a statutory requirement or a rule, regulation, or order of the department or a county board of health.

Statutes for the control of venereal disease, however, provide that any person who violates a venereal disease control statute, or a rule or regulation promulgated pursuant to such a statute, is guilty of a misdemeanor. (S. 31-17-8) There is apparently no penalty for the violation of a departmental order.

5. Hypodermic Syringes and Needles

Under Georgia's controlled substances law, it is unlawful for any person or corporation other than a licensed pharmacist or a practitioner licensed to dispense legend drugs to sell or otherwise distribute a hypodermic syringe or needle designed or marketed primarily for human use. (S. 16-13-32) A first offense under this provision is a misdemeanor; the second offense is a misdemeanor of a high and aggravated nature, while a third or subsequent offense is a felony subject to imprisonment for one to five (1-5) years and a fine of not more than $5,000.

B. Public Health Law and AIDS

Designated as a "notifiable disease," cases of AIDS must be reported to health officials, along with the patient's name, address, age, race, and sex. Such reports are deemed confidential, and are not open to public inspection.

Since AIDS has not been defined as a venereal disease or sexually transmissible disease, individuals with AIDS or suspected of having the disease would be subject only to those control measures generally applicable to other non-venereal communicable diseases or conditions.[1] Imposition of compulsory examinations would not be authorized without statutory amendment, nor would premarital or prenatal screening. If AIDS is declared to be "likely to endanger the health of others," the department and county health may isolate or segregate patients, or require quarantine or surveillance of carriers and persons exposed to or suspected of being infected with the disease until they are free of the infectious agent. (S. 31-12-4) Arguably, quarantine should not be allowed based only upon HTLV-III antibody positivity, but could be imposed only if the virus is present, since it is the virus, not the antibody, which is the infectious agent.

There has been no AIDS-specific legislation enacted.

C. Proposed AIDS-Specific Legislation

Four pieces of AIDS-related legislation have been proposed before the state legislature:

(1) H.B. 1187, sponsored by representatives McKinney, Wall, Bannister and Bennett, would define AIDS as a venereal disease, making it subject to the more stringent control measures applicable to such diseases.

(2) H.B. 1189, by the same sponsors, would amend the laws for the control of hazardous conditions and preventable diseases to prohibit the operation of bathhouses in which homosexual activity is permitted.

Under the legislation, "homosexual activity" is defined as any sexual act involving the sex organs of a male and the mouth or anus of another male. The department and county boards of health would be authorized to enjoin the operation of bathhouses as public nuisances.

(3) H.B. 1190, also by the same sponsors, would require marriage license applicants to submit to an approved HTLV-III antibody test before obtaining a license. If the test is positive, a license would not be issued unless, in the opinion of a certifying physician, the applicant is not infected with the virus or, if infected, is not in a communicable stage.

(4) S. 387 would require notification to morticians of the existence of infectious disease.[1]

D. Guidelines Adopted

The Georgia Task Force on AIDS recommends that the children with AIDS/ARC or any indication of AIDS virus infection should be allowed to attend school in accordance with the guidelines established by the CDC and the American Academy of Pediatrics.[2] The Task Force endorses CDC recommendations regarding restricted environments for preschool children who lack control of their bodily secretions or who display potentially hazardous behavior, and recommendations for HTLV-III/LAV screening by adoption and foster care agencies. Finally, the Task Force recommends that mortuarial personnel follow CDC developed guidelines relating to AIDS.

References

1. AIDS Policy & Law, Vol. 1, No. 2 (Feb. 12, 1986) at 7.

2. Georgia Task Force on AIDS, Consensus Statements (November 20, 1985).

X. Colorado

Statutes: Colo. Rev. Stat. 14-2-6 (Premarital Examination)

Colo. Rev. Stat. 21-1-639-640 (Care of Infected Persons)

Colo. Rev. Stat. 25-1-645 (Prevention of Spread of Disease)

Colo. Rev. Stat. 25-1-647 (Notice by Householder)

Colo. Rev. Stat. 25-1-649 (Notice by Physician)

Colo. Rev. Stat. 25-1-650 (Investigation by Health Officer)

Colo. Rev. Stat. 25-4-401 et seq. (Venereal Diseases)

Regulations: Rules and Regulations Pertaining to Communicable Disease Control

Introduction

Colorado, like the majority of jurisdictions surveyed for this report, has not recently revised its basic disease control statutes. The statutes include provisions regarding the control of communicable diseases "declared to be dangerous to the public health," as well as provisions geared to specific dangerous diseases such as tuberculosis and venereal diseases (defined to include syphilis, gonorrhea, chancroid, granuloma inguinale, and lymphogranuloma venereum).

The existing statutes for local control of communicable diseases are derived from the Law of 1893, and retain some of the flavor of public health measures then current: there is still strong emphasis on diseases such as smallpox which posed a significant public health threat before the development of effective vaccines. Although the statutory provisions for the control of diseases dangerous to the public health are expressly applicable to venereal diseases, there are separate venereal disease control statutes derived from the Laws of 1919. These statutes authorize control measures, such as compulsory examinations, which are not explicitly authorized for non-venereal communicable diseases.

Colorado has not enacted any AIDS-specific legislation. The communicable disease rules and regulations have been amended to require the reporting of cases of AIDS, positive HTLV-III antibody tests, and positive HTLV-III/ARV/LAV viral cultures.

A. Public Health Powers

1. Generally

State supervision over the public health laws is exercised by the department of health ("department"). The department is authorized to promulgate rules and regulations necessary for the control of communicable diseases in general and venereal diseases in particular. By statute, the department is required to issue rules and regulations providing for the control of persons isolated or quarantined for venereal disease. (S. 25-4-406) These rules are binding on all county and municipal health officers.

Local health boards are required to "use all possible care to prevent the spreading of the infection" when there is smallpox or any other disease dangerous to the public health within their respective jurisdictions. (S. 25-1-645) It is the duty of the local health officer to, among other things, investigate possible cases of communicable disease and isolate individuals so long as there is a danger of their communicating the disease to others; notify schools concerning families in which contagious diseases are found; give public notice of infected places; and supervise funerals of persons dead from a communicable disease dangerous to the public health. (S. 25-1-650) The local health official is required to monitor outbreaks of dangerous disease and keep the board informed of such occurrences.

2. Reporting Requirements

The department has by regulation identified those diseases which are declared to be dangerous to the public health and which must be reported to appropriate health officials. (R.1) Reports must include the patient's name, age, sex, address, and the name and address of the responsible physician, along with additional information such as telephone number and place of employment as needed to locate the patient for follow-up.

Individual reporting responsibilities are set out by statute and regulation. Under the general communicable disease control statutes, a householder who knows that any member of his or her family has smallpox or any other disease dangerous to the public health must notify the local board of health; failure to do so is punishable by a fine of up to one hundred dollars ($100). (S. 25-1-647) A physician who knows that a person he or she has examined is infected with smallpox, cholera, diphtheria, scarlet fever, or any other disease dangerous to the public health must notify the local health board and the householder, hotel keeper, keeper of a boarding house, or tenant within whose rooms the infected individual is located. (S. 25-1-649) Failure by a physician to report is punishable by a fine of not less than five dollars ($5) nor more than one hundred dollars ($100).

The communicable disease regulations expand upon the individual reporting responsibilities established by statute, requiring that persons in charge of schools (including school nursing staff) and licensed day care centers. (R.2) In addition, laboratories are required to report cases of disease based upon a finding of certain "highly diagnostic results."

Separate reporting provisions applicable solely to venereal disease have also been enacted. Any physician, intern, or other person who diagnoses, prescribes for, or treats a case of venereal disease, and any superintendent or manager of an institution where there is a case of venereal disease, must report the case to health authorities (S. 25-4-402) The physician is not required to name the infected individual. If, however, the physician believes that the individual's condition, circumstances, or habits make him or her a menace to the health of any other person, the physician may report the name, and may also disclose the diagnosis to the spouse of the individual, the person engaged to marry the individual or the parents or guardian of an infected minor. Reporting or disclosure required or authorized under the statute does not constitute libel or slander, nor does it violate a right of privacy or privileged communication.

Confidentiality

There is no confidentiality statute applicable to communicable diseases generally. The communicable disease control regulations, however, provide that all records and reports submitted to the department in compliance with the regulations are deemed confidential medical information, "to be used by the Department as source material for problem analysis and necessary disease control efforts." (2.8) Individual identifiers must be deleted before information is released to the public. Consultation with the attending physician or medical facility is required before the department or local health officials may undertake follow-up efforts.

Colorado law recognizes specific circumstances where a patient's right to confidentiality is overcome by another individual's right to be informed of danger. A physician is required by statute to disclose the presence of an individual with any disease dangerous to the public health to persons at the premises where the infected individual is located. (S. 25-1-649) In the case of a venereal disease, a physician is authorized to disclose the diagnosis to the individual's spouse of fiance if the individual, in the physician's judgment, represents a menace due to his or her condition, circumstances, or habits. (S. 25-4-402).

3. Personal Control Measures

Compulsory Examination and Treatment

There is no statute which explicitly authorizes compulsory examination of individuals suspected of being infected with a non-venereal communicable disease. Such authority may be implied, however, by the local health officer's duty to investigate whenever he or she receives reliable notice or has good reason to believe that there is a case of smallpox, diphtheria, scarlet fever, or other communicable disease dangerous to the public health within the jurisdiction. (S. 25-1-650)

Compulsory examinations are expressly authorized under the venereal disease control statutes. Health officers may, if in their judgment it is necessary to protect the public health, examine individuals "reasonably suspected" of being infected with venereal disease, detaining the individual until the results are known. (S. 25-4-404) Venereal disease examinations are required for all individuals confined in any public hospital for the insane, institution for the mentally deficient, certain state schools for girls and boys, home for dependent children, reformatory or prison, or private or charitable institution where a person may be confined by court order. (S. 25-4-405)

Premarital Examination

The Colorado premarital examination requirement differs from that found in most of the other jurisdictions; syphilis testing is not required. Each female marriage license applicant under the age of forty-five must submit to an examination, including a standard serological test for rubella immunity and Rh type. (S. 14-2-106) The physician who oversees the testing must inform the woman of the results and their medical significance. The results of the serological test do not affect subsequent issuance of the marriage license.

Prenatal Screening

A physician or other person permitted by law to attend a pregnant woman must obtain a blood sample for syphilis testing. (S. 25-4-201) Every birth or still-birth certificate must indicate whether the test was made, but may not state the results. (S.25-4-203) It is a misdemeanor for a physician and surgeon or other person attending a pregnant woman during the period of gestation or at delivery to fail to obtain a sample for testing unless the pregnant woman refuses. (25-4-204)

Regulation of Foodhandlers

A person who is infected with a communicable disease which can be transmitted by foods, or who has a boil or an infected wound, may not work in a food service or milk producing establishment in any capacity in which there is a likelihood that he or she will contaminate the food or food contact surfaces with pathogenic organisms or transmit diseases to other persons. (R.5)

Placarding

A local health officer who "receives reliable notice or has good reason to believe that there is ... a case of smallpox, diphtheria, scarlet fever, or other communicable disease dangerous to the public health" shall give public notice by placarding the premises. (S. 25-1-650).

Isolation and Quarantine

Under the statutes providing for control of communicable disease, a local health officer who receives reliable notice or has good reason to believe that there is within his or her jurisdiction a case of smallpox, diphtheria, scarlet fever, or other communicable disease dangerous to the public health, shall order the "prompt and thorough isolation of those sick or infected with such disease so long as there is danger of their communicating the disease to other persons." (S. 25-1-650) The statute does not prescribe any procedural requirements for the imposition of isolation.

The local board of health is required to "make effectual provisions in the manner deemed best for the safety of the [local] inhabitants by removing [a] sick or infected person to a separate house, if it can be done without danger to his health...." (S. 25-1-639) If the person cannot be safely removed, he or she may be kept at home, and the other inhabitants of the neighborhood removed. (S. 25-1-640)

Detention of individuals who are not known to be sick or infected is expressly authorized as an incident to compulsory examinations for venereal disease. If it is necessary to protect the public health, the health official may detain the individual until the results are known, and may isolate or quarantine persons infected with venereal disease. (S. 25-4-404) Persons who have venereal disease at the expiration of a term of imprisonment or institutional confinement must be isolated and treated until cured; in lieu of isolating such individuals, the department may require that they report for treatment to a licensed physician.

4. Public Health Crimes

It is unlawful for any person who has "knowledge or reasonable grounds to suspect that he is infected with a venereal disease" to willfully expose or infect another, or to knowingly perform an act which exposes to or infects another person with venereal disease. (S. 25-4-401)

There is no comparable provision generally applicable to diseases categorized as dangerous to the public health.

5. Violations and Penalties

Any person, firm, or corporation violating the venereal disease control statutes, or failing or refusing to obey any lawful order issued pursuant to the statutes is guilty of a misdemeanor, punishable by a fine of not more than three hundred dollars ($300), and/or by imprisonment in the county jail.

B. Public Health Laws and AIDS

Public health officials at the department believe that the existing public health, communicable disease control, and sexually transmitted disease statutes provide adequate authority to "sanction virtually all actions which might be necessary" to protect the public health.[1] AIDS-specific legislation would only serve to draw unwarranted distinctions between AIDS and other life-threatening communicable diseases. Such special legislation might not enhance public health's ability to control disease but could heighten the hysteria and misunderstanding about the illness.

The department has taken specific regulatory action, declaring AIDS to be a disease dangerous to the public health. Cases are reportable based upon a physician's diagnosis, with or without confirmatory lab results; laboratories are required to report cases based on repeatedly positive ELISA tests (or a confirmatory Western Blot test), or on a positive HTLV-III/ARV/LAV viral culture. (R.3) Thus, based on laboratory evidence, an individual who is antibody or virus positive would be reportable as a case of AIDS.

An individual with AIDS would be subject to any personal control measures generally applicable to diseases declared dangerous to the public health. It does not appear that compulsory examination would be authorized, nor would it be appropriate necessarily to exclude individuals with AIDS from food handling occupations since the disease is not food borne. An individual with AIDS could be subject to isolation and treatment if, in the judgment of the local health officer, there is a danger that he or she may communicate the disease to others. (See S. 25-1-650) Since the disease is not spread by casual contact, isolation could not be based solely on a diagnosis. AIDS is not a highly infectious disease, and danger of communication would arise only if the individual acts in a way which would expose others to the disease, e.g., by engaging in unsafe sexual intercourse or sharing contaminated hypodermic needles. Thus isolation would have to be based upon a combination of the presence of the disease and unsafe conduct by the affected individual.

Although the department appears to rely partially on venereal disease statutes as a source of authority for the control of AIDS, our analysis indicates that, in their current form, venereal disease control measures would be inapplicable. Venereal disease is expressly defined by statute to include syphilis, gonorrhea, chancroid, granuloma inguinale, and lymphogranuloma venereum. (S. 25-4-401) Although AIDS has been defined as a dangerous disease, it has not been defined as a venereal disease. Therefore, the control measures authorized for venereal disease--compulsory examination of suspected individuals, isolation premised on presence of the disease rather than individual conduct--could not be applied in the AIDS context.

C. Proposed AIDS-Specific Legislation and Regulations

The department has proposed no AIDS-specific legislation and there are no proposed regulatory provisions pending. A protocol for contact tracing is currently under consideration.

A bill, H.R. 1290, requiring physicians to report cases of AIDS or the presence of the "viral infection which causes AIDS" and authorizing the quarantine of persons with AIDS was pulled by its sponsor after the House and Senate were unable to reach a compromise on amendments.[2]

The bill would have made such reports confidential, and subject to release only under prescribed circumstances.[3] Compulsory examination and detention would have been allowed if shown to be necessary to protect the public health. The measure had the support of the Colorado Department of Health.[2]

D. Guidelines Adopted

We received no guidelines from health officials in Colorado.

References

1. Letter from Fred Wolf, Director of the Colorado STD Control Program, to William Curran, dated January 28, 1986 (discussing statutes applicable to AIDS).

2. Lack of accord kills Colorado bill. AIDS Policy and Law 1986; 1(9):2 (May 21, 1986).

3. AIDS Policy and Law 1986; 1(3):8 (February 26, 1986).

XI. Connecticut

Statutes: Conn. Gen. Stat. Ann. 19a-5 [as amended by 1985 Conn. Pub. Acts 155] (Reporting).

Conn. Gen. Stat. Ann. 19a-25 (Confidentiality)

Conn. Gen. Stat. Ann. 19a-207 (Quarantine—Local Regulations)

Conn. Gen. Stat. Ann. 19a-215 (Reporting)

Conn. Gen. Stat. Ann. 19a-220 (Enforcement)

Conn. Gen. Stat. Ann. 19a-221 (Quarantine)

Conn. Gen. Stat. Ann. 19a-229 (Appeal of order)

Conn. Gen. Stat. Ann. 19a-230 (Penalties)

Conn. Gen. Stat. Ann. 46b-26 (Premarital screening)

Regulations: Conn. Agencies Reg. 19-13-A2 through 19-13-A15 (Public Health Code)

Introduction

Connecticut law establishes broad statutory authority to require communicable disease reporting, compulsory examination, and quarantine of infected individuals who present a danger to others. The statutory provisions are supplemented by detailed regulations promulgated by the department of health services ("department"). Connecticut has not enacted AIDS-specific legislation, although it has recently provided by statute for the reporting of laboratory findings, and has updated its authority to confine individuals infected with a communicable disease.

A. Public Health Powers

1. Generally

The commissioner of health services ("commissioner") "shall employ the most efficient and practical means for the prevention and suppression of disease, and shall administer the health laws and public health code." (S. 19a-5) The commissioner has overall responsibility for the operation of the department, and he or she has authority over local health directors. When provisions of the general statutes or regulations of the public health code are not being enforced effectively at the local level, the commissioner may take necessary actions to ensure appropriate enforcement.

2. Reporting Requirements

In Connecticut, the commissioner has the duty to "secure information and data concerning the prevention and control of epidemics and conditions affecting the public health," and to compile such information for dissemination throughout the state. (S. 19a-5) New statutory language, added to the section in May, 1985, requires the commissioner to annually issue a list of reportable diseases and reportable laboratory findings, and to disseminate the list along with reporting forms to each licensed physician and clinical laboratory in the state. The language was added to simplify the process of making a disease reportable, removing it from the more cumbersome process required to amend or revise a regulation. No annual list has been issued as yet, although a preliminary draft has been prepared for review.[1]

Regulations promulgated by the department set out a list of diseases deemed to be "reportable." (R. 19-13-A2) In addition, the department's regulations require that diseases which are not enumerated but which present "a special problem" are to be "reported and controlled in accordance with special instructions of the state department of health or...the local director of health." (R. 19-13-A7)

Section 19a-215 of the Connecticut General Laws requires every physician to file a written report of each case of cholera, yellow fever, typhus fever, leprosy, smallpox, diphtheria, typhoid fever, scarlet fever, syphilis, gonorrhea, chancroid, or "other communicable diseases occurring in his practice"; the statute does not define "communicable disease." Cases of syphilis, gonorrhea, and chancroid are reportable by name, age, address, and occupation; a physician who diagnoses a case of primary or secondary syphilis or acute gonorrhea must report to the local health director the name, address, sex, and disease of an individual suspected of being the source of the infection, if that information can be obtained from the patient.

More explicit reporting requirements are set out in the department's regulations. Every physician or professional attendant "having under his care or observation a person affected with or apparently affected with a reportable disease" must report to the local health director or authority the patient's full name, age, address, sex, and occupation, as well as the name and date of onset of the disease. (R. 19-13-A3) If the patient is hospitalized, the name of the hospital must also be reported. The local health director must report or ensure the reporting to the state health services department of each "case" of reportable disease, and must report the occurrence of specified diseases in food or beverage production or handling establishments. Any "carrier of the infectious agent of any communicable disease" must also be reported by name, age, sex, and occupation. (R. 19-13-A11)

Regulations specify other individuals, in addition to physicians, who are required to report diseases. They include:

(1) the person in charge of any hospital, dispensary, or other institution delivering medical care;

(2) the parent, guardian, or householder of a child affected or apparently affected with the disease;

(3) the householder, proprietor, or keeper of any hotel, boarding house, lodging house, or any premises used for lodging where a case of the disease occurs;

(4) the teacher, school nurse, or principal of any private, parochial, public, or church school attended by any person affected or apparently affected with disease;

(5) the person in charge of any camp;

(6) the master or any other person in charge of any vessel lying within the jurisdiction of the state;

(7) the owner or person in charge of any dairy farm or other establishment producing, handling, or processing milk, cream, frozen desserts, other foods and non-alcoholic beverages for sale or distribution; and

(8) the master or any other person in charge of any aircraft landing within the jurisdiction of the state. (R. 19-13-A5)

Contact Tracing

In instituting measures for the control of reportable diseases, the local health director shall make "such investigations as he may deem necessary and shall secure all data which may assist him in establishing adequate control measures." (R. 19-13-A8) This regulation would authorize contact tracing.

Confidentiality

There is explicit statutory protection of the confidentiality of records concerning morbidity and mortality. All information obtained by the department in connection with studies of morbidity and mortality, or collected by other persons, agencies or organizations for the purpose of reducing morbidity or mortality, is confidential and may be used solely for the purposes of medical or scientific research. (S.19a-25) The information is not admissible as evidence in any action of any kind in any court or before any other tribunal, board, agency, or person, and it may not be disclosed in any way by the department or by any other person except as necessary for research purposes. The commissioner is directed to adopt regulations to ensure confidentiality of disclosures.

The communicable disease reporting statute explicitly recognizes the confidentiality of reports of cases of spyhilis, gonorrhea, and chancroid. (S.19a-215) Reports of cases are confidential and not open to public inspection; information obtained from a case about the source of the infection is also deemed to be strictly confidential, and the person's identity may not be divulged except as necessary or control of syphilis, gonorrhea, or chancroid.

3. Personal Control Measures

Compulsory Examination

When the control or release of a case, contact, or carrier of a reportable disease is dependent on laboratory findings, the local health director shall secure cultures or specimens for examination. (R. 19-13-A8) If there are reasonable grounds to believe that a person has been exposed to a communicable disease, the local director "may make such examinations... as he deems necessary and proper for the protection of the public health and the prevention of the spread of disease." (R. 19-13-A10) Conviction for an offense involving "sexual promiscuity or illicit sex relations" constitutes reasonable grounds for examination under the regulation. A routine medical examination, including tests for syphilis or gonorrhea, is required of every prisoner whose conviction involves sexual promiscuity or illicit sex relations.

Premarital Screening

Connecticut requires each marriage license applicant to submit to a standard laboratory blood test for syphilis; if the test is positive, no license may be issued without a physician's statement that the applicant is not infected with syphilis or is not in a communicable stage. (S. 46b-26) The statute also requires a female applicant who is less than fifty years of age and is capable of pregnancy to submit to a standard laboratory test for rubella immunity. She must be informed of the results of the test and the consequences of a lack of immunity, but is not required to receive a rubella immunization prior to issuance of a license.

Observation

Carriers of the infectious agent of a "communicable disease," whether transient, convalescent, or chronic, are to be maintained under observation "until repeated laboratory examinations of appropriate specimens show the absence of the infectious agent." (R. 19-13-A11) The regulation does not define what "observation" may entail, nor does it define communicable disease.

Regulation of School Attendance

In the event of a "communicable disease" outbreak in any public, private, parochial, or church school, the local health director is required to control the outbreak by individual examination of pupils, teachers, and other persons associated with the outbreak, and to "employ such other means as are necessary to determine the source of the infection or to provide for the segregation of infected persons." (R. 19-13-A8) A child who has been excluded from school as a case, contact, or carrier of a communicable disease may be permitted to re-enter school when, in the opinion of the local director, he or she is no longer infectious.

Quarantine and Confinement

Local health officials are required to enforce or assist in enforcing the public health code and any regulations adopted by the commissioner. (S. 19a-207) Local jurisdictions may adopt sanitary rules and regulations consistent with the state public health code. In any emergency when local health is menaced, or when local health officials fail to comply with the department's recommendations, the department may enforce quarantine regulations necessary to protect the public health.

The Connecticut legislature in 1985 amended the state's public health law relating to quarantine. Under the revised law, a local health director may order the confinement of an individual if he or she has reasonable grounds to believe that the individual is infected with a "communicable" disease and is unable or unwilling to act in a manner so as not to expose other persons to the danger of infection.

A "communicable" disease is defined under the statute as a disease or condition, the infectious agent of which may pass or be carried directly or indirectly, from the body of one person or animal to the body of another person or animal.

To quarantine an individual, the director must first determine that he or she poses a "substantial threat" to the public health and that the action is necessary to protect or preserve the public health. (S.19a-221) The order of confinement must be in writing and specify:

(1) the name of the individual to be confined;

(2) why the director believes that the individual is infected with a communicable disease, poses a substantial public health threat, and needs to be confined;

(3) the effective period of the order, not to exceed fifteen (15) days;

(4) the place of confinement; and

(5) other terms or conditions as necessary.

In addition, the order must inform the individual that he or she has a right to a hearing and, if a hearing is requested, the right to be represented by counsel. Counsel will be provided at state expense if the individual cannot afford to pay for counsel.

A confined individual has a right to a court hearing within seventy-two (72) hours after filing a written request. A three judge panel will conduct the hearing to determine whether (1) the individual is infected with a communicable disease; (2) the individual poses a substantial threat to the public health; and (3) the confinement of the individual is necessary and represents the least restrictive alternative available. The director must demonstrate the basis for the confinement by clear and convincing evidence. The court may order continued confinement until the individual no longer poses a public health threat, or it may release the respondent subject to terms and conditions deemed appropriate to protect the public health.

An individual confined under the statute may at any time petition for termination or modification of the order. The court on its own motion must hold annual hearings to determine whether the conditions justifying confinement or restrictions continue to exist, and may modify its order if a different remedy becomes appropriate.

4. Violations

Any person who violates any legal order of a director of health or board of health, for which no other penalty is provided, will be fined not more than $100 or imprisoned for not more than three months or both. (S.19a-230)

Any person who violates any statutory reporting provision, including the confidentiality provisions, shall be fined not more than $25. (S.19a-215)

B. Public Health Laws and AIDS

The department is 1983 issued Circular Letter #18-26[2] which ordered mandatory reporting of AIDS as a disease which presents a "special problem." For reporting purposes, the department has adopted the CDC Surveillance definition. Cases, suspected cases, and carriers are reportable.

As a reportable disease, AIDS will be subject to control on the same basis as any other reportable disease. Several public health statutes are potentially applicable to the control of AIDS, including the reporting statutes (S. 19a-5 and 19a-215), and the statute authorizing local health authorities to adopt quarantine regulations. (S. 19a-207)[3] In addition, it would appear that S. 19a-221, providing for the quarantine of certain persons, would also be applicable in the AIDS context. Provisions authorizing observation or exclusion from school would not be applicable since they relate specifically to "communicable" rather than "reportable" diseases, and AIDS has not been defined as communicable.

Regulations authorizing compulsory examination and lab testing to determine the presence of reportable disease would also be applicable to AIDS. (R. 19-13-A8)

C. Proposed Legislation and Regulations

At the present time, no additional AIDS-specific statutes, regulations, or guidelines are being considered or have been proposed.[4]

D. Guidelines Adopted

The department has adopted no CDC guidelines other than the surveillance definition for reporting purposes.[5] The department of education has issued guidelines regarding the education of children with AIDS or associated conditions.

References

1. Telephone interview with Peter D. Galbraith, Chief of the Connecticut Bureau of Health Promotion (Feb. 13, 1986).

2. Connecticut Department of Health Services, Circular Letter #18-26 (dated October 14, 1983) (Mandatory Reporting of Acquired Immune Deficiency Syndrome (AIDS)).

3. Letter from Peter D. Galbraith, Chief of the Connecticut Bureau of Health Promotion, to William Curran and Larry O. Gostin (dated January 15, 1986) (regarding state legislation, regulations, guidelines, and court decisions related to AIDS).

4. Id.

5. Id.

XII. Federal Law

Statutes:
    42 U.S.CA. 247c (Grants:AIDS)

    42 U.S.CA. 247d (Public Health Emergency)

    42 U.S.C.A. 249 (Medical Care of Quarantined and Detained Persons)

    42 U.S.C.A. 252 (Medical Examination of Aliens)

    42 U.S.C.A. 264 (Control of Communicable Diseases)

    42 U.S.C.A. 271 (Penalties)

Regulations:
    21 CFR 1240.3 et seq. (Control of Communicable Disease-FDA)

    42 CFR 34.1 et seq. (Medical Examination of Aliens)

    42 CFR 71.1 et seq. (Foreign Quarantine-CDC)

Introduction

Federal health provisions for the control of communicable diseases are geared toward preventing the introduction of diseases from foreign countries into the United States, and limiting the interstate spread of disease by regulating travel and conditions of commerce. The federal scope is more limited than that of the individual states; rather than exercising broad powers over communicable disease in general, federal law focuses on a narrower range of diseases. More general communicable disease reporting, surveillance, prevention, and control requirements were left to the states, to be addressed through the exercise of their police powers.

The basic declaration of the federal government's authority and obligation to act to prevent communicable diseases is found in the Public Health Services Act ("PHS Act"), which was enacted in 1944. The PHS Act contains a general statement establishing the scope of federal authority, which is to be implemented by appropriate regulations. Additional authority for disease control measures is found in the immigration laws, which establish the government's power to exclude aliens who have certain communicable diseases.

The federal government has enacted legislation pertaining to grants for AIDS-related projects. In addition, numerous guidelines have been issued by the Centers for Disease Control (CDC).

A. Public Health Powers

1. Generally

Under the Public Health Service Act, the department may make and enforce such regulations as are necessary to prevent the introduction, transmission, or spread of communicable diseases from foreign countries into the states or possessions, or from one state or possession into any other. (S.264) To implement this authority, the CDC has issued regulations governing foreign quarantine (R. 71.1 et seq.), and the Food and Drug Administration (FDA) has promulgated regulations governing the interstate control of communicable diseases. (R. 1240.3 et seq.)

The federal government also has express authority pursuant to immigration laws to investigate the health status of aliens seeking to enter the United States. Aliens afflicted with any dangerous contagious disease are excluded from admission to the United States.[1]

The department is required by statute to provide physical and mental examinations of aliens, and has issued regulations governing such examinations. (S. 252; R. 34.1 et seq.)

Federal provisions for the control of communicable disease do not preempt state or local health laws. Federal officers are to observe and aid in the execution of quarantines and other restraints established by state health laws. (S.97) If local efforts are insufficient to control the interstate spread of communicable disease, however, the commissioner of food and drugs may "take such measures as he deems reasonably necessary, including inspection, fumigation, disinfection, sanitation, pest extermination, and destruction of animals or articles believed to be sources of infection." (R. 1240.30)

2. Reporting Requirements

The CDC regulations require reports of death or illness which occur prior to arrival or while a carrier is in port. Section 71.21 requires the master of a ship and the commander of an aircraft to report any death or ill person on board within a prescribed time before arrival. An ill person is defined as an individual who has a temperature of 100° F. or greater, accompanied by a rash, jaundice, or glandular swelling, or which has persisted for more than 48 hours; or who has diarrhea. (R. 71.1) The master of a ship with more than thirteen passengers must also report the number of cases of diarrhea which occurred during the cruise (R. 71.21), and the master of any carrier must immediately report any death or ill person on board during a stay in port. (R. 71.35)

The FDA regulations require the master of any vessel or the person in charge of any conveyance engaged in interstate traffic on which a suspected case of communicable disease develops to notify the local health authority at the next port, station or stop. (R. 1240.45)

3. Personal Control Measures

Compulsory Examination

The Surgeon General may provide for the apprehension and examination of certain individuals entering the United States or traveling in interstate travel who are believed to be infected with a communicable disease. (S. 264) A carrier and its passengers will not be inspected unless the director determines that failure to inspect will present a threat of the introduction of communicable diseases as may exist when the carrier has an ill person on board. (R. 71.31) The regulations do not specify what a medical examination would entail.

There is separate authority under the immigration laws for compulsory medical examination of aliens. For the purposes of determining whether aliens belong to any excluded class because of a specified disease or mental or physical defects or disabilities, they may be detained for observation and examination. (S. 1222)

An alien may be excluded because he or she is afflicted with any "dangerous communicable disease," as defined by regulation, or has physical defect, disease, or disability that a consular or immigration officer determines may affect the ability of the alien to earn a living, unless the alien affirmatively establishes that he or she will not have to earn a living. (S. 1182)

The department is required to provide for making the required physical and mental examination. (S. 252) Regulations governing the medical examination of aliens define "dangerous contagious diseases" as chancroid, gonorrhea, granuloma venereum, infectious syphilis, and active tuberculosis. (R. 34.2) The regulations specify the scope of examinations, and require that certificates be issued following the examination stating whether the alien has a dangerous contagious disease; a physical defect, disease, or disability which amounts to a "substantial departure from normal physical well-being"; or any other defect, disease, or disability. (R. 34.7 - 34.10).

Travel Restrictions

The FDA regulations authorize imposition of travel restrictions on individuals with communicable diseases. An individual with any communicable disease in a communicable period is prohibited from interstate travel without a health permit if such a permit is required under the law of the place of destination. (R. 1240.40) An individual who has or has been exposed to cholera, plague, smallpox, typhus, or yellow fever may not engage in interstate travel without a permit issued by the Surgeon General. (R. 1240.50)

Isolation, Detention, and Surveillance

The PHS Act prohibits apprehension, detention, or conditional release of individuals "except for the purpose of preventing the introduction, transmission, or spread of such communicable diseases as may be specified from time to time in Executive Orders of the

President upon recommendation of the National Advisory Health Council and the Surgeon General." (S. 264) Executive Order No. 12452 lists the following as quarantinable communicable diseases: cholera or suspected cholera, diphtheria, infectious tuberculosis, plague, suspected smallpox, yellow fever, and suspected viral hemorrhagic fevers (Lassa, Marburg, Ebola, Congo-Crimean, and others not yet isolated or named).[1]

In the process of amending the list of diseases to be included in the Executive Order, the Council, in 1982, recommended the deletion of a number of diseases because they no longer constituted serious enough threats to the public health to warrant the use of detention and isolation measures as authorized by the Public Health Service Act; these diseases included anthrax, chancroid, chicken pox, dengue, favus, gonorrhea, granuloma inguinale, hemolytic streptococcal infections, infectious hepatitis, leprosy, lymphogranuloma venereum, meningococcal meningitis, poliomyelitis, psittacosis, relapsing fever, ringworm of the scalp, syphilis, trachoma, typhoid fever, and typhus.[2] The Council recommended the addition of suspected viral hemorrhagic fevers, which are highly communicable and fatal diseases, for which there is no specific treatment.[3]

The CDC foreign quarantine regulations, revised in 1985, define the personal control measures applicable at the federal level:

(1) "Detention" is the temporary holding of an individual for a time period determined by the CDC director;

(2) "Isolation" is the separation of an individual or group from other individuals, other than the health staff on duty, to prevent the spread of infection; and

(3) "Surveillance" is the temporary supervision of a person who has or may have been exposed to a communicable disease. (R. 71.1)

Under these regulations, an arriving person may be detained, isolated, or placed under surveillance by the director if there is reason to believe that the individual is infected with or has been exposed to one of the quarantinable communicable diseases. (R. 71.32) Where surveillance is authorized, the director may require isolation if he or she considers the risk of transmission of infection to be exceptionally serious. (R. 71.33) An individual who has been ordered isolated may be held in any facility suitable for isolation and treatment.

The FDA regulations governing interstate control of communicable diseases do not include isolation, detention, or surveillance provisions. Originally promulgated in 1956, the regulations specify only that they are inapplicable to the apprehension, detention, or conditional release of individuals except for the purpose of preventing the introduction, transmission, or spread of quarantinable communicable diseases. (R. 1240.54)[4]

The immigration laws authorize detention of aliens for the purpose of determining whether they fall within an excludable class. (S. 1223) Aliens arriving at a port of the United States are also subject to the isolation, detention, and surveillance measures applicable under the CDC's foreign quarantine regulations. (R. 34.12)

4. Penalties

Any person who violates the foreign quarantine regulations, or who disregards quarantine rules or regulations is subject to a fine of not more than one thousand dollars ($1,000), and/or by imprisonment for not more than one year. (S. 271; R. 71.2)

B. Public Health Laws and AIDS

Federal law explicitly authorizes the Secretary of Health and Human Services, acting through the director of the CDC, to make grants to public and nonprofit private entities for information and education programs, and for the diagnosis, prevention, and control of AIDS. (S. 42, Section 247c(d)) Information gathered in connection with the examination, care, or treatment of an individual by a program funded under this section shall not be disclosed without the individual's consent, except as necessary to provide services to him or her or as may be required by state or local law. (S. 42, Section 247c(e)(5)) Information which does not identify individuals may be released in summary, statistical, or other form, or for clinical or research purposes.

Additional federal law authorizes the Secretary to take "appropriate action" to respond to a "public health emergency," including making grants and entering into contracts and investigating the cause, treatment, or prevention of a disease or disorder that presents a public health emergency. (S.42, section 247d) The law requires that the Secretary, before making the determination, consult with the director of the National Institutes of Health, the Administrator of the Alacohol, Drug Abuse, and Mental Health Administration, the Commissioner of the FDA, or the Director of the CDC.

Personal control measures authorized under the current CDC regulations—isolation, detention, and surveillance—are not applicable to AIDS. The authority to impose such measures is limited to the communicable diseases specified by Executive Order No. 12452 and section 71.32 of the regulations. (S. 264) AIDS was not included in the list of covered diseases when it was revised in 1983, and thus is not subject to these control measures. Similarly, the FDA regulations would not authorize isolation, detention, or surveillance of individuals who have or are suspected of having AIDS.

Other restrictions, however, would apply in the AIDS context. AIDS is a communicable disease as defined by the regulations, and so would be subject to travel restrictions which apply under section 1240.40. A person with AIDS in the communicable period would be prohibited from traveling from one state or possession to another without a permit from the health officer of the state, locality, or possession of destination, if such a permit is the required law of the place of destination.

Finally, the personal control measures applicable under the immigration laws and implementing regulations—detention and exclusion—may be applicable to AIDS. Detention and exclusion are allowed to determine if an alien has one of the excludable dangerous contagious diseases identified in section 34.2 of the regulations governing medical examination of aliens. (S. 1182) AIDS has not been included on the list. However, exclusion is also allowed if, in the opinion of the consular officer at the time of application for a VISA, or in the opinion of the Attorney General at the time of application for admission, the alien has a physical defect, disease or condition which may affect the alien's ability to earn a living. AIDS may arguably fall within that category. Automatic exclusion would not be warranted for individuals who may have AIDS-associated illnesses (but not full-blown AIDS) or who are HTLV-III/LAV antibody positive; there is no reasonable basis at this point for determining that these conditions would hinder the individual's ability to earn a living.

The Justice Department has issued a 49-page legal opinion which concluded that the Rehabilitation Act of 1973 does not prohibit an employer from firing an individual who has AIDS or shows signs of infection if the dismissal is based upon fear, real or perceived, that the individual will spread the disease.[5] The opinion declares that Section 504 of the Act, which prohibits discrimination on the basis of handicap in any program or activity that receives federal funds, does not reach decisions based upon a fear of contagion.

C. Proposed Legislation and Regulations

Representative William E. Dannemeyer (R. California) has introduced five bills "aimed at reducing the spread of AIDS."

(1) H.R. 3646 would deny federal funds to any hospital or other health care facility that denies a physician, nurse, or other health care delivery personnel the opportunity to wear protective garments while dealing with patients with AIDS.

(2) H.R. 3647 would deny federal funds to any hospital or other health care facility which knowingly permits a physician, dentist, nurse, or other health care delivery personnel who has AIDS to practice in the hospital or facility.

(3) H.R. 3648 would prohibit any city, town, or other political jurisdiction from receiving federal revenue sharing funds if it permits the operation of any public bath which is owned or operated by an individual who knows or has reason to know that the bath is hazardous to the public health, or who knows or has reason to know it is used for sexual relations between males.

(4) H.R. 3649 would make it a crime for a person to intentionally donate blood if he knows that he has AIDS; has had sexual relations with a male since 1977; is an IV drug user; or has received a blood transfusion within the past year. A violator would be subject to imprisonment of not more than 10 years.

(5) H. Con. Res. 224 declares the sense of Congress that public elementary and secondary schools should not permit students with AIDS or ARC to attend classes, and that such schools should make alternative arrangements for such students to receive education.

D. Guidelines

The CDC has issued the following guidelines and recommendations:

(1) AIDS: Precautions for clinical and laboratory staffs (1982);

(2) AIDS: Precautions for health care workers and allied professionals (1983);

(3) Recommendations for presenting transmission of infection with human T-lymphotropic virus type-III/lymphadenopathy-associated virus in the workplace (1985);

(4) Education and foster care of children infected with human T-lymphotropic virus type III/lymphadenopathy-associated virus (1985);

(5) Recommendations for assisting in the prevention of perinatal transmission of human T-lymphotropic virus type III/ lymphadenopathy-associated virus and acquired immunodeficiency syndrome (1985);

(6) Recommendations for preventing possible transmission of human T-lymphotropic type III/lymphadenopathy-associated virus from tears; and

(7) Provisional public health service interagency recommendations for screening donated blood and plasma for antibody to the virus causing acquired immunodeficiency syndrome (1985).

References

1. Executive Order No. 12452, Dec. 22, 1983. (48 F.R. 56927)

2. 48 F.R. 36144 (Aug. 9, 1983).

3. Id.

4. The FDA regulations contain the list of quarantinable communicable diseases as it existed prior to the revision by Executive Order No. 12452.

5. U.S. finds grounds for firing AIDS carriers. Boston Globe at 1 (June 24, 1986).

XIII. Summary Findings Pertaining to AIDS

Reporting: AIDS

All of the states reviewed in this chapter require the reporting of cases and suspected cases of AIDS; confirmed cases meeting the surveillance definition are reportable to the CDC.

Seven of the states have amended their regulations to make AIDS reportable (Colorado, Georgia, Illinois, Massachusetts, New Jersey, New York, and Texas). In the remaining four states, AIDS has been declared reportable by notice issued under general provisions for the reporting of "unusual diseases" (California and Pennsylvania), or as a "special problem" (Connecticut), or as a reportable disease dangerous to the public (Florida).

None of the states has defined AIDS--by statute or regulation--as a venereal or sexually transmitted disease.

Reporting: HTLV-III/LAV Tests

Only Colorado explicitly requires the reporting of positive HTLV-III/LAV antibody tests which are repeatedly reactive or Western Blot confirmed.

New Jersey law requires reporting of laboratory findings which indicate or suggest the existence of a "reportable disease;" AIDS falls within this category.

Confidentiality: AIDS

Eight states have general disease reporting confidentiality statutes or regulations which apply to AIDS reports and records (California, Colorado, Connecticut, Georgia, Illinois, New York, Pennsylvania, and Texas).

Two states have confidentiality statutes applicable only to venereal diseases (Florida and New Jersey). Massachusetts has no specific public health confidentiality statute.

Confidentiality: HTLV-III/LAV Antibody Testing

Two states explicitly prohibit by statute unauthorized disclosure of HTLV-III/LAV antibody test results (California and Florida).

Illinois regulations provide for confidential disclosure of test results, and Massachusetts regulations require that laboratories performing the test establish written procedures to assure confidentiality.

There are no test-related provisions in the remaining jurisdictions.

Compulsory Examination

None of the states explicitly authorizes compulsory examination to diagnose or confirm a diagnosis of AIDS.

Florida authorizes county health officers to require an examination if notified of a "disease condition" where the nature of the disease and the circumstances warrant.

Three states by statute authorize compulsory examinations to diagnose "communicable diseases;" AIDS has not been specifically defined as a communicable disease in any of these states, however. (Connecticut, New Jersey, and Pennsylvania).

Screening: Blood

Three of the jurisdictions require by statute or regulation that blood donations be screened for HTLV-III/LAV antibodies (California, Illinois, and New York).

Screening: HTLV-III/LAV Antibody Testing

None of the jurisdictions reviewed has established mandatory testing requirements either by statute or regulation.

Four states have explicitly provided for the establishment of alternative test sites (California, Florida, Illinois, and New York).

Screening: Premarital or Prenatal

None of the jurisdictions currently requires either premarital or prenatal screening for HTLV-III/LAV antibodies.

Exclusion of Foodhandlers

None of the state has enacted AIDS-specific restrictions applicable to foodhandlers.

Exclusion from School

None of the jurisdictions requires automatic exclusion of school age children who have AIDS or HTLV-III/LAV infection.

Guidelines adopted in five states recommend that any exclusion be based on a case by case review to determine the existence of special circumstances (e.g. biting behavior) which could increase the likelihood of disease transmission (New Jersey, Connecticut, New York, Pennsylvania, Texas).

Quarantine and Isolation

None of the jurisdictions has explicitly authorized the application of quarantine or isolation measures to individuals with AIDS, suspected carriers, or their contacts.

Connecticut law would allow quarantine of an individual with AIDS who was proven to be unable or unwilling to refrain from conduct which threatened the health of others. In Colorado, where AIDS has been declared a disease dangerous to the public health, local health officers may isolate an individual with a communicable disease dangerous to the public health for so long as there is a danger of communicating the disease to others.

In six jurisdictions which generally authorize isolation or quarantine to control communicable diseases, AIDS has not been explicitly defined as a communicable disease, and so is not subject to these provisions (California, Georgia, New Jersey, New York, New York City, and Pennsylvania).

Two jurisdictions which specify by regulation the particular control measures applicable to reportable or other diseases have not specified isolation or quarantine measures applicable to AIDS patients or contacts (Florida and Massachusetts).

Two jurisdictions authorize quarantine only for specifically designated diseases, and have not included AIDS on the applicable list (Texas and the federal government).

Public Health Crimes

No AIDS-specific criminal sanctions have been enacted in any of the jurisdictions surveyed.

In Texas, knowingly exposing others to a communicable disease is a crime; AIDS is defined as a communicable disease in that state.

Nine of the jurisdictions have no criminal sanctions expressly applicable to an individual with comunicable disease (other than venereal disease) who knowingly exposes another to infection (Colorado, Connecticut, Florida, Georgia, Massachusetts, New York, New York City, Pennsylvania, and the Federal Government).

CHAPTER 2

Proposed Legislation

Of the jurisdictions responding to our survey, excluding the jurisdictions reviewed in Chapter 1, AIDS-related legislation has been proposed in fourteen states and in the District of Columbia. To provide an overview, Chapter 2 will present a brief state-by-state description of the legislative proposals we have notice of.

Alabama

(1) H. 21 would require all marriage license applicants to submit to a physical examination and an approved laboratory test for AIDS, and to file a physician's certificate that they are not infected with AIDS as a prerequisite to obtaining a license. A probate court judge could waive the requirement for emergency causes as defined by the state board of health.

Misrepresentation of any facts, or issuance of a license without a certificate, or other noncompliance with the requirements is a misdemeanor, subject to a fine and/or imprisonment.

(2) H. 25 would require the quarantining of any inmate in a county jail or state penitentiary who is diagnosed as an AIDS virus carrier.

Alaska

No proposed legislation received.

Arizona

Proposed legislation, not yet filed, would prohibit discrimination based on AIDS in employment; rental housing; the use of business establishments, including health care services; access to state facilities and services; and access to educational institutions. A person who violates the provisions is liable for actual damages, costs, reasonable attorney fees, and at the court's discretion, punitive damages.

Arkansas

No proposed legislation received.

Delaware

H.B. 395 clarifies the power of the Department of Correction to review medical histories, complete medical histories, complete medical examinations, perform appropriate laboratory tests, and treat persons committed to its care, to prevent the spread of infectious diseases among prisoners and staff.

H.B. 434 would reestablish serological testing requirements in Delaware, requiring each marriage license applicant to submit to serological testing for antibodies or other evidence of AIDS, and to certify that he or she is not infected with AIDS. Certificates, laboratory reports, applications, and related information would be confidential, and could not be disclosed to any person other than the appropriate physician and the state board of health.

Misrepresentation, wrongful issuance of a license, and other noncompliance is subject to a fine and/or imprisonment.

H.B. 435 would require the reporting of AIDS by name, address (including city and county), age, sex, name and address of responsible physician, and other information as necessary to identify the patient. Cases are reportable based on a physician's diagnosis, whether or not supporting laboratory data is available. A case is also deemed reportable by a laboratory if there is a positive HTLV-III/LAV/ARV antibody test, or a positive viral culture.

All records and reports are confidential medical information to be used by the department as source material for problem analysis and necessary disease control efforts; individual identifiers must be removed.

H.B. 485 would make it a felony to engage in prostitution if the individual is infected with HTLV-III/LAV.

H.B. 485 would authorize HTLV-III/LAV antibody testing of any individual arrested for prostitution.

S.B. 322 would amend the Uniform Anatomical Gift Act to authorize physicians, surgeons, funeral directors, or eye bank technicians who are authorized to remove donated parts to draw blood samples in order to screen tissue for medical purposes.

District of Columbia

The District of Columbia Council unanimously passed legislation (6-343) which prohibits insurers from denying coverage or altering benefits because an individual has refused to be tested or has received a positive test result for the probable causative agent for AIDS. The bill prohibits companies from basing underwriting decisions on age, marital status, area of residence, occupation, sex, or sexual orientation, and establishes a 5-year prohibition on insurers' use of any test to discover HTLV-III/LAV exposure in rate setting or benefit decisions. The bill awaits signature of the major and subsequent consideration by Congress.

Hawaii

No proposed legislation received.

Idaho

The state department of health and welfare is proposing a statutory amendment to designate AIDS as a venereal disease; no legislation has been filed at this time.

Indiana

H.B. 1059 would establish the AIDS prevention and treatment study commission to (a) propose legislation to prevent the spread of AIDS; (b) study and make recommendations concerning the incidence, prevalence, and spread of AIDS, ARC, and HTLV-III infection; (c) study and make recommendations concerning the availability and costs of research and services for the prevention and treatment of AIDS, ARC, and HTLV-III infection; and annually monitor and report on the progress made in preventing the spread of HTLV-III infection.

Iowa
No proposed legislation received.

Kansas
No proposed legislation received.

Kentucky
Proposed legislation, not yet filed, would define AIDS as a sexually transmitted disease, and declare all information, records, and reports concerning persons infected with or suspected of being infected with or tested for or identified in an epidemiological investigation for STDs to be strictly confidential. Access would be limited to personnel of local health departments and the Cabinet for Human Resources. Records would not be subject to disclosure by subpoena or subpoena ducestecum. Violations would be subject to a fine of $50 to $100.

Louisiana
The State AIDS Task Force has forwarded a package of proposals to the State Health Officer. The first proposal is for anti-discrimination legislation and then a system of contact tracing. If money is available, mandatory reporting of positive serologic tests will be put into effect. The State Public Health Department is recommending against screening and quarantine.

S.B. 661, as introduced in May, 1986, would allow the head of the state health department to obtain an arrest warrant for a person who has a contagious disease. There is no provision for a hearing.

H.B. 1708 would create an AIDS trust fund, and would provide a tax writeoff for individuals contributing to the fund.

Maine

S.P. 818 would prohibit discrimination against any individual because the individual or a family or household member has AIDS, ARC or other medical condition resulting from AIDS or ARC viral positivity or seropositivity. It is applicable to employment, real estate sales and rentals, availability of goods and services from any business establishment, and the use of state or municipal services or facilities. The bill would also prohibit any person from requiring another to be tested for a condition covered by the legislation.

A person violating the provisions is liable for actual damages and a civil penalty equal to $1,000 or three times the amount of actual damages, whichever is greater; cost; attorneys fees; and equitable relief.

S.P. 818 would also establish the "Committee to Advise the Department of Human Services on AIDS."

It would limit disclosure of test results to the subject, designated health providers, persons authorized by the subject, health care providers who process donated human body parts, and research facilities. No insurer may request an individual's test history, or condition coverage or rates on testing. A violator is liable to the subject for actual damages and costs, plus a civil penalty of up to $1,000 for a negligent violation or $5,000 for an intentional violation.

S.P. 825 would define AIDS and related conditions as a dangerous communicable disease. It directs the department of human services to promulgate rules for the identification of occupations and employment situations with significant opportunity for exposure to blood and other body fluid or waste; procedures for the identification of persons with AIDS or ARC; and procedures for notification and precautionary measures concerning AIDS. The bill would require notice to any person disposing of the body of an individual who was diagnosed as having AIDS or ARC.

<u>Maryland</u>

Twenty to thirty AIDS-related bills have been filed in the current legislative session ranging from reporting of seropositive lists to workman's compensation for fire fighters who acquire AIDS in the course of their work. The Governor's Task Force on AIDS introduced only one piece of legislation which proposes to strengthen the confidentiality provisions of the Maryland law. The bill would make medical records available only upon a court order and then the record would be sealed by the court.

The Task Force has also drafted an anti-discrimination statement which is currently being reviewed by the Governor.

Michigan

(1) H.B. 5247 would require the department of corrections to test prisoners being incarcerated prior to being placed in any state correctional facility and to isolate prisoners diagnosed as having AIDS.

(2) H.B. 5272 would allow insurance companies to ask health or life insurance applicants AIDS-related questions and/or to require AIDS tests of applicants.

(3) H.B. 5276 would require all individuals who wish to be married to be tested for AIDS prior to issuance of a marriage certificate.

(4) H.B. 5279 would require individuals, either male or female, who are arrested for prostitution or solicitation to be tested for AIDS. If the person tests positive and is diagnosed as having AIDS, this information should be provided to the judge who sets the accused's conditions of release pending trial.

(5) H.B. 5281 would require the public health department to interview all persons diagnosed as having AIDS to determine who their sexual contacts have been. The department is further required to

contact these individuals, counsel them concerning their possible exposure to AIDS, and provide them with information on AIDS testing and interpretation of test results.

(6) H.C.R. 458 requests the governor to create a council to ascertain the facts about AIDS, and to develop a comprehensive state policy.

Minnesota

No proposed legislation received.

Mississippi

No proposed legislation received.

Missouri

No proposed legislation received.

Montana

No proposed legislation received.

Nebraska

No proposed legislation received.

Nevada

No proposed legislation received.

New Hampshire

Proposed legislation would establish a unified statutory system for the control of communicable and sexually transmitted diseases.

New Mexico

No proposed legislation received.

North Carolina

No proposed legislation received.

North Dakota

No proposed legislation received.

Ohio

H.B. 704 would declare AIDS to be a contagious disease and require reporting by name, address, age, sex, and race. The bill:

(1) Requires isolation of patients with AIDS until a physician certifies that the patient has recovered and is no longer communicable; and

(2) Prohibits school-age children with AIDS from attending public or private school until released from isolation by the board of health.

Oklahoma

No proposed legislation received.

Oregon

No proposed legislation received.

Rhode Island

S. 2765 would provide for the award of three times the normal weekly compensation benefit to health care workers who contact AIDS while performing their normal jobs.

South Carolina

No proposed legislation received.

South Dakota

No proposed legislation received.

Tennessee

Two pieces of proposed legislation are expected to be passed by the legislature and forwarded to the governor for approval. The first would require screening of all blood donations for HTLV-III/LAV infection; untested blood could be used in an emergency. The bill would permit directed blood donations for family members and others. The second bill wold make it a misdemeanor for an individual who knows that he or she has AIDS or has had a positive HTLV-III/LAV test to donate blood.

Utah

No proposed legislation received.

Vermont

No proposed legislation received.

Virginia

The department of health reports two legislative proposals: the first would require the department to notify school authorities of the names of children with AIDS, and the second would require premarital testing for HTLV-III/LAV antibodies.

Washington

No proposed legislation received.

West Virginia

No proposed legislation received.

Wisconsin

No proposed legislation received.

Wyoming

No proposed legislation received.

CHAPTER 3

Scientific Foundations

Acquired Immunodeficiency Syndrome (AIDS) is the most serious communicable disease epidemic in contemporary times; the effort to reduce its spread has been declared to be the U.S. government's top health priority.[1,2] It is unique in its combination of components: The syndrome and its destruction of the individual's immune system cannot currently be prevented by vaccine or effectively treated;[3] HTLV-III/LAV, the etiologic viral agent, is noted for its phenotypic variability and ability to mutate easily, making development of vaccines or treatment difficult; there is no known finite incubation period so that carriers of the virus are believed to be chronically infectious; and members of the major risk groups (gay and bisexual men and intravenous drug users) are already vulnerable to social prejudice and private discrimination, creating special problems for public health officials seeking to identify individuals who carry the virus and who may be be capable of transmitting it. AIDS therefore poses an incomparable challenge for health policy makers who must seek methods of reducing the spread of the disease and ensuring the public health which are consistent with protection of the individual.

The public health response to AIDS must be thoroughly grounded in the state of the art scientific knowledge on the nature and communicability of the disease. There is already a massive body of scientific literature on AIDS and associated conditions, and new information is being reported with astonishing rapidity. In Chapter 3, we will briefly review the scientific literature relating to the etiology and transmission of AIDS as a prelude to our analysis of the major public policy options available to public health officials and legislators.

Development of a Case Definition

Cases of what would later be identified as AIDS were first reported in the United States in 1981, with the reporting of five patients, all gay men, who died from Pneumocystis carinii pneumonia, an opportunistic lung infection caused by a protozoan parasite.[4] Other patients developed a rare neoplasm, Kaposi's sarcoma, and similar cases of unusual opportunistic disease and infection were reported thereafter.[5] The cases were remarkable because they involved young, previously healthy gay men, who developed opportunistic diseases typically occurring only in individuals with severely compromised immune systems. Because the first cluster of cases involved gay men, the condition was designated as the "gay-related immune deficiency" (GRID).[6] The designation "AIDS" was chosen after it became apparent that incidence of the syndrome was not limited to gay men.[7]

The CDC developed its initial case definition of AIDS for national reporting purposes in 1982.[7] This surveillance definition was developed for precision, consistency in interpretation, and specificity in order to provide useful data on disease trends, and was endorsed by the World Health Organization for use in countries where appropriate technologies are available.[8] Although there have been subsequent revisions,[9-12] the basic definition remains the same. Adult AIDS is defined as a reliably diagnosed disease which is at least moderately indicative of an underlying cellular immunodeficiency when no known cause for reduced resistance to that disease is present. This surveillance definition was developed before HTLV-III/LAV was identified as the probable causative agent, and development of the HTLV-III/LAV antibody tests has made it possible to include additional serious conditions in the syndrome where the patient is seropositive.[12] Because of the complexity of diagnosing AIDS in children, a provisional case definition for pediatric AIDS has been developed.[13]

The CDC case definition of AIDS was narrowly drawn to facilitate consistent disease reporting and surveillance. As more has been learned about HTLV-III/LAV infection, broader classifications have been suggested which would encompass the range of manifestations from asymptomatic infection to full-blown AIDS.[14-15] The CDC has published for comment a classification system developed with the advice of a panel of expert consultants.[16]

The CDC system is intended to serve broad public health purposes, including disease reporting and surveillance, epidemiologic studies, prevention and control activities, and public health policy and planning. It would classify patients diagnosed with HTLV-III/LAV infection into four (4) mutually exclusive groups according to the clinical expression of disease. The classifications and definitions used would be expected to evolve as more is understood about clinical and laboratory findings attributable to HTLV-III/LAV infection.

The Epidemic

From June 1, 1981 to the present day, over 21,000 patients meeting the surveillance definition for AIDS have been reported to the CDC; over 50% of these patients have died.[17] Cases have now been reported in all fifty states and the District of Columbia.

Distribution by sex, age, and race has remained relatively stable. According to figures released in early 1986 by the CDC, 93% of patients are male, and 90% are 20 to 49 years of age; sixty percent are white, 25% are Black, and 14% are Hispanic.[18] Ninety-four percent of these patients fall within recognized risk groups: 65% are gay or bisexual men with no history of intravenous (IV) drug use; 17% are heterosexual IV drug users; 8% are gay or bisexual men with a history of IV drug use; 2% are recipients of transfused blood or blood components; and 1% each are hemophiliacs, and the heterosexual partners of persons with AIDS or at risk for AIDS. Only 6% of the adult cases have not been classified by any recognized risk factor.

The majority of pediatric patients (75%) are from families in which one or both parents had AIDS or were at increased risk for contracting the syndrome. Of the remaining cases, 14% received transfusions before the onset of illness; 5% are hemophiliacs; and 6% were not classified. The case fatality rate for pediatric patients is 59%.

It has been estimated that for every person who meets the CDC definition of AIDS, there are between fifty and one hundred who have the infection.[19] If the infection-to-AIDS ratio is correct, then 1,000,000 to 2,000,000 people in the United States have been infected with the virus. Moreover, some predictive models indicate that over 12,000 additional cases of AIDS will be reported within the next twelve months.[20] Others have given more cautious estimates of increased prevalence of the virus and the disease, suggesting that the curve will flatten out due to a saturation of the risk groups;[21] these commentators note that there has been a relatively steady one percent of the population of AIDS cases which are outside known risk groups, indicating that, in the United States, the disease may not move to non-risk groups as has occurred in other countries.

Etiology: HTLV-III/LAV/ARV

French researchers in 1983 isolated a retrovirus, the lymphadenopathy-associated virus (LAV) from a patient with lymphadenopathy;[22] subsequent research identified the presence of LAV in patients in the United States.[23-24] In 1984, U.S. researchers independently isolated a similar retrovirus, designated human T-lymphotropic virus type III (HTLV-III), which has also been isolated in patients with AIDS or at increased risk for AIDS.[25-26] AIDS-associated retroviruses (ARV) have also been identified in patients with AIDS in San Francisco.[27] Although there is some variation between HTLV-III, LAV, and ARV in the strains,[28] they are believed to be essentially the same agent.[29] An increasing body of epidemiologic data supports the hypothesis that these retroviruses are etiologic agents in AIDS.[30-31]

Testing for Antibodies

There is currently no diagnostic test for AIDS, although tests have been developed to identify antibodies to the virus. In 1985, an enzyme-linked immunosorbent assay (ELISA) test was licensed by the Food and Drug Administration to screen blood and plasma collected for transfusion or manufactured into other products.[32] A reactive result indicates that the individual has been exposed to the virus and has mounted an immunologic response (serum antibodies). However, because the ELISA is not an antigen test, a positive result does not necessarily indicate that the person currently harbors the virus.

Although originally intended only as a means of protecting the nation's blood supply, experience with the ELISA test led the CDC to recommend its use not only to screen blood, but also for the diagnosis and differential diagnosis of clinical illness.[33-34] Use of the test has been recommended as a means of preventing perinatal transmission[35] and to help drug abuse related and sexual transmission of the virus by infected persons.[36]

A test is considered reasonably "sensitive" if it registers positive in a high proportion of patients with the condition tested for; and reasonably "specific" if it registers positive in a low proportion of healthy individuals. Excluding borderline results, the range of sensitivity of the ELISA test has been shown to be 93.4-99.6% and the range of specificity 98.6-99.6%.[37-40] Seroepidemiologic studies within each of the major risk groups, including hemophilia patients,[41-44] gay men and parenteral drug users,[45-47] show high rates of positivity. A preliminary report shows a lower prevalence among IV drug users under treatment in California.[48] Positivity among heterosexual men and women who are not members of known risk groups is extremely low.[29,37-39]

The full significance of a positive ELISA test result remains unclear, however. A number of commentators have expressed concern over the reliability and ethical considerations involved in use of the test.[49-51] Reactive test results may be due to subclinical infection, to immunity, or to an active carrier state, or may represent false positive reactions such as cross-reactivity to antigens or other viruses.[37] "False positives" are test results which show an immunologic response to HTLV-III/LAV when in fact there is no such response. The rate of false positives probably depends upon the prevalence of antibody in the tested population, with higher prevalence resulting in less false positives.[38] The range of false positive rates for the ELISA is estimated to be between 0.17-0.89% of the total population tested. Out of every one hundred persons who test positive, perhaps one-half to more than two-thirds may be false positives.[38-39]

To confirm whether a positive test result is a "true" positive, a confirmatory ELISA test can be performed. In a study of 131 blood banks and centers, less than one-third of the initially reactive blood units were repeatedly reactive.[52] A second ELISA test can reduce the number of false positives, but will not eliminate them.[33] A more expensive ($100, compared with $2-3) and technically more difficult confirmatory test, the Western Blot, can be performed. The Western Blot test identifies antibodies and proteins of a specific molecular weight.[53]

Virus Transmissability

Theoretically, it should be possible to isolate HTLV-III/LAV in any body fluid which contains lymphocytes. Scientists have successfully isolated and cultured live viruses from the blood and semen,[54-55] saliva,[56] tears[57], cerebrospinal fluid,[58-59] neural tissues,[58] and brain[59] of patients with AIDS or AIDS related-symptoms, or from infected asymptomatic individuals. More recently, researchers have isolated HTLV-III/LAV from cervical secretions of women at risk for AIDS,[60] and ARV from genital secretions of women with antibodies to the virus.[61] HTLV-III/LAV has not, as yet, been isolated from breast milk, urine, or feces.

Live viruses can transmit disease, but the presence of a live virus in low concentrations in a body fluid is not necessarily significant. The HTLV-III/LAV is quite fragile and difficult to communicate. Almost all cases of transmission in the United States have occurred through one or more of four distinct routes: close sexual contact involving the exchange of body fluids, intravenous drug administration with contaminated needles, use of contaminated blood and blood products, and passage of the virus from infected mothers to their newborns.[19] Epidemiologic studies have identified specific behavioral risk factors which increase the likelihood of transmission, such as increased number of sexual partners and receptive anal intercourse or other practices associated with rectal trauma. Heterosexual transmission of the virus has been well documented.[62-65] Male to female transmission is thought to be more efficient and is epidemiologically significant in the United States. Data suggesting female to male transmission has been reported from Central Africa,[66-68] and from the United States[69] which emphasizes the role of female prostitutes in this form of transmission. More recently, correspondence in the New England Journal of Medicine reported a single instance of sexual transmission of HTLV-III from an infected man to his wife, who then, it is believed, transmitted the virus to another man through frequent vaginal intercourse and heavy mouth kissing.[70]

There is increasingly strong evidence indicating that the virus is not transmitted through casual contact. Studies showing the extreme rarity with which infection is transmitted from prolonged and close household contact illustrate that mere exposure to and touching of persons who have been infected poses no meaningful risk of virus transmission.[64,71]

There is also evidence demonstrating the difficulty of transmitting the virus even in higher risk settings such as hospitals and laboratories where there is a greater opportunity for contact with patients with AIDS or associated conditions. The most obvious point of concern perhaps is needlestick accidents; evidence shows that HTLV-III/LAV transmission, resulting from an isolated parenteral response is extremely low.[72-75] Health care workers also do not appear to have contracted the virus from contact with patients from other causes such as cuts, open wounds, or attending to sanitary needs of patients, although future occurrences cannot be ruled out. The CDC has received a report of a child with transfusion-associated infection whose mother appears to have been infected while providing nursing care that involved extensive unprotected exposure to the child's blood and body secretions and excretions.[76] We will return to the potentially "higher risk" setting of hospitals later in the report.

The Clinical Spectrum

The surveillance definition of AIDS developed by the CDC is only a narrow point on a wide spectrum of illness which is still not fully understood.[19,77] Although the great majority of individuals exposed to the HTLV-III/LAV will be asymptomatic (with viremia or antibody or both), the virus is known to cause a non-specific syndrome characterized by lymphadenopathy (a disease process affecting the lymph nodes), prolonged unexplained fever, myalgia (muscular pain), fatigue or lethargy, gastrointestinal symptoms, sore throat and diarrhea.[78] Clinical manifestations of HTLV-III/LAV infection which do not fall within the CDC case definition are often referred to as AIDS- related complex (ARC).

Studies have confirmed that HTLV-III/LAV is neurotropic as well as lymphotropic.[79-80] Acute infection of the central nervous system occurs with seroconversion to HTLV-III/LAV antibody.[58] The presence within the blood-brain barrier of a specific immunoglobulin to HTLV-III/LAV has also been documented in patients with neurolgic complications of AIDS or ARC.[81]

The occurrence in immunosuppressed patients of central nervous system disease caused by a number of other organisms is well known.[82] We now know that certain patients with HTLV-III/LAV infection have neurologic disease but no clinical manifestations of immunodeficiency.[83] HTLV-III/LAV, then, is probably directly responsible for some of the neurologic syndromes found in patients with HTLV-III/LAV infections--such as chronic meningitis (inflammation of the membranes of the brain or spinal cord), dementia (organic brain syndrome marked by progressive mental deterioration), and encephalopathy (a disease of the brain); although the exact incidence is not known, as many as 60% of AIDS patients will develop dementia.[84-85] Neurologic complications also occur in infants and children with HTLV-III/LAV infection.[86]

The clinical manifestations of HTLV-III/LAV-related neurologic disease can range from asymptomatic to chronic progressive mental deterioration. Early symptoms may be indistinguishable from depression; it should be recognized that knowledge of infection with a potentially fatal virus provides ample psychological impact to cause reactive depresion. This depressive syndrome is characterized by forgetfulness and poor concentration, psychomotor retardation, decreased alertness, apathy, withdrawal, and loss of libido. AIDS-related dementia is often characteristic of a progressive senile dementia with loss of recent memory, confusion, and difficulty with novel experience. At the most extreme, neurologic disease results in profound dementia, seizures, coma and death.[87-93]

Evidence indicates that HTLV-III/LAV infection of the brain probably persists throughout life. The persistence of viral infection would be further promoted by the immunosuppression caused by HTLV-III/LAV.[81] The brain, therefore, may provide a sanctuary for HTLV-III/LAV.[59,81,84] The special features of persistent infection in the brain, together with the difficulty of medication across the blood-brain barrier, will make it difficult, if not impossible, to counter HTLV-III/LAV infection in the central nervous system.[94]

Natural History of Infection

AIDS, then, is a continuum of disease manifestations. The phenomenon is so recent that science does not yet fully understand the natural history of the disease. Current studies are underway to discover the process and time periods involved for infected, asymptomatic persons to develop acute lymphadenopathy syndrome, ARC, and then, perhaps "frank" AIDS. In several different studies, the proportion of seropositive persons in whom "frank" AIDS developed during follow-up periods of one to five years ranged from 4 to 20 percent.[3,19,95-97] In one follow-up study, 29% of patients with generalized lymphadenopathy had progressed to frank AIDS over a period of 4 1/2 years.[98] Research is also underway to explore the process of seroconversion. A study of a cohort of homosexual men in New York City indicates that the highest incidence of seroconversion occurred within the last several years, even though these men indicated a decrease in their sexual activity.[99]

The occurrence of AIDS in previously healthy young people suggests that the AIDS-related virus may be sufficient to cause the disease. Other theories point to co-factors which may be involved in the disease process. The demonstrated greater susceptibility of infants to the AIDS-related virus may result from the immaturity of the neonatal immune system.[77] It is possible, but not yet demonstrated, that other factors which suppress the immune system may affect the disease process. Such factors could include the medical use of steroids or antineoplastic agents, other coexisting immunosuppressant diseases, severe protein-calorie malnutrition, or even old age. A recent three-year prospective study of homosexual men supports the hypothesis that intercurrent infection, such as a recent episode of sexually transmitted disease, may be an important cofactor in the acquisition of infection and subsequent disease progression.[95] Similar unconfirmed hypotheses have focused on a specific or nonspecific "overload" of the immune system impairing its function in vulnerable patients.[100]

Whatever the disease process may turn out to be, for public health purposes it must be assumed at this time that individuals who are infected with the AIDS-related virus are capable of transmitting the infection. It does not matter whether the individual is asymptomatic or manifesting the symptoms of ARC or frank AIDS. A legal policy analysis cannot logically distinguish those who harbor the virus from those who can transmit it.

References

1. Message from Secretary Heckler and Letter from Commissioner Young. FDA Drug Bulletin. 1985; 15:26.

2. U.S. Public Health Service. Facts about AIDS. 1984:1.

3. Francis DP, Petricciani JC. The prospects for and pathways toward a vaccine for AIDS. N Eng J Med 1985; 313:1586-90.

4. CDC. Pneumocystis pneumonia--Los Angeles. MMWR 1981; 30:250-2.

5. CDC. Kaposi's sarcoma and Pneumocystis pneumonia among homosexual men--New York City and California. MMWR 1981; 30:305-8.

6. Stryker J. AIDS: Panic and public policy. Health Span 1985; 2:3-15.

7. CDC. Update on acquired immune deficiency syndrome (AIDS)--United States. MMWR 1982;31:507-14.

8. WHO. Acquired immune deficiency syndrome: Meeting of the WHO laboratory centres on AIDS. Weekly Epi Rec 1985; 43:333-4. Ibid. 1985;35:270-1.

9. Jaffe HW, Bregman DJ, Selik RM. Acquired immune deficiency syndrome in the United States: The first 1,000 cases. J Infect Dis 1983; 148:339-45.

10. Jaffe HW, Selik RM. Acquired immune deficiency syndrome: A disseminated aspergillosis predictive of underlying cellular immune deficiency? J Infect Dis 1984; 149:829.

11. Selik RM, Haverkos H, Curran JW. Acquired immune deficiency syndrome (AIDS): Trends in the United States 1978-1982. Am J Med 1984; 76:493-500.

12. CDC. Revision of the case definition of acquired immunodeficiency syndrome for national reporting--United States. MMWR 1985; 34:373-4.

13. CDC. Update: Acquired immunodeficiency syndrome (AIDS)--United States. MMWR 1984; 32:688-91.

14. Haverkos HW, Gottlieb MS, Killen JY, et al. Classification of HTLV-III/LAV related diseases (letter). J Infect Dis 1985; 152:1095.

15. Redfield RR, Wright DC, Tramont EC. The Walter Reed staging classification for HTLV-III/LAV infection. N Eng J Med 1986; 314:131-2.

16. CDC. Classification system for human T-lymphotropic virus type III/lymphadenopathy-associated virus infections. MMWR 1986; 35:334-9.

17. PHS predicts: AIDS to cause 54,000 deaths a year by 1991. The Nation's Health 1986; 16(7):1.

18. CDC. Update: Acquired immunodeficiency syndrome--United States. MMWR 1986; 35:17-21.

19. Curran JW, Meade Morgan W, Hardy AM, et al. The epidemiology of AIDS: Current status and future prospects. Science 1985; 229:1352-7.

20. Hardy AM, Allen JR, Meade Morgan W, et al. The incidence rate of acquired immunodeficiency syndrome in selected populations. JAMA 1985; 253:17-22.

21. Sandberg S, Sherman H. Final report on a mathematical model of the AIDS epidemic developed under contract with the Massachusetts Department of Public Health, 1985.

22. Montagnier L. Lymphadenopathy-associated virus: From molecular biology to pathogenicity. Ann Int Med 1985; 103:689-93.

23. Barre-Sinoussi F, Chermann JC, Rey F, et al. Isolation of T-lymphotropic retrovirus from a patient at risk for acquired immune deficiency syndrome (AIDS). Science 1983; 220:868-71.

24. Barre-Sinoussi F, Mathur-Wagh U, Rey F, et al. Isolation of lymphadenopathy associated virus (LAV) and detection of LAV antibodies from U.S. patients with AIDS. JAMA 1985; 253:1737-9.

25. Gallo RC, Salahuddin SZ, Popovic M, et al. Frequent detection and isolation of cytopathic retroviruses (HTLV-III) from patients with AIDS and at risk for AIDS. Science 1984; 224:500-3.

26. Popovic M, Sarngadharan MG, Read E, et al. Detection, isolation, and continuous production of cytopathic retroviruses (HTLV-III) from patients with AIDS and pre-AIDS. Science 1984; 224:497-500.

27. Levy JA, Hoffman AD, Kramer SM, et al. Isolation of lymphocytopathic retroviruses from San Francisco patients with AIDS. Science 1984; 225:840-2.

28. Benn S, Rutledge R, Folks T, et al. Genomic heterogeneity of AIDS retroviral isolates form North America and Zaire. Science 1985; 230:949-51.

29. Landesman SH, Ginzburg HM, Weiss SH. The AIDS epidemic. N Eng J Med 1985; 312:521-5.

30. Levy JA, Shimabukuro J. Recovery of AIDS-associated retroviruses from patients with AIDS or AIDS-related conditions and from clinically healthy individuals. J Infect Dis 1985; 152:734-38.

31. Gallo RC, Wong-Staal F. A human T-lymphotropic retrovirus (HTLV-III) as the cause of the acquired immunodeficiency syndrome. Ann Int Med 1985; 103:679-89.

32. CDC. Human T-lymphotropic virus type III/lymphadenopathy-associated virus antibody testing at alternative sites. MMWR 1986; 35:284-7.

33. CDC. Update: Public Health Service workshop on human T-lymphotropic virus type III antibody testing-United States. MMWR 1985; 34:477-8.

34. Panel urges test for AIDS be seen as diagnostic tool. Boston Globe at p. 3 (February 25, 1986).

35. CDC. Recommendations for assisting in the prevention of perinatal transmission of human T-lymphotropic virus type-III/ lymphadenopathy-associated virus and acquired immunodeficiency syndrome. MMWR 1985; 34:721-6, 731-2.

36. CDC. Additional recommendations to reduce sexual and drug-abuse related transmission of human T-lymphotropic virus type III/lymphadenopathy-associated virus. MMWR 1986; 35:152-5.

37. Sarngadharan MG, Popovic M, Bruch L, et al. Antibodies reactive with human T-lymphotropic retrovirus (HTLV-III) in the serum of patients with AIDS. Science 1984; 224:506-8.

38. Petricciani JC. Licensed tests for antibody to human T-lymphotropic virus type III: Sensitivity and specificity. Ann Int Med 1985; 103:726-9.

39. Schorr B, Berkowitz A, Cumming PD, et al. Prevalence of HTLV-III antibody in American blood donors. N Eng J Med 1985; 313:384-5.

40. Weiss SH, Goedert JJ, Sarngadharan MG, et al. Screening for HTLV-III (AIDS agent) antibodies: Specificity, sensitivity, and applications. JAMA 1985: 253:221-5.

41. Ragni MV, Tegtmeier GE, Levy JA, et al. AIDS retrovirus antibodies in hemophiliacs treated with factor VII or factor IX concentrates, cryoprecipitate, or fresh frozen plasma: prevalence, seroconversion rate, and clinical correlations. Blood 1986; 67:592-7.

42. Evatt BL, Gomperts ED, McDougal JS, et al. Incidental appearance of LAV/HTLV-III antibodies in hemophiliacs and the onset of the AIDS epidemic. N Eng J Med 1985; 312:483-6.

43. Goedert JJ, Eyester ME, Sarndagharan MG, et al. Antibodies reactive with human T-cell leukemia viruses in the serum of hemophiliacs receiving factor VIII concentrate. Blood 1985; 65:492-5.

44. Melbye M, Froebel KS, Madhok R, et al. HTLV-III seropositivity in European hemophiliacs exposed to factor VIII concentrate imported from the U.S.A. Lancet 1984; 2:1444-6.

45. CDC. Antibodies to a retrovirus etiologically associated with acquired immune deficiency syndrome (AIDS) in populations with increased incidences of the syndrome. MMWR 1984; 33:377-9.

46. Robert-Guroff M, Weiss SH, Giron JA, et al. Prevalence of antibodies to HTLV-I, -II, and -III in intravenous drug abusers from an AIDS endemic region. JAMA 1986; 255:3133-7.

47. Spira TJ, Des Jarlais DC, Marmor M, et al. Prevalence of antibody to lymphadenopathy-associated virus among drug detoxification patients in New York. N Eng J Med 1984; 311:467-8.

48. Levy N, Carlson JR, Hinrichs S, et al. The prevalence of HTLV-III/LAV antibodies among intravenous drug users attending treatment programs in California: a preliminary report [Letter]. N Eng J Med 1986; 314:446.

49. Levine C, Bayer R. Screening blood: Public health and medical uncertainty. In: AIDS: The Emerging ethical dilemmas. Hastings Center Report 1985:8.

50. Marwick C. Use of the AIDS antibody test may provide more answers. JAMA 1985; 253:1694-9.

51. Osterholm MT, Bowman RJ, Chopek MW, et al. Screening donated blood from plasma for HTLV-III antibody: Facing one more crisis. N Eng J Med 1985; 312:1185-9.

52. CDC. Results of human T-lymphotropic virus type III test kits reported from blood collection centers--U.S., April 22--May 19, 1985. MMWR 1985; 34:375-6.

53. Young FE. "Dear Doctor" Letter, Feb. 19, 1985.

54. Zagury D, Bernard J, Leibowitch J, et al. HTLV-III in cells cultured from semen of two patients with AIDS. Science 1984; 226:449-51.

55. Ho DD, Schooley RT, Rota TA, et al. HTLV-III in the semen and blood of a healthy homosexual man. Science 1984; 226:451-3.

56. Groopman JE, Salahuddin SZ, Sarngadharan MG, et al. HTLV-III in saliva of people with AIDS-related complex and healthy homosexual men at risk for AIDS. Science 1984; 226:447-8.

57. Fajikawa LS, Salahuddin SZ, Palestine AG, et al. Isolation of human T-cell leukemia/lymphotropic virus type III (HTLV-III) from the tears of a patient with acquired immune deficiency syndrome (AIDS). Lancet 1985; II:529.

58. Ho DD, Rota TR, Schooley RT, et al. Isolation of HTLV-III from cerebrospinal fluid and neural tissues of patients with neurologic syndromes related to the acquired immunodeficiency syndrome. N Eng J Med 1985; 313:1493-7.

59. Levy JA, Shimabukuro J, Hollander H, et al. Isolation of AIDS-associated retroviruses from cerebrospinal fluid and brain of patients with neurological symptoms. Lancet 1985; 2:586-8.

60. Vogt MW, Witt DJ, Craven DE, et al. Isolation of HTLV-III/LAV from cervical secretions of women at risk for AIDS. Lancet 1986; 8480:525-7.

61. Wofsy CB, Cohen JB, Haver LB, et al. Isolation of AIDS-associated retrovirus from genital secretions of women with antibodies to the virus. Lancet 1986; 8480:527-9.

62. CDC. Heterosexual transmission of human T-lymphotropic virus type III/lymphadenopathy associated virus. MMWR 1985; 34:561-3.

63. Redfield RR, Markham PD, Salahuddin SZ, et al. Frequent transmission of HTLV-III among spouses of patients with AIDS-related complex and AIDS. JAMA 1985; 253:1571-3.

64. Jason JM, McDougal JS, Dixon G. HTLV-III/LAV antibody and immune status of household contacts and sexual partners of persons with hemophilia. JAMA 1986; 255:212-15.

65. Lederman MM. Transmission of acquired immunodeficiency syndrome through heterosexual activity. Ann Int Med 1986; 104:115-16.

66. Piet P, Quinn TC, Taelman H, et al. Acquired immune deficiency syndrome in a heterosexual population in Zaire. Lancet 1984; II:65-9.

67. Clumeck N, Van de Perre P, Cargel M, et al. Heterosexual promiscuity among African patients with AIDS. N Eng J Med 1985; 313:182.

68. Kreiss JK, Koech D, Plummer FA, et al. AIDS virus infection in Nairobi prostitutes: spread of the epidemic to East Africa. N Eng J Med 1986; 314:414-8.

69. Redfield RR, Markham PD, Salahuddin SZ, et al. Heterosexually acquired HTLV-III/LAV disease (AIDS-related complex and AIDS): Epidemiologic evidence for female to male transmission. JAMA 1985; 254:2094-6.

70. Calabrese LH, Gopalakrishna KV. Transmission of HTLV-III infection from man to woman to man [letter]. N Eng J Med 1986; 314:987.

71. Friedland GH, Saltzman BR, Rogers MF, et al. Lack of transmission of HTLV-III/LAV infection to household contacts of patients with AIDS or AIDS-related complex with oral candidiasis. N Eng J Med 1986; 314:344-349.

72. CDC. Update: Prospective evaluation of health care workers exposed via the parenteral or mucous-membrane route to body fluids from patients with acquired immunodeficiency syndrome--United States. MMWR 1985; 34:101-3.

73. Weiss SH, Saxinger WC, Rechtman D, et al. HTLV-III infection among health care workers: Association with needle-stick injuries. JAMA 1985; 254:2089-93.

74. McCray E, et al. Occupational risk of the acquired immunodeficiency syndrome among health care workers. N Eng J Med 1986; 314:1127-32.

75. Stricof RL, Morse DL. HTLV-III/LAV seropositivity following ia deep intromuscular needlestick injury [letter]. N Eng J Med 1986; 314:1115.

76. CDC. Apparent transmission of human T-lymphotropic virus type III/lymphadenopathy-associated virus from a child to a mother providing health care. MMWR 1986; 35:76-78.

77. Amman AJ. The acquired immune deficiency syndrome in infants and children. Ann Int Med 1985; 103:734-7.

78. Fauci AS, Macher AM, Longo DL, et al. Acquired immunodeficiency syndrome: Epidemiologic, clinical, immunologic, and therapeutic considerations. Ann Int Med 1984; 100:92-106.

79. Shaw GM, Harper ME, Hahn BH, et al. HTLV-III infection in brains of children and adults with AIDS encephalopathy. Science 1985; 227:177-82.

80. Harris AA, Segreti J, Levin S. Central nervous system infections in patients with the acquired immune deficiency syndrome (AIDS). Clin Neuropharm 1985; 8:201-10.

81. Resnick L, diMarzo-Veronese F, Schupbach J, et al. Intra-blood-brain barrier synthesis of HTLV-III specific IgG in patients with neurologic symptoms associated with AIDS or AIDS-related complex. N Eng J Med 1985; 313:1498-504.

82. Levy RM, Bredesan DE, Rosenblum ML. Neurological manifestations of the acquired immunodeficiency syndrome (AIDS): Experience at UCSF and review of the literature. J Neurosurg 1985; 62:475-95.

83. Carne CA, Tedder RS, SMith A, et al. Acute encephalopathy coincidence with seroconversion for anti-HTLV-III. Lancet 1985; II:1706-8.

84. Goldstick L, Mandybar TI, Bode R. Spinal cord degeneration in AIDS. Neurology (Cleveland) 1985; 35:103-6.

85. Barnes, DM. AIDS-related brain damage unexplained. Science 1986; 232:1091-3.

86. Belman AL, Ultmann MH, Horoupian D, et al. Neurological complications in infants and children with acquired immune deficiency syndrome. Ann Neurol 1985; 18:560-6.

87. National Institute of Mental Health. Coping with AIDS: Psychological and social considerations in helping AIDS patients and others with HTLV-III infection. (In press).

88. Bredesen DE, Messing R. Neurological syndromes heralding the acquired immune deficiency syndrome (abstract). Ann Neurol 1983; 14:141.

89. Britton CB, Marquardt MD, Koppel B, et al. Neurological complications of the gay immunosuppressed syndrome: Clinical and pathological features (abstract). Ann Neurol 1982; 12:80.

90. Britton CB, Miller JR. Neurological complications in acquired immunodeficiency syndrome (AIDS). Neurol Clin 1984; 2:315-39.

91. Horoupian DS, Pick P, Spigland I, et al. Acquired immune deficiency syndrome and multiple tract degeneration in a homosexual man. Ann Neurol 1984; 15:502-5.

92. Horowitz, SL, Benson DF, Gottlieb MS, et al. Neurological complications of gay-related immunodeficiency disorders (abstract). Ann Neurol 1982; 12:80.

93. Snider WO, Simpson DM, Nielson S, et al. Neurological complications of acquired immune deficiency syndrome: Analysis of 50 patients. Ann Neurol 1983; 14:403-18.

94. Black PH. HTLV-III, AIDS and the brain. N Eng J Med 1985; 313:1538-9.

95. Jaffe HW, Hardy AM, Meade Morgan W, et al. The acquired immunodeficiency syndrome in gay men. Ann Int Med 1985; 103:662-4.

96. Goedert JJ, Sarngadharan MG, Biggar RJ, et al. Determinants of retrovirus (HTLV-III) antibody and immunodeficiency conditions in homosexual men. Lancet 1984; II:711-16.

97. Weber JN, Wadsworth J, Rogers LA, et al. Three year perspective study of HTLV-III/LAV infection in homosexual men. Lancet 1986; 8491:1179-82.

98. Mathur-Wagh U, Mildvan D, Senie RT. Follow-up at 4 1/2 years on homosexual men with generalized lymphadenopathy. N Eng J Med 1985; 313:1542-3.

99. Melbye M, Biggar RJ, Ebbesen P, et al. Long-term seropositivity for human T-lymphotropic virus type III in homosexual men without the acquired immunodeficiency syndrome development of immunologic and clinical abnormalities. Ann Int Med 1986; 104:496-500.

100. Krieger T, Caceres CA. The unnoticed link in AIDS cases. Wall St. Journal. Oct. 24, 1985.

CHAPTER 4

Regulatory Efforts on AIDS: Legal and Constitutional Foundations

The protection and preservation of the public health is among the chief ends of government.[1] In the exercise of police powers all states have enacted statutes and regulations which provide for personal control measures designed to restrict the spread of infectious diseases.[2] Such measures may include testing and screening for the presence of a carrier or disease state, requirements to report to public health departments, contact tracing, medical examination and treatment, and restrictions on the movement of named individuals or those within specified geographical areas.

This chapter of the report will examine the likely approach of the courts in reviewing these personal control measures. We will first look at the public health law cases, most of which were decided in the early part of the century. For the most part we find these cases to be unreliable precedent because they precede the substantial development of a more searching judicial inquiry of state action which deprives individuals of constitutionally protected rights. The early cases do lay down certain substantive limitations on public health powers which would constitute the minimum courts would require today: (1) the true purpose of the legislation is public health and is not a disguised form of prejudice; (2) that there is some discernible "public health necessity" supported by scientific evidence; (3) the place of quarantine itself does not pose a significant health risk;

and (4) that there is a reasonable relationship between the measure adopted and the objective of reducing the spread of infectious disease. These four enduring principles will be discussed. They will be followed by the modern equal protection analysis we believe would be applied in the context of AIDS. We conclude that only personal control measures which infringed upon a constitutionally protected interest such as the freedom to travel or privacy would attract the highest level of judicial scrutiny. They would, accordingly, not be upheld unless the measures were clearly necessary to achieve a compelling public purpose; and the means used must be the least restrictive alternative.

A. The Public Health Cases

Most of the relevant public health cases were decided around the turn of the century and early 1900's. The cases provide ample support for the exercise of police powers designed to protect the public health.[3] The hallmark of the early public health cases was the deference consistently shown by the courts to the will of the legislature. The adoption of public health measures was regarded as presumptively valid;[4] the states would be given substantial latitude in determining the measures which were necessary. The courts uniformly took the view that they would not substitute their judgment for that of the legislature, and that the "manner and mode" of regulatory efforts was solely within the ambit of the states' police powers.[5]

The major impetus for the judicial activity in the field was the sporadic presence of epidemics of venereal disease,[6] tuberculosis,[7] smallpox,[8] scarlet fever,[9] leprosy,[10] cholera,[11] and bubonic plague.[12] The response of the courts must be measured by the perceived urgency of the times to control the "menace" of these epidemics.[13] It was within this context that private rights were to be subordinated to the public interest, and individuals were bound to conform their conduct for the social good.[14] As one court put it, quarantine does not frustrate constitutional rights because there is no liberty to harm others.[15] Although some courts recognized that personal control measures cut deeply into private rights, they would not allow the assertion of those rights to thwart public policy.[16] This preference for social control over individual autonomy emerged as a major characteristic of judicial rulings of the time.[17]

Many early judicial opinions, asserted that the courts simply had no power to review the exercise of police powers:[18] "where the police power is set in motion in its proper sphere, the courts have no jurisdiction to stay the arm of the legislative branch...."[19] In their haste to give effect to any state action designed to promote health and welfare, these courts abdicated their traditional role as guarantor of constitutional rights first asserted by the U.S. Supreme Court in Marbury v. Madison. The Court in Marbury would not countenance government with "unlimited" unreviewable powers.[20] The U.S. Supreme Court has subsequently made clear that "there are, of necessity, limits beyond which the legislature cannot go" in exercising its police powers to protect the public health.[21]

The duty to exercise the states' police powers to prevent the spread of infectious disease remains to the present, and would lead the courts to give considerable leeway to state legislatures in the formulation of public policy. But several early public health cases also set a few clear boundaries in the exercise of the police power. These can be presumed to be the <u>minimal</u> courts would be expected to apply at the present time in relation to AIDS. As such they are worth briefly stating.

1. True Purpose

Clearly, contemporary courts would regard the preservation of the public health as a proper concern of state legislatures. But the courts would be expected to look beyond the nominal statutory intent to discover the true legislative purpose.[22] The courts would not be bound by "mere forms," nor misled by "mere pretenses" under the guise of police powers.[23] They would require the motivation of the legislature to be directed towards health and welfare, and not allow a disguised form of discrimination. If police powers exercised for the ostensible purpose of controlling AIDS were shown to be guided by prejudice or irrational fear the courts would not uphold the statute. Nor could the state, under the guise of protecting the public, arbitrarily interfere with private business, or impose unusual and unnecessary restrictions upon lawful activities; whether they have done so in a particular case is a judicial question.[24] Were there to be any doubt as to the actual purpose behind AIDS legislation the courts would be expected to delve deeply into the legislative history and full statutory scheme to discover the true legislative intent.

2. Public health necessity

The constitutional foundation for the exercise of police powers is "public necessity."[25] But early public health cases provide confusing, and sometimes contradictory, statements on the issue,[26] making it difficult to harmonize their disparate holdings. One court posed the question with tantalizing acuity: Can quarantine of a person be ordered by the Board of Health notwithstanding the fact that the patient's attending physician certified that his life would be endangered by the quarantine, or the fact that it would not be effective or advisable as a public health measure? The court, without explanation, never answered its own penetrating question.[27]

Some early public health cases illustrate the harm that can occur from imposing control measures that aren't clearly supported by scientific evidence. In Kirk v. Wyman, an elderly woman with anaesthetic leprosy was quarantined even though there was "hardly any danger of contagion."[28] She had lived in the community for many years, attended church services, taught in school and mingled in social life without ever communicating the disease. The court thought it "manifest that the board were well within their duty in requiring the victim of it to be isolated" when the "distressing nature of the malady is regarded."[29] The courts' preparedness to support the public health department was not diminished by the fact that Mrs. Kirk's disease was not curable and that the quarantine would be indefinite. Nor did the court in State v. Rackowski require any more than "common knowledge" in deciding whether or not a person had scarlet fever.[30]

In Ex parte Company the court upheld a quarantine regulation which included a provision that "all known prostitutes and persons associated with them shall be considered as reasonably suspected of having a venereal disease."[31] Those who "by conduct and association" contract such disease as makes them a menace to the health and morals of the community" must submit to control measures.[32] The court did not appear unduly concerned to discover whether or not Martha Company had venereal disease.

In People v. Strautz the court accepted similar assumptions. "Suspected" prostitutes were considered "natural subjects and carriers of venereal disease," making it "logical and natural that suspicion be cast upon them and necessity dictate a physical examination of their persons."[33] The court was unclear as to the evidence that should be required to establish a reasonable belief that a person engaged in prostitution.

Several earlier cases were much clearer in requiring a demonstration of public health necessity and, in particular, medical proof that individuals were in fact infectious.[34] Ex parte Shepard specifically rejected the proposition that mere suspicion of a venereal disease is sufficient to uphold a quarantine order.[35] Similarly, in Ex parte Arata the court required that reasonable ground must exist to support the claim that the person is afflicted with venereal disease: "Mere suspicion unsupported by facts giving rise to reasonable or probable cause will afford no justification at all for depriving persons of their liberty.[36]

Smith v. Emery presents the clearest statement by a court as to the need for medical evidence to support control measures: "The mere possibility that persons might have been exposed to such disease [smallpox] is not sufficient, but they must "have been exposed to it, and that the conditions actually exist for a communication of the contagion...." Further, these issues are to be determined by "medical science and skill," and not "common knowledge."[37]

Modern courts would almost certainly require a clear public health justification for any personal control measure; the exercise of such a measure in a particular case would require scientific support that the person actually was in an infectious condition; that circumstances existed whereby the infection could be communicated; and that the measure would be effective in eliminating or reducing the risk of contagion.[38]

3. The requirement of a safe environment for quarantine

Those who harbor a communicable virus can be made to submit to compulsory measures which are for the common good. The question arises whether this social welfarist notion can be extended so far that the control measure itself poses a health risk for the subjects. In effect, can a person be quarantined in conditions which pose an unnecessary risk to his or her health? In Jew Ho v. Williamson[39] (discussed further at page 244 infra) the court was heavily influenced by evidence that confinement of large groups of people together in an area where bubonic plague was suspected placed all those under the quarantine at increased risk of contracting the disease.

The court in Kirk v. Wyman was quite prepared to uphold a quarantine despite the absence of proof that the form of leprosy from which Mary Kirk was suffering was contagious. Nevertheless, the court would not subject her to an unsafe environment. She was to be quarantined in a pesthouse which was "a structure of four small rooms in a row, with no piazzas, used heretofore for the isolation of negroes with smallpox, situated within a hundred yards of the place where the trash of the city...is collected and burned." The court drew the conclusion that "even temporary isolation in such a place would be a serious affliction and peril to an elderly lady, enfeebled by disease, and accustomed to the comforts of life."[40] The public health department was compelled to wait until it had finished building Miss Kirk a "comfortable cottage" outside the city limits. (One wonders why the court felt that it was reasonably safe to allow Miss Kirk her freedom until some future date; in the interim Miss Kirk would still be allowed full association within the city).

A more modern court was less rigorous in reviewing the conditions of quarantine. In Ex parte Martin the court supported giving the health officers discretion as to the place of quarantine. The county jail was designated as a place of quarantine of people with venereal disease despite uncontested evidence that it was overcrowded and had been condemned by a legislative investigating committee. The court supported the Attorney General's position that, "While jails, as public institutions, were established for purposes other than confinement of diseased persons, occasions of emergency or lack of other public facilities for quarantine require that jails be used."[41]

The use of jails as places of quarantine, together with the absence of any rigorous requirement to demonstrate that persons were actually infectious with venereal disease, leads to the inference that punishment was an underlying public purpose. Punishment is not an appropriate concept in public health because there is no specific finding that a criminal offence has been committed. Public health departments have an obligation not to do unnecessary harm by providing unsafe or punitive environments for subjects of a quarantine. Indeed, the essence of quarantine should be that the quid pro quo for loss of liberty is the obligation to provide the finest possible care and conditions for those who must forego their individual rights for the collective good.

4. Substantial relationship between control measures and public health objectives

The U.S. Supreme Court in Jacobson v. Massachusetts, in obiter dicta, placed substantive limitations on public health powers: The state must refrain from acting in "an arbitrary, unreasonable manner," or "going so far beyond what was reasonably required for the safety of the public."[42] This standard of review of the police power is deferential. The court would support any reasonable state regulatory measure which was not wholly irrational, indiscriminate or enacted in bad faith. While the Court did not as yet require "least restrictive means" in the early 1900's, it did state that the methods adopted must not be unreasonably intrusive.[43] A statute enacted to protect public health must have a "real or substantial relation to those objects," and cannot be "a plain palpable invasion of rights."[44] Thus, the means must clearly be designed to achieve a legitimate public health goal. Even though the intent of the legislature may be valid and beneficent, the methods adopted must be able to achieve that goal.

The "arbitrary, oppressive and unreasonable" standard has found expression for several decades in the courts' jurisprudence. The test was sufficient to strike down the most invidious public health measures as occurred in Jew Ho v. Williamson. There the Federal District Court refused to uphold the quarantine of an entire district of San Francisco containing a population of more than 15,000 persons. The court inquired whether the measure was reasonable and necessary. Bubonic plague is most easily communicated in conditions of overcrowding and unsanitary surroundings. "It must necessarily follow that, if a large territory is quarantined, intercommunication of the people within that territory will rather tend to spread the disease than to restrict it."[45] The court embarked upon a searching scrutiny of means adopted which was uncharacteristic of early public health cases but accurately predictive of contemporary judicial analysis. The court noted that this species of quarantine would enlarge the sphere of the disease and increase its danger and destructive force; that the evidence to show the existence of plague and the circumstances of its transmission was slight; and the fact that the quarantine was made to operate exclusively against the Chinese community demonstrated an "evil eye and an unequal hand." The "reasonable means" test continued to be applied by the courts through the 1950's and 1960's particularly in relation to the quarantine of tuberculosis patients.[46]

More representative of current constitutional analysis is New York State Association for Retarded Children v. Carey concerning hepatitis B, which is transmitted much in the same way as HTLV-III. The Court determined that mentally retarded children who were carriers of serum hepatitis could not be excluded from attending regular public school classes as "the Board was unable to demonstrate that the health hazard...was anything more than a remote possibility."[47] This remote possibility did not justify the action taken considering the detrimental effects of isolating carrier children.

The early cases, then, do delineate four baseline standards of judicial review: (1) the true purpose of the legislation must be for the public health; (2) the measures must be grounded upon a "public health necessity" supported by medical evidence in the particular case; (3) the environment of quarantine must be reasonably safe; and (4) there is a substantial relationship between the means adopted and the public health objective to be achieved.

These four standards should be the minimum present in a contemporary judicial analysis relating to AIDS. But we would anticipate a more rigorous examination under modern equal protection and due process standards. Inherent in the reasoning of modern courts are the different levels of scrutiny undertaken depending upon the constitutionally protected interests or class that is burdened by the control measure. Thus, despite the traditional deferential posture of the courts, it would be a mistake to assume judicial complacency in reviewing compulsory powers against persons infected with HTLV-III. Almost all of the relevant cases were decided during a period which preceded the remarkable evolution in constitutional decision-making which has occurred since the civil rights movement. We review this new constitutional analysis in the section that follows.

B. Modern Equal Protection Analysis Applied in the Public Health Context

The Fourteenth Amendment of the United States Constitution guarantees both due process and equal protection of the laws.[48] The due process clause has been construed to have both a procedural and substantive component. The procedural component requires the state to use fair procedures in arriving at a decision which interferes with any constitutionally protected liberty interest. We address this procedural question later in the chapter. We begin by examining the substantive limitations inherent in the due process and equal protection clauses of the Fourteenth Amendment. These substantive provisions set the parameters as to what states may and may not do under the Constitution. While procedural due process requires fair procedures associated with state decisions, substantive due process and equal protection may limit the kinds of powers states may exercise at all.

There is a significant overlap between substantive due process and equal protection; and courts can usually cast the same set of facts into an analysis using either clause. The courts view substantive questions before them quite differently depending upon the personal interest that is being invaded. There are fairly specific rights which have been regarded as "fundamental," such as the freedom to travel,[49] to marry[50] and certain privacy rights.[51] Today, only liberties specifically deemed by the court to be fundamental are afforded a higher level of judicial protection under substantive due process. For "non-fundamental" rights, substantive due process requires only that infringements have some rational connection with a permissible government goal. This is a highly permissive test which is much akin to the Jacobson line of cases already described earlier in this chapter.

Modern courts have tended to cast substantive issues in equal protection terms. The equal protection clause usually is construed as having a sharper bite. Accordingly, we focus on equal protection in this report, recognizing that the framework for analyzing that clause is markedly similar to its sister provision--substantive due process.

1. Minimum rationality

The constitutional guarantee of equal protection of the laws does not require the state to treat all people the same. What it does require is some comprehensible rationale for differential treatment of similarly situated people.[52] Thus, if control measures against mentally retarded children are taken to prevent the spread of hepatitis B, the courts will inquire why those measures were not also taken against dentists who have a reservoir of infection similar to the mentally retarded.[53] A legislature can legitimately seek to differentiate between groups for valid reasons such as a more efficient promotion of the public health. However, the state cannot exercise a "naked preference" for one group over another simply because that group is politically favored[54]--e.g., dentists over mentally retarded children. Under equal protection analysis, then, "the courts must reach and determine the question whether the classification drawn in a statute is reasonable in light of its purpose."[55] The courts have developed rigid tests of the relevance of a classification to the statutory purpose. Since the 1960's the courts have applied a two tier test, and, depending upon the level of scrutiny used, the result is highly predictable. The U.S. Supreme Court is now subtly moving from that position; it has developed what some have called a middle tier and has even begun to signal that it will be shifting to a more flexible approach.[56]

The first level of equal protection analysis is often termed "minimum rationality." Here, the classification must have some rational connection with a permissible government objective.[57] The latest Supreme Court ruling on this test stated that where individuals in a group affected by a statute have distinguishing characteristics relevant to interests a state has the authority to implement, the equal protection clause requires only that the classification drawn by the statute be rationally related to a legitimate state interest.[58] This is a highly deferential test and, for the most part, once the court decides that it will use a minimal level of scrutiny, it signals its result. The test, then, is outcome determinative, and highly permissive. Courts will only overturn legislation if the state has acted in a wholly unreasonable, unnecessary and arbitrary manner.[59] The current Supreme Court feels it is appropriate to give the legislature wide latitude[60] particularly in relation to social and economic measures. It is not for the Court "to closely scrutinize legislative choices as to whether, how and to what extent those interests should be pursued."

Public health is a legitimate government objective. If legislatures purport to act for the public health, and if the enactment does not trigger stricter scrutiny, it is highly likely that the courts would uphold the measure. The courts' chief concern in such instances is to ensure that public health was the true legislative purpose and that there is not some other agenda based upon prejudice or raw political preference. Current state requirements to report CDC defined AIDS, for example, depending upon the specific regulatory provisions, may not impinge upon any constitutionally protected interests. If the court were to apply a test of minimum rationality, in all probability current reporting requirements would be upheld. There is a reasonable relation between the goal (epidemiological data on the presence of AIDS in the population) and the method (reporting of the disease).

2. Strict scrutiny

a. "Fundamental Rights" and Privacy

Just as "minimum rationality" signals a deferential posture by the judiciary, so too does heightened scrutiny signal the courts' determination to strike down the statute. The court uses a higher level of review where state action interferes with fundamental liberties. "Fundamental" liberties have a specific meaning in law, and encompass only those so held by the U.S. Supreme Court. These include the right to travel,[61] to marry,[62] and to certain privacy interests such as freedom to choose whether to bear children.[63] The rights to travel, to marry and to privacy are each potentially relevant to constitutional analysis of public health powers in the AIDS context. As AIDS is a blood born infectious disease, methods of preventing its spread could involve restricting movement or sexual freedoms. The right to privacy is potentially implicated where information about a person's health status is kept on record, or will be reported or where public health officials trace their sexual contacts. The U.S. Supreme Court has already held that privacy encompasses "an individual interest in avoiding disclosure of personal matters."[64]

Only those privacy interests designated by the courts are deemed fundamental. The courts have traditionally restricted privacy protections to those intimate activities broadly linked with matters of procreation and family life.[65] As the Court stated in Roe v. Wade, privacy represents "some extension to activities relating to marriage ... procreation... contraception, family relationships,... and childbearing and education."[66]

As the judicial trend has been to link privacy rights with intimate decisions relating to marriage, family and birth, this could bode poorly for its application to AIDS. As sexual controls will often be applied against homosexuals where there are no traditional familial and childrearing interests, the court could be reluctant to extend privacy rights into this form of relationships. Yet, the court has made clear already that privacy belongs to individuals rather than family units[67] and that the right can extend beyond the traditional family context.[68]

There has been extensive scholarly argument in favor of a right to privacy inherent in homosexual relationships.[69] The courts, however, have been slow to accept this argument. In Doe v. Commonwealth's Attorney[70] the Supreme Court summarily affirmed the judgment of a three-judge district court upholding the constitutionality of a Virginia sodomy statute. Several courts have regarded the Supreme Court's summary affirmation as controlling and have refused to strike down similar statutes.[71] The 11th Circuit Court of Appeals in Hardwick v. Bowers[72], however, did find a constitutionally protected interest in "private consensual sexual behavior among adults."[73] The Bowers case, however, was recently overturned by the United States Supreme Court.[74] Justice White, writing for the Court, found that the constitutional right to privacy would not "extend a fundamental right to homosexuals to engage in acts of consensual sodomy." The Court decision appears to place private consensual homosexual activity outside the constitutionally protected privacy doctrine of the Court. This will make it extremely difficult to sustain a constitutional argument in relation to public health measures impinging upon intimate sexual activities such as in sexual contact tracing or the closure of bathhouses. It does not, however, create a constitutional license for discriminatory policies in the guise of public health measures.

b. Special Protection for Suspect Classifications

Heightened scrutiny under the Equal Protection clause can be achieved not only by showing that the enactment infringes a fundamental right but also if it creates a suspect classification. Any classification based upon race,[75] alienage[76] or national origin[77] is regarded as suspect because it is so seldom relevant to the achievement of any state interest. Statutes grounded upon such considerations "are deemed to reflect prejudice and antipathy—a view that those in the burdened class are not as worthy or deserving as others."[78]

It is to be emphasized that a classification is not subject to close scrutiny simply because it affects an historically vulnerable or discriminated against minority. There is no heightened review to differential treatment based upon age,[79] disability, mental illness or infirmity.[80]

A major question arises in the AIDS context as to whether homosexuality is a suspect classification. If it were to be so held it could potentially invalidate any control measure drawn on the basis of sexual preference such as a screening requirement which was limited to gays, or the closure of gay meeting places, leaving similarly situated heterosexual establishments untouched. Highly persuasive arguments that homosexuality should be a suspect class have been put forward.[81] Gays have no distinguishing characteristics from the rest of the population and are not as a class any less capable of contributing to and engaging in society than any other group. The lack of any distinguishing characteristics makes sexual orientation akin to race. It could be argued that, as the prevalence of HTLV-III infection is significantly higher among gays than in the general population, public health measures (such as screening) could conceivably draw a classification on the basis of sexual preference. If homosexuality were regarded as suspect, it is doubtful the court would allow this because the public health measure would affect many gays who were not infected and would not engage in behavior likely to transmit the virus. The closest analogy would be if a compulsory measure to control sickle cell anemia were applied against all Black people. To burden an entire 'disfavored' class where most of its members do not require control measures could too easily be based upon the wrong reasons; the court would be expected to examine such measures most carefully.

c. Effects of Heightened Scrutiny

Heightened scrutiny which flows from the infringement of a fundamental right[82] or the creation of a suspect class[83] is a strong signal that the statute will be invalidated. These enactments will only be sustained if they are suitably tailored to serve a compelling state interest. The means used must also be the least restrictive necessary to achieve the compelling public purpose.

i. Suitably tailored to serve a compelling state interest

Any personal control measure applied to AIDS which restricted freedom of movement would attract the highest level of judicial review. Preservation of the public health might well be regarded as a compelling state interest. But the courts would also require a "tight fit" between means and ends. The public health measure adopted must be clearly necessary to achieve the compelling purpose. The means could not, in particular, be too sweeping so as to apply to those who pose no real danger of spreading the infection. This would be the case in a general quarantine of all AIDS patients or carriers. Although it might be a fair assumption that all such people were infectious, it does not follow that all would create a danger of contagion by their behavior. As the measure affects liberty and therefore triggers strict scrutiny, it is doubtful it would be upheld as a constitutionally valid exercise of public health powers.

ii. Under-inclusion

Under-inclusion occurs when a state benefits or burdens persons in a manner that furthers a valid public purpose but does not confer the same benefit or burden on others who are similarly situated. A quarantine measure which was limited to patients with CDC defined AIDS would exclude HTLV-III carriers, even though they are equally infectious. The courts often do not hold that under-inclusion is violative of equal protection because the legislature should be free to remedy parts of a public health problem without tackling it all. The legislature is also free to recognize degrees of harm and to state where the harm is most acute or where the measures could be more effective. For example, a court would not strike down a limited quarantine measure solely because of its under-inclusiveness. Sometimes the courts will find that under-inclusion is so arbitrary as to deny equal protection.[84] This could occur, for example, if a control measure were to be applied only to homosexual school teachers who had AIDS and not to "straight" people in the schools who could similarly communicate the infection.

iii. Over-inclusion

An over-inclusive classification includes not only those who are similarly situated with respect to the purpose but others who are not. Thus, a control measure whose purpose was to reduce the activities of those who posed a threat of the spread of HTLV-III would be over-inclusive if applied to all homosexuals and users of intravenous drugs, since only a small segment of those groups actually pose such a threat.[85]

When the state action is burdensome as in the context of personal control measures, over-inclusion is less tolerable than under-inclusion, "for while the latter fails to impose the burden on some who should logically bear it the former actually does impose the burden on some who do not belong to the class."[86] Accordingly, courts are more likely to invalidate statutes which restrict the rights of more people than absolutely necessary.

iv. Least restrictive alternative

Under strict scrutiny, not only must the statute avoid affecting more people than necessary, it also must avoid using measures on anyone which are more intrusive than necessary. Thus, a statute cannot be overly intrusive. If the public health objective could be achieved as well, or better, by less intrusive or restrictive measures, then those should be used. Non-lawyers sometimes have difficulties with the principle of the least restrictive alternative. Public health measures have often been predicated on the notion that it is best to err on the side of caution. Under this philosophy, "health" comes before "rights", and if a control measure might promote the public health it should be used without exploring less restrictive alternatives.

As a manner of risk management it is understandable that if the almost certain result of contracting AIDS is death, aggressive use of public health powers at an early stage may be justified. The principle of the least restrictive alternative is not necessarily inconsistent with this view. It does not require a less effective measure be used merely because it is less intrusive. It only requires a less intrusive measure if it is equally, or more, effective.

3. Intermediate Standard of Scrutiny

Although the Supreme Court avoids using the term, it has developed some form of intermediate standard of review which is not as permissive as the "rational relation" test, nor as rigorous as "strict scrutiny." Legislative classifications based on gender or illegitimacy call for a middle standard of review. Gender generally provides no reasonable ground for differentiated treatment. "What differentiates sex from such nonsuspect statuses as intelligence or physical disability...is that the sex characteristic frequently bears no relation to ability to perform or contribute to society."[87] Illegitimacy is also beyond the individual's control and bears "no relation to the individual's ability to participate in and contribute to society."[88]

Where such "quasi-suspect classifications" are used statutes "will survive equal protection scrutiny to the extent that they are substantially related to a legislative state interest.[89] Statutes which deprive individuals of important, but not fundamental, rights also receive intermediate scrutiny.[90]

The major relevance of the intermediate standard of review in the AIDS context would appear to be whether homosexuality would be regarded as a suspect classification, a subject already discussed at pages 253-254 supra. In addition the question arises whether any of the privacy or other rights affected by a public health measure would be regarded as sufficiently important to warrrant more careful review. Any state action, for example, which seriously threatened the livelihood of the person or his ability to obtain health insurance could provoke the court into a less deferential form of review. But the past record of the court does not give any clear signs as to how these might be treated.

4. <u>The Rigidity of Traditional Equal Protection Analysis: Toward a More Flexible Equal Protection</u>

The equal protection analysis developed by the courts is open to the criticism that it is a highly mechanistic approach--if certain key classes are drawn or fundamental rights affected the court's analysis cuts with a sharp blade; if no such key factors are at work the court is almost obsequious in its relations with the legislature. In its rational relation test the court has demanded only the loosest fit between the classification and the relevant public objective even in cases in which the reasonable legislative motives are hard to ascertain. Such results have led to "understandable skepticism about whether the rationality constraint...is any constraint at all."[91] Only a few rights are said to be "fundamental" and a few classes "suspect," generating an infrequent mechanistic constraint on public policy.

Recent court decisions, notably <u>City of Cleburne, Texas v. Cleburne Living Center</u>, have begun to strip down the artificial tiers of scrutiny developed by the court over decades. The <u>Cleburne</u> court struck down a zoning ordinance excluding group homes for mentally retarded people. Although the court found no reason to raise its standard of review, it nevertheless searched deep in the record to conclude that there was no rational basis for believing that mentally retarded people would pose a special threat to the city's legitimate interests.

While the reason for its more searching analysis of public justifications was not apparent in the majority opinion, Justice Stevens, joined by Chief Justice Burger argued that where a class is subjected to a "tradition of disfavor" by public law, and where there are no characteristics of the disadvantaged class justifying disparate treatment, a "rational basis" test should have some bite. Should this line of thought be brought to bear on AIDS legislation, we might see the court providing a more careful review of the statute than otherwise would be expected under the lowest level of scrutiny.

A good illustration of the impact of the court's analytic framework on the probable outcome would be the Colorado statute requiring the reporting of a positive HTLV-III antibody test. This test reporting requirement probably fails to implicate any fundamental interest or create any suspect class. Traditional "minimal rationality" would require only a reasonable relation to a valid state interest; i.e., the need to collect epidemiological data to monitor the spread of HTLV-III. Usually the court would go no further in its "minimalist" review. Yet if the court were to comb through the record as it did in Cleburne it might well conclude that such reporting statutes were unnecessary for the purpose and that the less extensive requirement of reporting the disease status would suffice. (See pp. 338-341 infra).

At present we would predict a more permissive, judicial approach. However, one suspects that ultimately the decision would rest upon the court's judgment as to the legislative motives. Were the court to conclude that the measure was provoked more by fear or prejudice than reason, it would exercise more control.

C. Conclusion

Public policy makers can be virtually assured of judicial and political support for compulsory public health measures to control the spread of AIDS which are carefully based upon the current state of scientific understanding. Such measures would not be required "to resort to close distinctions or to maintain a precise scientific uniformity,"[92] no matter how much this is desirable. What policy makers may not do--even under the judiciary's "minimum rationality" review--is to base their measures on "vague, undifferentiated fears...of some portion of the community" or on "irrational prejudice."[93] Nor may public health regulators succumb to "a bare...desire to harm a politically unpopular group."[94] Even stricter scrutiny will be applied to public health measures which affect liberty, autonomy or privacy of human beings. These measures should not be promulgated without searching examination as to public health need, specificity of the targeted population and adherence to the principle of the least restrictive alternative.

References

1. State v. Rackowski, 86 A. 606, 607-08 (S.Ct. Conn. 1913).

2. See chapters 1 and 2 supra.

3. See, e.g., Jacobson v. Massachusetts, 197 U.S. 11, 25 (1905) and cases cited therin; Ex parte Johnson, 40 Cal. App. 242, 180 P. 644 (1919); Ex parte Company, Ex parte Irvin, 139 N.E. 204, 206 (S. Ct. Ohio 1922); In re Smith, 146 N.Y. 68, 40 N.E. 497, 28 L.R.A. 820 (Ct. App. N.Y. 1895); Jew Ho v. Williamson, 103 F. 10 (1900); Lawton v. Steele, 152 U.S. 133 (1894).

4. Varholy v. Sweat, 15 So.2d 267, 269-70 (S. Ct. Fla. 1943); State v. Rackowski, 86 A. 606, 608 (S. Ct. Conn. 1913) (and cases cited therein); Highland v. Schulte, 82 N.W. 62, 64 (S. Ct. Mich. 1900); Hurst v. Warner, 102 Mich. 238 (1894); Allison v. Cash, 137 S.W. 245 (Ky, 1911).

5. Jacobson v. Massachusetts, 197 U.S. 11, 25 (1905).

6. Ex Parte Martin, 188 P.2d 287 (Cal.App.3 Dist. 1948); State ex rel. Kennedy v. Head, 185 S.W.2d 530 (Tenn. 1945); Varholy v. Sweat, 153 Fla. 571, 15 So.2d 267 (1943); City of Little Rock v. Smith, 204 Ark. 692, 163 S.W.2d 205 (1942); Ex Parte Caselli, 62 Mont. 201, 204 P. 364 (1922); Ex Parte Arata, 52 Cal.App.380, 198 P. 814 (1921); Ex Parte Shepard, 51 Cal.App.49, 195 P. 1077 (1921); Ex Parte McGee, 105 Kan. 574, 185 P. 14 (1919); State ex rel. McBride v. Superior Court, 103 Wash. 409, 174 P. 973 (1918); Ex Parte Company, Ex Parte Irvin, 106 Ohio St. 50, 139 N.E. 204 (1922).

7. Greene v. Edwards, 265 S.E.2d 661 (W.Va. 1980); Application of Halko, 54 Cal. Rptr. 661 (1966); Jones v. Czapkay, 6 Cal. Rptr. 182 (1960); White v. Seattle Local Union No. 81, Amalgamated Meat Cutters and Butcher Workmen of North America, 337 P.2d 289 (Wash. 1959).

8. Crayton v. Larrabee, 220 N.Y. 493, aff'd 147 N.Y.S. 1105 (1917); Allison v. Cash, 137 S.W. 245 (Ky. 1911); Hengehold v. City of Covington, 108 Ky. 752, 57 S.W. 495 (1900); Henderson County Board of Health v. Ward, 107 Ky. 477, 54 S.W. 725 (1900); Highland v. Schulte, 123 Mich. 360, 82 N.W. 62 (1900); Smith v. Emery, 42 N.Y.S. 258, 11 App.Div.10 (1896); City of Richmond v. Henrico County Supervisors, 83 Va. 204, 2 S.E. 26 (1887); Beckwith v. Sturdevant, 42 Conn. 158 (1875); In Re Smith, 146 N.Y. 68, 40 N.E. 497 (Ct. App. N.Y. 1895); Spring v. Inhabitants of Hyde Park, 137 Mass. 554, 50 Am.Rep. 334 (1884); Harrison v. Mayor & City Council of Baltimore, 1 Gill. 264 (Md. 1843).

9. People v. Tait, 103 N.E. 750 (1913); State v. Rackowski, 86 Conn. 677, 86 A. 606 (1913).

10. Kirk v. Wyman, 83 S.C. 372, 65 S.E. 387 (1909).

11. Rudolphe v. City of New Orleans, 11 La.Ann. 242 (1856).

12. Jew Ho v. Williamson, 103 F. 10 (N.D. Cal. 1900).

13. City of Little Rock v. Smith, 163 S.W.2d 705,707 (S.Ct. Ark. 1942).

14. State ex rel. McBride v. Superior Court, 103 Wash 409, 174 P. 973 (1918).

15. Kirk v. Wyman, 65 S.E. 387 (S.Ct. S.C. 1909).

16. Ex Parte McGee, 105 Kan. 574, 185 P.14, 8 A.L.R. 831,835 (1919).

17. See e.g., City of Little Rock v. Smith supra ("private rights...must yield in the interest of security"; VD "affects the public health so intimately and so insiduously that considerations of delicacy and privacy may not be permitted to thwart measures necesary to avert the public peril"); Mugler v. Kansas, 123 U.S. 623 (1887) (power to quarantine "so as to bind us all must exist somewhere; else, society will be at the mercy of the few, who, regarding only their appetites or passions, may be willing to imperil the security of the many, provided only they are permitted to do as they please"); Irwin v. Arrendale, 159 S.E.2d 441 (Ct.App.Ga. 1967) (individuals must submit to reasonable public health measures for the common good).

18. State ex rel. McBride v. Superior Court, 103 Wash. 409, 174 P. 973,976 (1918); Aaron v. Broiles, 64 Tex. 316 (1885); Hurst v. Warner, 102 Mich. 238 (1894).

19. Ex Parte Caselli, 204 P. 364 (1922).

20. Marbury v. Madison, 1 Cranch 137,176, (1803).

21. Mugler v. Kansas, 123 U.S. 623 ( ).

22. See Health Department of City of New York v. Rector, etc. of Trinity Church, 145 N.Y. 32, 39 N.E. 833 (1895).

23. See City of Cleburne, Texas v. Cleburne Living Center, 105 S.Ct. 3249 (1985).

24. Lawton v. Steele, 152 U.S. 133 (1894). See Jew Ho v. Williamson, 103 F.102 (1900).

25. E.g., Chu Lung v. Freeman, 92 U.S. 275,280 ("the right of a state to protect the public health can only arise from a vital necessity for its exercise, and cannot be carried beyond the scope of that necessity"); Rock v. Carney, 185 N.W. 798,799 (Mich. 1921); Wilson v. Alabama G.S.R. Co, 28 So. 567 (Miss. 1900); Jacobson v. Massachusetts, 197 U.S. 11,28 (1905). But see, Kaul v. City of Chehalis, 27 P.2d 352 (Wash. 1954).

26. Compare Jew Hew v. Williamson, 103 F. 10 (N.D. Cal. 1900).(searching scrutiny of necessity) with Viemeister v. White, President, 197 N.Y. 235, 72 N.E. 97 (1904) ("what the people believe is for the common welfare must be accepted as tending to promote the common welfare, whether or not it does in fact or not") quoted with approval in Jacobson v. Massachusetts, 197 U.S. at 35.

27. Hengehold v. City of Covington, 57 S.W. 495 (Ky. 1900).

28. Kirk v. Wyman, 65 S.E. 387,390 (S.Ct. S.C. 1909).

29. Kirk v. Wyman, at 390.

30. State v. Rackowski, 86 A. 606 (S.Ct. Conn. 1913).

31. Ex parte Company, Ex parte Irvin, 106 Ohio St. 50, 139 N.E. 204,205 (S.Ct. Ohio 1922). See Ex parte Johnson, 40 Cal. App. 242, 180 P. 644 (1919).

32. Ex parte Company, Ex parte Irvin, 139 N.E. at 206.

33. People v. Strautz, 386 Ill. 360, 54 N.E. 2d 441,444 (1944). See ex parte Caselli, 204 P. 364 (1922); State ex rel. Kennedy v. Head, 185 S.W.2d 530 (Tenn. 1945); State v. Hutchinson, 18 So.2d 723 (Ala. 1944).

34. People v. Tait, 30 N.E. 750 (S.Ct. Ill. 1913); Railroad Company v. Husen, 95 U.S. 465,471-73 (1877); Ex parte Martin, 188 P.2d 287 (Ct.App.Cal. 1948) (public health officials must have "probable cause" to quarantine pending an opportunity for further investigation or examination); Ex parte Dillon, 186 P. 170 (Ct.App. 2Dist 1919).

35. Ex parte Shepard, 51 Cal. App. 49, 195 P. 1077 (1921).

36. Ex parte Arata, 198 P. 814,816 (1921). See In re Smith, 40 N.E. 497 (Ct.App. N.Y. 1895).

37. Smith v. Emery, 42 N.Y.S. 258,260 (1896).

38. See Comment, Fear itself: AIDS, herpes and public health decisions, 3 Yale Law & Policy Review, 479 (1985).

39. Jew Ho v. Williamson, 103 F. 10 (N.D. Cal. 1900).

40. Kirk v. Wyman, 65 S.E. 387,391 (S.Ct. S.C. 1909).

41. Ex parte Martin, 188 P.2d 287,291 (Ct.App. Cal. 1948).

42. Jacosbon v. Massachusetts, 197 U.S. 11,28 (1905). See People ex rel. Baker v. Strautz, 54 N.E.2d 441,443 (Ill. 1944); People v. Tait, 103 N.E. 750,752 (1913).

43. See Kirk v. Wyman, 65 S.E. at 390 ("The courts consider, first, whether interference with personal liberty was reasonably necessary to the public health, and second, if the means used and the extent of the interference were reasonably necessary for the accomplishment of the purpose to be attained.")

44. Jacobson v. Massachusetts, 197 U.S. at 31. See Rock v. Carney, 185 N.W. 798,799,800 (Mich. 1921) (methods must bear some true

relation to the real danger and be reasonable, having in mind the end to be attained); Wilson v. Alabama G.S.R. Co., 28 So. 567 (Miss 1900) (Broad restriction of movement was unreasonably related to determining who was diseased or who was a carrier of yellow fever).

45. Jew Ho v. Williamson, 103 F. 10,22 (N.D. Cal. 1900).

46. See In re Halko, 246 C.A. 2d 553, 54 Cal.Rptr. 661 (1966); Moore v. Draper, 57 S.2d 648 (1952).

47. New York State Association for Retarded Children v. Carey, 612 F.2d 644,650-51 (2d Cir. 1979).

48. For a general discussion of these principles in various contexts, see e.g., City of Cleburne, Texas v. Cleburne Living Center, 105 S.Ct. 3249 (1985); Note, Developments--Equal Protection, 82 Harv. L. Rev. 1065 (1969); Note, Developments--The Family, 93 Harv. L. Rev. 1156, 1161-93 (1980); Note The Supreme Court 1982 Term, 97 Harv. L. Rev. 4, 70-118 (1983); L. Tribe, American Constitutional Law (1978); Note, Parental Rights and the Habilitation Decision for Mentally Retarded Children, 94 Yale L.J. 1715, 1729-37 (1985).

49. Shapiro v. Thompson, 394 U.S. 618 (1969).

50. Zablocki v. Redhail, 434 U.S. 374 (1978).

51. E.g., Griswold v. Connecticut, 381 U.S. 479 (1965).

52. Plyer v. Doe, 457 U.S. 202,216 (1982).

53. New York Association of Retarded Children v. Carey, 612 F.2d 644 (Second Cir. 1979). See D. Rothman & S. Rothman, The Willowbrook Wars (1984).

54. See Sastein, Naked Preferences and the Constitution, 84 Colum. L. Rev. 1689,1710-18 (1984).

55. McLaughlin v. Florida, 379 U.S. 184,191 (1964).

56. See further p. *infra*.

57. Schweiker v. Wilson, 450 U.S. 221,230 (1981); Vance v. Bradley, 440 U.S. 93 (1979).

58. City of Cleburne, Texas v. Cleburne Living Center, 105 S.Ct. 3249, 3255 (1985).

59. See Zobel v. Williams, 457 U.S. 55,61-63 (1982); United States Department of Agriculture v. Moreno, 413 U.S. 528,535 (1973).

60. United States Railroad Retirement Board v. Fritz, 449 U.S. 166,174 (1980); New Orleans v. Dukes, 427 U.S. 297,303 (1976).

61. Shapiro v. Thompson, 394 U.S. 618 (1969).

62. Zablocki v. Redhail, 434 U.S. 374 (1978).

63. Griswold v. Connecticut, 381 U.S. 479 (1965). Other "fundamental" rights include the right to vote, Harper v. Virginia Board of Elections, 383 U.S. 663 (1966); and the right to criminal appeals, Douglas v. California, 372 U.S. 353 (1963).

64. See Whalen v. Roe, 97 S.Ct. 869 (1977).

65. See Note, Developments--The Family, 93 Harv. L. Rev. 1156,1163-64 (1980).

66. Roe v. Wade, 410 U.S. 113,152-53 (1973) (abortion). See Zablocki v. Redhail, 434 U.S. 374 (1978) (marriage); Skinner v. Oklahoma, 316 U.S. 535 (1942) (procreation); Carey v. Population Services Int'l, 431 U.S. 678 (1977) (contraception); Griswold v. Connecticut, 381 U.S. 479 (1965) (contraception); Moore v. City of E. Cleveland, 431 U.S. 494,499 (1977) (family relationships); Pierce v. Society of Sisters, 268 U.S. 510,535 (1925)(rearing and education of children); Meyer v. Nebraska, 262 U.S. 390 (1923) (rearing and education of children); Cleveland Bd. of Educ. v. La Fleur, 414 U.S. 632 (1974)(childbearing).

67. See Planned Parenthood v. Danforth, 428 U.S. 52 (1976) (husband's consent to wife's abortion held to be an unwarranted intrusion on wife's right to abortion). See also Eisenstadt v. Baird, 405 U.S. 438,453 (1972); Eichbaum, Toward an Autonomy-Based Theory of Constitutional Privacy: Beyond the Ideology of Familial Privacy, 14 Hav. C.R.-C.L. L. Rev. 361,366 (1979).

68. See Carey v Population Services Int'l., 431 U.S. 678 (1977) (procreative rights extend to the unmarried); Roe v. Wade, 410 U.S. 113 (1973) (abortion rights extend to unmarried women).

69. Richards, Unnatural Acts and the Constitutional Right to Privacy: A Moral Theory, 45 Fordham L. Rev. 1281 (1977); Richards, Sexual Autonomy and the Constitutional Right to Privacy: A Case Study in Human Rights and the Unwritten Constitution, 30 Hastings L.J. 957 (1979); Richards, Homosexuality and the Constitutional Right to Privacy, 8 Rev. of L. & Soc. Change 311 (1980); Saphire, Gay Rights and the Constitution: An Essay on Constitutional Theory, Practice, and Dronenburg v. Zech, 104 Dayton L. Rev. 767 (1985); Delgado, Fact, Norm, and Standard of Review--The Case of Homosexuality, 104 Dayton L. Rev. 575 (1985).

70. Doe v. Commonwealth's Attorney, 425 U.S. 901, 96 S.Ct. 1489 (1976).

71. Baker v. Wade, 769 F.2d 289 (1985); Dronenburg v. Zech, 741 F.2d 1388,1398 (D.C. Cir. 1984).

72. Hardwick v. Bowers, 760 F.2d 1202 (11th Cir. 1985).

73. See Carey v. Population Services International, 431 U.S. 678,688, n.5, 694 n.17 (1977).

74. Bowers v. Hardwick, 54 U.S.L.W. 4919 (June 24, 1986).

75. Korematsu v. United States, 323 U.S. 214 (1944).

76. Graham v. Richardson, 403 U.S. 365 (1971).

77. Oyama v. California, 332 U.S. 633 (1948).

78. City of Cleburne, Texas v. Cleburne Living Center, 105 S.Ct. 3249,3255 (1985).

79. Massachusetts Board of Retirement v. Murgia, 427 U.S. 307,313 (1976).

80. City of Cleburne, Texas v. Cleburne Living Center, 105 S.Ct. 3249,3258 (1985).

81. See Note, The Constitutional Status of Sexual Orientation: Homosexuality as a Suspect Classification, 98 Harv. L. Rev. 1285 (1985); Note, An Argument for the Application of Equal Protection Heightened Scrutiny to Classifications Based on Homosexuality, 57 S. Cal. L. Rev. 797 (1984).

82. Kramer v. Union Free School District No. 15, 395 U.S. 621 (1969); Skinner v. Oklahoma ex rel. Williamson, 316 U.S. 535 (1942).

83. McLaughlin v. Florida, 379 U.S. 184 (1964); Graham v. Richardson, 403 U.S. 355 (1971).

84. See Note, Developments—Equal Protection, 82 Harv. L. Rev. 1065, 1084-85 (1969).

85. See Hirabayshi v. United States, 320 U.S. 81 (1943); and Korematsu v. United States, 323 U.S. 214 (1944) where similar over-inclusive classifications were permitted due to the exigent circumstances of wartime.

86. Note, Developments—Equal Protection, 82 Harv. L. Rev. 1065,1086 (1969).

87. Frontiero v. Richardson, 411 U.S. 677,686 (1973). See Reed v. Reed, 404 U.S. 71 (1971).

88. Mathews v. Lucas, 427 U.S. 495,505 (1976). See Levy v. Louisiana, 391 U.S. 68 (1968).

89. Mills v. Habluetzel, 456 U.S. 91,99 (1982).

90. See Vlandis v. Kline, 412 U.S. 441 (1973) (higher education at an affordable cost); Bell v. Burson, 402 U.S. 535 (1971) (driver's license); United States Dept. of Agriculture v. Murry, 413 U.S. 508 (1973) (government benefits such as food stamps).

91. Sunstein, Naked Preferences and the Constitution, 84 Colum L. Rev. 1689,1714 (1984).

92. Allied Stores of Ohio, Inc. v. Bowers, 358 U.S. 522,527 79 S.Ct. 437,441 (1959).

93. City of Cleburne, Texas v. Cleburne Living Center, 105 S.Ct. 3249,3258-59 (1985).

94. United States Dept. of Agriculture v. Moreno, 413 U.S. 528,534, 93 S.Ct. 2821,2826 (1973).

CHAPTER 5

Testing and Screening Programs

A. Introduction

This chapter will focus on testing procedures designed to determine whether a person has been exposed to the AIDS related virus. The overriding purpose of testing is to identify those individuals or tissue products which are potentially infectious. The goal of the chapter is to assess the legal and public policy justifications for and against application of the screening programs to specific populations or for specific purposes. The chapter establishes a general legal standard for assessing the justification for various screening programs, and then applies that standard to major proposals currently being considered at the federal or state levels.

1. Operational Definitions of "Testing" and "Screening"

We use the term _testing_ to refer to the application of the diagnostic ELISA procedures and supplemental diagnostic tests to individuals. The usual settings for testing are when an individual desires to know of his antibody status for personal reasons and when a physician needs the test for legitimate clinical reasons. Each of these is a voluntary use of the diagnostic procedure and always requires informed consent. Individuals can be tested without their consent where the state has a strong interest in finding or confirming antibody status. Mandatory clinical examinations, diagnostic testing and treatment are not uncommon public health measures have been applied frequently to persons reasonably suspected of having venereal disease.

We use the term <u>screening</u> to refer to the systematic application of the ELISA and supplemental procedures to specific targeted populations. Implicit in the concept of screening is the sorting out of those who are seropositive from those who are not. Screening invites the conclusion that those found seropositive will be dealt with in some special way; e.g., that they will be excluded from certain activities or environments, or special actions will be taken. Indeed the primary legal or policy justification for systematic collection of such information is that some legitimate and necessary use will be made of it. Collection of sensitive data without clear rationale is always legally suspect. It is therefore difficult to separate legal analysis of screening from the critical consequences which are intended to accrue from the program.

Programs can either screen <u>people</u> with the primary purpose of identifying members of a population who are antibody positive or they can screen <u>bodily products</u>, with the primary purpose of protecting the recipients of those products from suspected contamination. In the latter situation there is no compulsion upon people to donate the products. However, once products are donated the screening becomes mandatory.

2. Reliability of the ELISA and Supplementary Tests

Some commentators have expressed concern over the reliability and ethical considerations involved in widespread use of the antibody test.[1] Reactive tests may be due to subclinical infection, to immunity, or to an active carrier state, or may represent false positive reactions such as cross-reactivity to antigens or other viruses.[2] "False positives" are test results which show an immunologic response to HTLV-III/LAV when in fact there is no such response. The rate of false positives depends upon the prevalence of antibody in the donor population with higher prevalence resulting in more meaningful test results.

If a positive finding on a single ELISA were to result in adverse consequences to the individual, these could be visited upon an unacceptably large number of people who were not carriers of the virus. Screening programs, therefore, should require strongly positive sequential testing with a repeatedly reactive ELISA, together with a supplemental test such as the Western Blot or an immunofluorescence assay (IFA). If sequential testing were required for screening programs, the reliability would be well within scientifically acceptable levels.[3]

B. Screening in the Aggregate

   1. Screening of Tissue Donors

Even without confirmatory testing the ELISA is within acceptable ranges where the results of the screening are applied in the aggregate and there is no impact on any identified individual. There is clear justification as a matter of public policy to use the assay to screen blood, tissues, organs and semen donors. Lactating mothers who contribute to milk banks may also be subject to screening procedures. Screening in this context is concerned with avoiding the contamination of products to be received by third parties. There should be no coercion involved in the decision to donate bodily tissue and the purpose of the test should not be to identify people who are infected outside the confines of the particular donation and future donations.

The American Red Cross and blood banks across the United States have instituted programs of required screening of blood and blood products. Several states have required such screening by statute. Most organ donation programs have also indicated that routine screening includes testing for the presence of HTLV-III. The Federal Food and Drug Administration issued proposed rules on routine screening for HTLV-III in blood and blood products on February 21, 1986. The rules require testing of each unit of human blood and blood products. Establishments must keep adequate records of test results and be able to trace contaminated products to individual donors, maintain confidentiality of the records, and maintain identification necessary to assure positive testing individuals could not donate blood or blood products in the future.

2. Screening within a Research Protocol

A further example of allowable screening is that carried out in important health research projects. Knowledge of the effects of HTLV-III infection on individuals and transmission of the virus is crucial. Research is an indispensable element in the strategy for combatting AIDS. Accordingly, no legal prohibitions should adhere which present unreasonable obstacles to screening within an ethically acceptable research protocol. We do not intend to examine the many legal and ethical requirements that should be applied in AIDS research. The Hastings Center has already published an admirable document on that subject.[4] Further, the U.S. government has issued guidelines to Institutional Review Boards concerning AIDS research.[5]

3. Informing Persons of the Results of HTLV-III Antibody Testing

There is clear support in ethical medical practice of informing nearly all patients of their medical condition as revealed in routine diagnostic procedures. Nevertheless a reasonable case can be made that informing a person of his HTLV-III antibody status is not always warranted. Sequentially positive antibody testing does no more than place the person within an undefined statistical range of probability of developing HTLV-III related disease. There are currently a number of studies seeking more data on the natural history of HTLV-III infection. All of the factors which can contribute to a change from seropositivity to lymphadenopathy syndrome and through to full blown AIDS are not yet fully understood. In these circumstances, it is legitimate to question whether information as to seropositivity is directly useful and beneficial to every patient. In health matters it should ordinarily be a choice of the patient as to the information he will or will not receive. A patient is entitled to be informed of all relevant information bearing upon his health. Where the information is inconclusive, that is not a sufficient justification for withholding it, but only a reason for careful explanation and, where wanted, counseling.

Information concerning HTLV-III infection, however, has importance beyond the patient's own welfare. A person who is sero positive is assumed to be infectious and thus personal choices have consequences beyond the individual concerned. A person acquiring knowledge that he or she may harbor an infectious and potentially fatal virus may be the foundation for behavior change. While it is certainly possible to assume that some people would alter their behavior whether or not they had knowledge of seropositivity, such assumptions are complacent in attempts to stop the spread of the virus.

Holders of information may also have a legal duty to inform the person that he is seropositive. The minimum the law would require is to inform the patient of the test results and the consequences of behavior likely to transfer the infection (see pp. 289-294 infra). The holder of such information may also have a duty to protect third parties. The minimum steps required to fulfill this duty would be to seek to influence the patient's future behavior in favor of reducing or eliminating danger to third parties.

C. Voluntary Testing

1. Personal Choice for Testing: Alternative Test Sites

Individuals in high risk groups have compelling personal reasons for wanting to know their antibody status. A positive test result may trigger changed behavior and a healthier life style. A positive test result also provides the occasion for focused education and counseling to help avoid spread of the infection.

In order to divert people from donating blood to discover their antibody status most states have established alternative test sites. Alternative test sites guarantee anonymity and provide a useful public service in encouraging individuals to find out more about their health and the potential for infecting others. Some states which have a requirement to report positive HTLV-III antibody tests, make an exception at alternative centers.

At such centers, individuals can usually avoid the reporting requirement by withholding their names. The test centers also provide professional services for informing, educating and assisting people in respect of appropriate future life choices. Accordingly, we see substantial advantages in encouraging those at high risk for HTLV-III infection to seek anonymous testing. We note that one state, Oregon, has a policy of refusing to allow anonymity at alternate test sites. This practice appears to us to detract significantly from the chief value of these sites; viz, to encourage people in high risk groups to seek the antibody test in a confidential site, thus avoiding the use of blood donation centers for this purpose.

2. Testing for Diagnostic or Other Clinical Purposes

The CDC definition of AIDS does not require a positive HTLV-III antibody test in most cases for diagnostic purposes. Nevertheless, HTLV-III infection has a wide clinical spectrum and identifying the cause of outward signs of immunosuppression can be clinically beneficial. An ELISA is now a well recognized supplementary diagnostic tool. Physicians should only order an ELISA for legitimate and necessary clinical purposes. The mere ordering of an assay may imply that the person is in a high-risk group, based upon personal history or mere suspicion by the clinician. Rigorous efforts should be taken by hospitals and their staff to assure confidentiality of test results, whether positive or negative. Some physicians and hospitals have adopted the practice of inserting results of the assay into clinical records by means of a confidential code.

Physicians and hospitals are well advised to limit sero testing to well documented clinical need for the data. A hospital should not assume that permission to draw blood for unspecified clinical testing of a patient clearly implies permission to administer an ELISA. Whenever an ELISA is to be performed the patient must give informed consent.[6]

3. Regulatory Issues in Use of the ELISA

The Federal Food and Drug Administration is responsible for regulating the use and labelling of new products. It has licensed the ELISA for use only as a method of screening blood and blood products, and the commercial companies that market the test label its use only for those purposes.

The ELISA is, however, widely used for purposes other than for which it has been licensed, notably as a diagnostic test for the presence of HTLV-III. More importantly, the Centers for Disease Control have specifically recommended the use of the test for screening of persons in high risk groups (see pp. 307-309 infra).

It is not uncommon or unlawful for a product to be used other than for the purposes for which it was licensed. Nevertheless, the fact that the U.S. Public Health Service has gone further than the FDA may be a confusing approach to standard setting. One option to maintain greater consistency would be for the commercial companies who market the ELISA to work with the FDA towards additional labelling of the product.

D. Population Screening

It is when the ELISA is proposed to be used beyond the situations described above that serious problems are presented. In this section we intend to develop a general test to be used in cases where screening is proposed. We will then set out several general reasons against population screening, including the absence of any effective medical intervention, the cooperation obtained thus far from high risk groups and the legal problems associated with population screening.

Finally, we will apply the general test proposed to a variety of selective screening programs and give justifications for and against their implementation. Whenever relevant we will refer to published guidelines by federal authorities and state proposals for screening. The test proposed has application to both voluntary and compulsory screening programs, but we will differentiate between these in the ensuing discussion. We will also seek to demonstrate the need for much clearer public justifications for compulsory applications of screening programs.

1. Proposed Criteria for Assessing Population Screening

There is no single formula which can provide all the correct answers as to whether screening of particular populations is appropriate public policy. Yet, to attempt to address each proposal without a systematic theory of analysis strikes us as somewhat haphazard and could reach inconsistent results. Accordingly we offer a general test to be applied in examining screening proposals. In most cases we would suggest that a reasoned positive response to each of the following criteria is desirable before concluding that screening is warranted, particularly if its application is to be mandatory:

    a. The selected population should have a reservoir of infection. The purpose is to ensure that the screening program does not affect disproportionate numbers of people who would have to submit to personally intrusive and unnecessary testing procedures. This criterion would clearly differentiate, say, between a program of screening within a treatment center for sexually transmitted diseases, and within a school. In the former it is possible to conclude that there may be a potentially high reservoir of infection while in the latter there are no reasonable grounds for believing this is the case.

b. The environment or setting within which the population operates poses a significant risk of communication of the infection.

The purpose is to demonstrate that, not only is there a reservoir of infection, but that the risks of transmission are real. The "public health necessity" which must form the basis of screening programs requires the existence of a setting where transfer is reasonably likely to take place. There is no public health justification for screening where the only expected association among people is casual. It is quite another matter where there is something inherent in the environment in which the population operates, which involves intimate contact or the possible exchange of bodily fluids.

c. Knowledge of the results of testing enables the authorities to take effective precautions to reduce the spread of the infection which could not otherwise be taken without that knowledge.

Assuming that all persons within a selected class were to be screened, what could be done with the resulting test information that could be effective in achieving the goal of reducing the spread of infection? Further, could the action have been taken in the absence of any screening program? This issue is fundamentally important because it requires a clear need for test results as the basis for action or precautions necessary to reduce the spread of HTLV-III. If the proposed action or precautions should actually be taken whether or not the test is given, then it raises the question as to whether systematic population screening is truly needed.

d. The critical consequences of the screening are not disproportionate to the benefits.

Screening programs carry the potential danger that they may result in the disclosure of personal information with adverse consequences for the patient. Also, screening may be intended as a condition precedent to other more intrusive public health powers. These are the critical consequences of screening. Screening programs, together with measures which follow, are usually designed to have some effect in reducing HTLV-III transmission. Yet, the human or social costs of the exercise of these powers may simply be disproportionate to their expected benefits. The balancing process entailed in the critical consequences criterion involves a judgment as to whether the health benefit of screening would outweigh the personal, social and economic costs for those who test positive. This critical consequences criterion would also legally require the use of less restrictive alternatives. Thus, if the public health objective of screening could be achieved with consequences which were less severe, intrusive or restrictive, then they are to be preferred.

2. General Legal and Policy Implications of Screening Programs

Justification for legally authorized selective screening must be based upon the undisputed achievement of protection of the public health which clearly outweighs the invasion of individual privacy and loss of occupation or profession which could result to individuals in these groups. At this time we see great difficulties in finding such a justification for compulsory screening programs. Since there is currently no treatment or vaccine for prevention, knowledge of carriers of the virus could not be utilized to alleviate a person's infectious condition or to suggest precautions in personal conduct that are not already well known among risk groups.

The spread of HTLV-III can be reduced through avoidance of intimate behavior which may result in transmission of the virus. The introduction of screening, particularly if it has a coercive element, may have the reverse effect of causing persons in known risk groups to avoid seeking testing and treatment on a voluntary basis.

The mere fact that highly sensitive information is collected and available builds a demand for its use by hospitals, insurance companies, employers, landlords and others. Ultimately the only rationale for collection of the data by public health officials is to use it together with other control measures. Thus, a burden falls on those seeking systematically to collect information to demonstrate that its use will be constructive to the public health and not disproportionately harmful to the individual. This burden of demonstrating a significantly positive benefit/cost ratio will be difficult to discharge given the current state of scientific knowledge.

The systematic screening of selective populations poses a plethora of legal and ethical quandaries--the requirement to obtain informed consent in any voluntary testing or screening program; the duty to keep the information confidential; and the sometimes contradictory duty to protect third parties who are in foreseeable danger of contracting the infection. We deal with each of these three legal issues in turn.

a. Informed consent

As a general rule, any medical procedure which involves the touching of a patient without the patient's authorization constitutes a battery. Physicians, therefore, may not infer consent to an ELISA solely on the basis of agreement to withdraw a sample of blood. In most jurisdictions failure to provide sufficient information for the patient to form a reasonable judgment about a medical procedure is an issue of negligence as opposed to battery. The most commonly applied standard of disclosure is whether the information is "material" to a reasonable person's decision to consent.[7] The results of an antibody test may be psychologically invasive to the patient and, if disclosed to others, could be detrimental to the patient's interests. Knowledge of the fact that the test is to be performed is thus clearly material to the patient. Thus, in the absence of any legally authorized mandatory screening program, permission to do an assay should be sought. In a health care context, physicians and hospitals are well advised to limit sero-testing to well documented clinical need for the data. A physician should not assume that permission to draw blood for unspecified clinical testing clearly implies permission to administer an ELISA. To obtain informed consent, the physician should explain the purposes of the testing, the range of reliability, and the potential for social harm if the results of the procedure were inappropriately disclosed. The patient may, of course, still wish the test to be performed, but the choice should be with the individual. Adequate information and counseling services should accompany these legal requirements.

b. <u>Confidentiality</u>

Confidentiality of the records of people infected with HTLV-III is of the greatest importance. HTLV-III infected individuals are found largely among groups who have long been subjected to persistent prejudice and discrimination. Unauthorized disclosure of their health status publicly associates individuals as members of these groups. Disclosure can lead to social opprobrium among family and friends and to loss of employment, housing and insurance.

Persons at risk of HTLV-III infection, therefore, have strong grounds for desiring personal privacy and confidentiality of medical information. Indeed their cooperation with public health authorities and treatment centers is largely dependent upon their expectation of confidentiality. AIDS control, in the absence of a therapeutic intervention, is currently dependent upon voluntary restraint from private, intimate behaviors most likely to spread the infection. The overriding public health objective at this time is to influence those infected with HTLV-III as to their future behavior. At the heart of that policy is confidentiality, for trust and compliance with public health programs are dependent upon an unbreachable confidential relationship.

The unauthorized disclosure of confidential information during the course of a physician/patient relationship is contrary both to medical ethics and law.[8] Most courts have imposed a legally enforceable duty of confidentiality and have grounded their decisions on the importance to public policy of a sphere of privacy between doctor and patient.[9] The Massachusetts Supreme Court most recently held that a "duty of confidentiality arises from the physician-patient relationship and that a violation of that duty, resulting in damages, gives rise to a cause of action sounding in tort against the physician."[10]

Exceptions to the principle of confidentiality have been recognized in a number of jurisdictions based upon overriding public interests. These public interests include: (1) situations where disclosure of an infectious condition is necessary to protect the public health, and (2) situations where a duty is imposed by law to disclose information, such as when information is required by subpoena.

Statutory protections of confidentiality are contained in most state public health statutes. The Centers for Disease Control has already contracted for a study of confidentiality statutes in relation to sexually transmitted diseases, and we do not intend to duplicate that effort. We note only that the strongest confidentiality protections apply to sexually transmitted diseases because of the deeply rooted personal values and moral overtones that are associated with sexually transmitted diseases. The CDC study suggests the following standards for a quality STD confidentiality statute:
- a specific subpoena exemption which protects all information and records held by the health department that relate to known or suspected cases of STD.

- a disclosure allowance that enumerates the conditions under which a release is permissible, specifying that patient consent is required for the release of any details.

- a testimony exemption that protects all state and local health department officers and employees from courtroom examination and which covers any records possessed of cases examined and/or treated by private medical sector facilities.

Statutes accomplishing many of these objectives are already in place in several states. One of the major elements of a sound confidentiality statute is its ability to protect records against court subpoena; some provisions such as in Illinois[11] and New York City[12] have been judicially construed to ensure that the privilege or exemption under law overrides judicial subpoena power. We support such statutes and urge the development of model confidentiality laws incorporating these elements applicable to HTLV-III infection.

There are several obstacles, however, to overcome in order to establish adequate statutory protections in relation to HTLV-III infection. While the strongest confidentiality protections generally apply to venereal or sexually transmitted diseases, few jurisdictions have classified AIDS as such. Most states classify the syndrome either as a communicable disease or simply as a reportable disease. Stricter control measures such as quarantine, however, are often specifically targeted at venereal disease. Therefore, inclusion of AIDS as an STD could strengthen confidentiality protections, but could also make individuals potentially subject to stricter compulsory measures.

Our survey uncovered six states (California, Florida, Illinois, New York, Wisconsin and Massachusetts) which have enacted specific legislation or regulations to protect the confidentiality of HTLV-III antibody test results. There is considerable variation in the confidentiality protection offered, even within these six states. California, for example, would protect the confidentiality of test results even from court subpoena, while Massachusetts regulations simply require laboratories to develop unspecified procedures for confidentiality.

    c. The duty to protect persons in foreseeable danger of contracting HTLV-III

Confidentiality is not a principle that will override any other legal duty owed by the holder of personal information. Many important court decisions have held that health care professionals are required to disclose information concerning a patient to those who are in foreseeable danger from that patient. The theory of liability to third parties is often said to have sprung from Tarasoff v. The Regents of California,[13] although the basic principles predate that case.

Ordinarily the law of tort does not establish a duty of care between a professional and a third party who has no relationship with the professional. In Tarasoff, a psychologist was found liable when one of his patients, having told him of his intentions, murdered a third party. The Tarasoff court carved out an exception to this common law rule in cases in which the professional stands in some "special relationship" to either the person whose conduct needs to be controlled (i.e., the patient) or in a relationship to the foreseeable victim of that conduct. The court concluded that once a therapist does in fact determine, or under applicable professional standards should have determined, that a patient poses a serious danger to others, he bears a special duty to the foreseeable victim.

In general, state jurisdictions have divided on the Tarasoff rule. Some have adopted Tarasoff, requiring a duty to protect foreseeably endangered third parties.[14] Others have created an allowable exception to the principle of confidentiality so that it is lawful for the professional, in his sound clinical judgment, to disclose confidences to protect third parties in clearly foreseeable danger.[15]

Three parameters of the Tarasoff principle are important to review. First, the duty of care extends only to third parties in foreseeable danger. To establish such a duty several courts have required a specific threat to a specific individual; i.e., a readily identifiable target.[16] Mere frequency of contact between the patient and a third party does not make the third party a foreseeable victim. The duty to protect "is not owed to statistically probable victims, but rather to specifically targeted victims."[17] It is clear, however, that all courts do not require an identifiable victim to establish liability.[18]

Second, the professional must have the ability to control the dangerous situation either by initiating procedures necessary for criminal or civil arrest or confinement or by warning those in a position to take protective measures.[19] If a professional has knowledge but no means at his disposal to prevent a foreseeable harm, he is not liable. This situation might arise where a hospital seeks to discharge a known prostitute with AIDS. Apart from informing the health department, the hospital has no control or power to prevent future dangerous sexual behavior which may be dangerous.

Third, the steps the professional will have to take to fulfill the duty to protect third parties are not entirely clear. Although the Tarasoff principle has been called the "duty to warn," a warning in itself may or may not be required; or, indeed, a warning may be regarded as insufficient to carry out the duty to protect. Much depends upon what a reasonable, similarly situated, professional would be expected to do. He may be expected to warn a foreseeable victim, inform the police or public health department, initiate procedures for civil confinement for mental illness or drug abuse, or simply to counsel the patient.

Most of the court decisions establishing a duty to protect third parties from contracting an infectious disease predate Tarasoff. Once a physician discovers or should have discovered that his patient has a contagious condition he must comply with relevant public health statutes and regulations, including any requirement to report the condition to the public health department.[20] But the physician's legal responsibilities may not end there.[21] The physician has a special relationship with his patient and owes a duty to protect those who are in foreseeable danger of contracting the infection.[22] In another important decision, the court observed:

> The relation of a physician to his patient and the immediate family is one of the highest trust. On account of his scientific knowledge and his particular relation, an attending physician is, in a certain sense, in custody of a patient infected with infectious or contagious disease. And he owes a duty to those who are ignorant of such disease, and who by reason of family ties or otherwise, are liable to be brought in contact with the patient, to instruct and advise them as to the character of the disease.[23]

The relevant court decisions in this area are usually concerned with a duty owed to family members or clinical attendants, such as nurses, to protect from an airborne infection. It is foreseeable that intimate associates may be harmed if they are not informed of the existence of an airborne infection. A blood borne infection, however, which results from HTLV-III is not so easily contracted.

The character of the duty to protect against exposure to an infectious condition has usually been framed as a "duty to advise." Those who have a foreseeable risk of contracting the infection must be advised of the nature of the infection, how it is spread and precautions that can be taken. The practical application of this "duty to advise" is not at all clear for the modern physician. Does this rule require a direct disclosure of confidential information to all third parties foreseeably at risk? Does it, in turn, require further questioning of the patient and contact tracing? Such a holding would virtually set aside any respect for the confidential relationship between physician and patient. One option to improve the situation would be to impose a threshold obligation only to advise the patient of his social responsibility to behave responsibly and to warn close contacts of his infection. A strict application of the Tarasoff line of cases would make a care-giver liable only if the patient specifically informed him of his intention not to heed the advice. Clearly if the patient declared an intention to engage in a high risk activity with an identified person, the physician's duty, minimally, would extend to warning that person.

In Gammill v. United States[24] a U.S. Army physician failed to inform the public in a nearby community about the outbreak of cases of hepatitis. Plaintiffs, who contracted the disease, claimed that the Army had a legal duty to disclose this risk to the public via the county health department. The court, however, held that there was no legal duty to warn the general public; before a duty to warn exists there must be awareness of specific risks to specific persons at risk for hepatitis. Because of the limited threat of spread of this particular condition, a reasonably specific (e.g., to a patient's close sexual contacts) and high degree of potential harm was required before the court would dispense with the obligation of confidentiality in this situation. The Gammill case has obvious application to situations involving spread of HTLV-III and would seem to establish a duty to warn only close or intimate associates. The warning may, perhaps, only be legally warranted when the patient, by his own statements or his general irresponsibility, exhibits no potential for conforming to reasonable health measures or for disclosing his positive status to intimate associates.

E. Screening of Selected Populations: Illustrative Cases

1. Compulsory Screening of Military Personnel

The only population, apart from blood donors, which has already been subject to systematic compulsory screening for HTLV-III antibodies are United States military personnel. On August 30, 1985, the Defense Department announced that it would test all new recruits for HTLV-III antibodies and that it would bar all those who test positive from the military. The test was expected to be given to some 328,000 recruits a year at a cost of nearly $1 million.[25] The army tested 270,000 recruits from October 15 to January 17, and had rejected 400. Exclusion from the military requires a doubly reactive ELISA. At the time the test for recruits was ordered, commanding officers were given discretion to order the test for existing troops.

The confidentiality of military test results became an issue shortly after the screening was implemented when some military installations "offered" the information to civilian health authorities. This breach of confidentiality led the Defense Department to assure publically that the test results would not be disclosed "except in response to a valid civilian health authority request."[26] Apparently, requests by health authorities for the data in accordance with their state laws are respected. As most state laws require the reporting only of CDC defined AIDS, reporting of test results is usually not requested. The Defense Department has since extended its program of screening by requiring all military personnel to be tested.[27]

The military has given a number of justifications for the introduction of a full scale screening program.[28] All military recruits receive live virus vaccines against several diseases and may fall victim to the attenuated virus itself; all military personnel receive multiple vaccines to which they may respond suboptimally. The military also deploys many of its personnel to areas where they may be at risk of acquiring serious diseases such as malaria, leishmaniasis and trypanosomiasis. Those who are immunosuppressed may be at greater risk from the military's vaccination and deployment program than the general population. Yet, those who are seropositive are not necessarily immunosuppressed; a positive ELISA often does not indicate that there is any current clinical problem. Moreover, immunosuppression can be determined more accurately from physical examination (e.g., unhealing sores or swollen lymph nodes) and examination of lymphocyte function as mediators of cellular immunity. Military personnel are, of course, not unique in their exposure to potentially harmful infectious agents.

The military's major public argument for compulsory screening is that most of their personnel are intended for possible combat duty. The military must plan for blood spillage in combat and using other personnel to act as blood donors in the field. When some active duty soldiers are infected with HTLV-III, there is a risk that the infection would spread rapidly. There is some evidence of a significant reservoir of infection within the military, and the Defense Department has an important public purpose in protecting personnel entering combat.

In the United States Navy, recruits testing positive were at first discharged on grounds of "erroneous enlistment" because the Navy maintained that they had the condition prior to joining the service. Judge Louis Oberdorfer in the Federal Court denied a petition for a preliminary injunction against these discharges. He noted, however, that the Navy had since changed its position and would now grant honorable discharges rather than entry level separations. The judge found the honorable discharge essentially reduces plaintiffs' alleged injury to loss of pay, allowances, and the ability to continue in active service.[29] Two of the discharged men have filed an administrative appeal with the Board for Correction of Naval Records.[30]

The decision by the U.S. military to institute a program of screening raises the question whether this could be extended to other analogous areas. The State Department and private military contractors, for example, travel abroad, and could transmit or contract the virus. The decision in the military should not set a precedent on the civilian sector, but should require separate and independent justification.

2. Compulsory Exclusion from Schools

Exclusion of children from school who harbor the AIDS related virus has been sought in a number of jurisdictions. Legal actions have already been decided in New York City[31] California[32] and Indiana[33], and two cases have been filed in New Jersey.[34] All of the cases are concerned with the removal of infected school children. A proposal has been made in Congress seeking to introduce a concurrent resolution expressing the view that public schools should not permit students with AIDS or ARC to attend regular classes and that such schools should make alternative arrangements for such students to receive education.[35] While the resolution is cast as a way of "respecting the education" of children with AIDS, its impact would be to isolate these children from their peers. Two further proposals that would prevent infected teachers and students from sharing classrooms with healthy peers have been introduced in the Florida legislature.[36]

a. Behaviors which efficiently transmit the virus: Sexual behavior and IV drug use in schools.

Epidemiologic evidence shows that there are four major methods of transmission of HTLV-III: use of contaminated needles, sexual transmission, transfusion of contaminated blood, and in utero or intrapartum transmission or transmission postnatally possibly from ingestion of breast milk. The great majority of children contract the virus from their infected mothers. None of these high risk behaviors are an inherent part of school activities and they can be virtually ruled out as possibilities for younger children. If evidence emerged that some schools had increasingly high reservoirs of infection, and that transmission was occurring through shared needles or sexual activities, further control measures to deal with these activities could be legally justified. It should be realized that these activities are prohibited already on school grounds.

b. Child to child casual contact

The focal point of public confusion is the risk of infection from casual contact in schools. The recent paper by Friedland et al demonstrates the absence of any contagion caused by casual contact even within the secretion rich environment of the family.[37] The Friedland study confirms earlier work.[38] CDC concludes that there is no risk of communication of the virus in a normal school environment.[39]

The potential for viral transmission in schools through child to child contact is extremely unlikely, without a single documented case occurring. Parental fears have been spurned by reports of live virus isolated in tears and saliva. Yet, more recent evidence shows the exceedingly low isolation rate in samples of saliva. All available evidence points to school children having the most remote possibility of contracting the virus on school grounds.

c. The consequences of exclusion from school: Discrimination against the handicapped

Balanced against the remote risk entailed in allowing infected children to attend school is the critical consequence of excluding them. Compelling a child to forego the enriching experience of social integration at school is a harsh consequence. Schooling is a constitutionally protected right and, even if basic education could be provided elsewhere, it robs the child of a right to association.

Exclusion of handicapped children, has been found to be a form of discrimination proscribed by federal and state law.[40] In <u>New York State Association for Retarded Children, Inc. v. Carey</u>,[41] the Second Circuit Court of Appeals held that exclusion or isolation of students merely because they have a medical condition (hepatitis B) that may pose a remote risk of transmission violates the Federal Rehabilitation Act. The Court held that such students were handicapped and were being excluded form participation in a federally assisted activity on the basis of that handicap. No substantial justification was found for that exclusion. The <u>Carey</u> court found that even separate educational facilities would discriminate against infected children as it would limit the extent to which the children can participate in school-wide activities such as meals, recesses, and assemblies. It would reinforce the stigma to which these children were already subjected.

It should be noted, however, that in <u>Kampmeiier v. Nyquist</u>[42] exclusion from a school activity was not found improper if there exists "a substantial justification for the school's policy." The burden of proving "substantial justification" was placed on the party seeking to justify exclusion.

The decision in <u>Carey</u> that there was no justification in excluding hepatitis B carriers from school should similarly apply in relation to children with HTLV-III. Since the risk of transmission of hepatitis B is probably greater than for HTLV-III, the rationale for exclusion of children with AIDS is even less apparent.

An earlier decision, <u>Arline v. School Board of Nassau County</u>[43] also supports the conclusion that exclusion from school would trigger the protection of the Federal Rehabilitation Act. The <u>Arline</u> court held that a teacher with a history of tuberculosis was protected against discrimination, noting:

> The Court is obliged...[to determine] whether the defendant's justifications reflect a well-informed judgment grounded in a careful and open-minded weighing of risks and alternatives, or whether they are simply conclusory statements that are being used to justify reflexive reactions grounded in ignorance or capitulation to public prejudice.

The U.S. Supreme Court has recently agreed to review the <u>Arline</u> decision.

d. <u>CDC Guidelines on Screening in Schools</u>

CDC guidelines have been published on "Education and Foster Care of Children Infected with HTLV-III/LAV."[44] These guidelines advise against mandatory screening as a condition for school entry. The guidelines also recommend that infected school-age children attend regular school and after-school day care.

CDC guidelines do recommend a restricted environment for "infected preschool-aged children and for some neurologically handicapped children who lack control of their body secretions or who display behavior such as biting, and those children who have uncoverable, oozing lesions." Such infected children should be cared for and educated in settings that minimize exposure to blood or body fluids.

CDC guidelines encouraging attendance of children in school are consistent with evidence of the small reservoir of infection and the minimal risk of contagion within the school system. The recommendation that pre-school children and children with biting behaviors and neurological problems should be excluded from school is not as clear. Much of the evidence of the lack of transmission in families involves very young children. There is little evidence that HTLV-III has been transmitted through biting in a classroom. While the virus has been cultured in saliva, no case of transmission through biting has been documented. The very low rate of isolation of the virus in saliva suggests it is unlikely that enough virus particles could be transmitted in the saliva from a bite. It is uncommon for aggressive biting to occur in very small children, and rarer for such bites to break the skin.

We cannot suggest that it is incorrect to adopt a prudential course in relation to young children in school. There is a clear need for more research discovering the level of risk of transmission through biting, open sores, excrement and other close person-to-person experiences. Until such research demonstrates the absence of a real risk, it cannot be said that temporary absence of pre-school or school children who bite or have uncontrolled presence of body fluids is wholly inappropriate or legally unjustified.

e. <u>Judicial review of decisions relating to the exclusion of children from school</u>

(i) <u>New York City</u>

CDC guidelines advise that children with AIDS should not be automatically excluded from primary and secondary school and that their educational placement should be reviewed on a case by base basis. This policy has been adopted in New York City whereby children with AIDS are seen by a special multidisciplinary panel to review their health and development, and to advise on an appropriate educational setting. The New York City review panel recently recommended that one seven-year old child with AIDS should continue in school and that the child's identity should remain confidential. The recommendation was accepted, and cause substantial protests by parents in Queens, where the child was going to school. An action was filed in a trial court in the County of Queens t reverse the city's decision. Later a re-constituted review panel found the boy did not have CDC defined AIDS but was infected with the virus.

The trial court in <u>District 27 Community School Board v. The Board of Education of the City of New York</u>[45] held that the New York City policy of non-exclusion was lawful. The court's powers of review in suc circumstances were found limited, and the court would not substitute it judgment for that of the Public Health Commissioner. The court concluded:

> Since "the apparent nonexistent risk of transmission of HTLV-III/LAV" in the school setting finds strong support in the epidemiologic data accumulated over the five years of experience with this disease..., and because the <u>automatic exclusion of children with AIDS from the regular classroom</u> would effect a purpose having no adequate connection with the public health..., it would usurp the function of the Commissioner of Health if this court adjudged, as a matter of law, that the non-exclusion policy was arbitrary and capricious or an abuse of discretion.... [The court] is dutibound to objectively evaluate the issue...and not be influenced by unsubstantiated fears of catastrophe.[46]

The court went further and found that exclusion of the child would have constituted discrimination under section 504 of the Federal Rehabilitation Act and would have violated the child's right to equal protection of the laws.

(ii) California

A Superior Court [trial] judge in Orange County, California, ruled on February 20, 1986, that a hemophiliac student who tested positive for HTLV-III antibody could return to school.[47] Judge Harmon Scoville found that the child was not suffering from AIDS and the virus was not contagious in a school setting.

(iii) Indiana

Officials of Western Middle School in Kokomo, Indiana, banned a fourteen-year old boy with AIDS from his seventh grade classes. The Indiana Board of Special Education Appeals referred the case to a county medical officer for determination. The county medical officer found that the child was handicapped through a combination of hemophilia and AIDS and that there was no medical justification for excluding the child from school. The child returned to school, but by the end of the day, Howard County Circuit Judge R. Alan Brubaker held that a state public health law applied to the case.[48] Judge Brubaker barred the student from class until he could hold a hearing on whether AIDS is a communicable disease within the state statute. At that hearing, the court held that the Indiana law prohibiting students with communicable diseases from attending school did not apply to this case.

(iv) New Jersey

Two cases were filed in New Jersey. In Board of Education of the City of Plainfield v. Cooperman[49] appeal has been taken from a decision of the State Board of Education directing the City of Plainfield to admit a five-year old child with HTLV-III infection to class in the same manner as any other child eligible for school attendance. The case is being heard together with the companion case of Board of Education of the Borough of Washington v. Cooperman.[50] The New Jersey school's policy follows CDC guidelines, and does not exclude AIDS children from school unless they are incontinent, excessive droolers, or have a documented history of aggressive behavior.

On March 25, 1986, the state education department's policy of admitting children with AIDS to schools was struck down by the Appellate Division of the Superior Court of New Jersey. The Court held that the Board of Education should have followed state administrative procedures including the holding of public hearings in adopting any policy on AIDS. The New Jersey School Board have announced their intention to appeal the court decision.

3. Screening of Food Handlers

The city of Houston had a proposal before its city council within the past six months which would have required screening of food handlers for communicable diseases with the purpose of preventing disease transmission through food. It is expected that the proposal will be rejected.

CDC guidelines state that all "epidemiologic and laboratory evidence indicates that blood-borne and sexually transmitted infections are not transmitted during the preparation or serving of food or beverages, and no instances of HBV [hepatitis B virus] or HTLV-III/LAV transmission have been documented in this setting."[51] CDC does not recommend routine serologic testing of food service workers. CDC does recommend general personal hygiene and food sanitation. Food contaminated with blood should be discarded, and individuals with the abnormal discharge of body fluids such as weeping sores should not work in food establishments. There seems to be no legal justification for going beyond CDC recommendations.

4. General Screening in High Risk Populations

Our national survey has not revealed any federal or state legislative proposals for widespread, systematic screening of high risk populations. However, very recently the U.S. Public Health Service has issued guidelines[52] recommending that voluntary periodic testing be offered at health care and public health facilities for HTLV-III among a large number of high risk groups:

-homosexual and bisexual men;
-present and past intravenous drug users;
-persons with signs and symptoms of AIDS or ARC;
-persons born in Haiti and countries in Central America where heterosexual transmission has been evidenced to transmit the virus;
-male and female prostitutes;
-sex partners of infected persons;
-hemophiliacs who have received blood-clotting products;
-newborn children of infected mothers.

These guidelines reach considerably beyond any other federally generated recommendations, which have been characteristically limited in scope and application. These new guidelines would apply to millions of people in the United States. A comprehensive voluntary screening program of this type will require extensive planning efforts and the use of resources and personnel to test individuals on a large scale. Much data will be generated presenting considerable problems of confidentiality concerning how the data are to be utilized. It may well be necessary to provide legal foundation for such a program in order to protect it from potential abuse.

If a program of widespread screening such as that recommended by the Public Health Service in this latest proposal were to be suggested on a compulsory basis, it would face considerable legal obstacles. The justification for use of compulsory powers would need to be spelled out clearly and would need to withstand inevitable constitutional challenge. As indicated in Chapter 4 of this Report, we doubt that such a proposal would survive constitutional scrutiny at this time.

5. Screening of Prostitutes

We have discovered several state proposals for compulsory screening of persons arrested or convicted in connection with prostitution. A proposal is before the Michigan House of Representatives which would require individuals, male or female, arrested for prostitution or solicitation to be tested for HTLV-III antibodies. If the person tests positive and is diagnosed as having AIDS, this information would have to be provided to the judge who sets the accused's conditions of release pending trial. A similar proposal has been recommended to the Georgia legislature. In North Carolina, the Department of Human Resources reports that it is considering directed screening of these persons.

Compulsory examination of prostitutes has a long and often sordid history which has been well documented in the field of venereal disease control. There is, however, a crucial distinction between measures in relation to venereal disease and proposed measures in relation to HTLV-III. In the former, there is a clear, effective and speedy therapeutic intervention which can clearly be justified as a measure of prevention of spread and cure for the individual. Compulsory treatment may be supported under the state's police powers and parens patriae powers. No such justification exists in relation to HTLV-III, for there is no medical intervention available which can eliminate the infection.

6. Screening at STD and Drug Dependence Treatment Centers

Another approach to preventing the spread of HTLV-III would be to provide voluntary screening at already established treatment centers for sexually transmitted diseases and at treatment and rehabilitation centers for drug dependent persons using intravenous drugs. The population at these centers is already identified and would require no additional search program. Attendance at the centers is voluntary and beneficial to the patients who receive treatment. Sero testing could be offered voluntarily to all patients and the results would traditionally be kept confidential along with other aspects of patient care at such centers. For those patients found positive for HTLV-III, educational and counseling services would be intensified. The centers would be alerted to watch for signs or symptoms of AIDS itself or AIDS-related complex and if such evidence were found, the patient could be referred for prompt treatment of these conditions.

If voluntary programs proved ineffective, however, consideration could be given to making such HTLV-III screening a required condition of continued treatment at such centers. This could be attempted on one of two levels. First, by making testing a condition precedent to entry into the program. Second, by utilizing or extending current statutory powers to medically examine persons reasonably suspected of having a sexually transmitted disease. Compulsory testing, however, might discourage use of the centers for venereal disease and drug dependence treatment.

Our state survey did not reveal any specific new legislation or regulations concerning screening at such centers. We have been told, however, that voluntary testing has been suggested at some centers.

Most do not perform the test themselves. Patients are merely expected to report their test results to the center if they so desire. Obviously, such a practice has problems of reliability and could not be made effective on a periodic basis of greatest benefit to patient care. On-site voluntary testing or certification by a public testing facility would be more reliable and useful for STD and drug dependence treatment centers.

7. Pre-marital Screening

The most obvious legislative trend which has emerged from our state survey is the proposal to introduce compulsory premarital screening for HTLV-III antibodies. Proposals for premarital screening were reported in Alabama, Georgia, Connecticut, California, Massachusetts, Michigan and New York. There is a similar proposal offered at the federal level.[53]

Such proposals are extensions to current requirements in most states for testing for sexually transmitted diseases, usually syphilis, before a marriage license can be issued. A public health benefit might be achieved by discouraging or preventing marriages where one of the partners is likely to infect the other through sexual activity, and where any future offspring are placed at serious risk. Positive test results for HTLV-III would be disclosed to both partners and knowldge of the results could motivate the couple to practice a "safer" form of sexual activity, or to refrain from the marriage at all.

To some public health authorities, another advantage of establishing a compulsory premarital screening program is the collection of extensive data on the spread of the virus. Currently, the health departments do collect and utilize the epidemiological data on sexually transmitted diseases obtained through premarital testing. We caution, however, that this collection of data on HTLV-III is not greatly useful without an available treatment program to follow it. Later in this report we will deal with the general issue of data collection resulting from HTLV-III screening programs.

The disadvantages of premarital testing have also been spelled out to us, particularly by states with low a incidence of HTLV-III. Such testing would be required of all applicants for a marriage license even though a very small proportion is likely to be infected. Further, knowledge of a positive test result will not prevent the spread of HTLV-III. Many partners will already have engaged in sexual intercourse and others will already be aware of, and have accepted the risk. Moreover, a single negative test result is no guarantee that the tested individual is not, in fact, infected.

So long as the results are held confidential and not disclosed to any third party, it may be in the interest of both parties to have this premarital information. Since there is no treatment for the condition of being seropositive, the legislation could not order treatment as a condition of approval of the marriage certificate.

It would be contrary to public policy to adopt a permanent bar to marriage by those found seropositive. Marriage is obviously not a precondition to heterosexual intercourse or pregnancy. Prohibiting marriages between a seropositive person and a non-infected person could not necessarily prevent infection. Furthermore, marriage has been determined by the U.S. Supreme Court to be a fundamental right.[54]

Voluntary testing, as a supplement to current compulsory programs of premarital screening for venereal disease, offers a less restrictive alternative to compulsory premarital screening for HTLV-III. The test could be offered free of charge with assured confidentiality of results.

8. Prenatal Screening

Legislation in many states currently requires physicians attending pregnant women to obtain a test for venereal disease, usually syphilis, and to report the results to the state or local health department. The pregnant woman usually must consent to the procedure. If the woman refuses, the refusal must be reported to the same public health authorities.

We have not found any American jurisdictions where testing for HTLV-III has been added to the above-indicated prenatal screening. We also have not found legislative proposals of this type during our state surveys. Since there are several proposals for adding HTLV-III testing to premarital screening laws, we might expect similar proposals in this field. The absence of treatment which could be instituted during pregnancy is an obvious reason militating against such an addition to the law.

9. Screening of Health Care Patients and Staff:

Health care settings pose special risks in the communication of any disease, including AIDS related infections. The source of the infection could rest either with the patient or the health care personnel.

It is because of the potential for transmission in the health care setting that several types of proposals for screening and other measures have been considered. Two of the proposed federal bills concern health care workers: forbidding discrimination against nurses or other health care professionals for using protective garments when treating AIDS patients; and prohibiting persons with AIDS from practicing in the health care industry.[55] We have discovered very few state-level legislative proposals for general screening or other special measures in the health care setting. However, many health care groups and hospitals have informally considered voluntary screening. Apart from the safety issues are concerns about legal liability. If a patient were to develop an AIDS related infection following a period of hospital care, knowing that person's serologic status prior to admission could clarify liability issues.

The major factors in determining whether a program of screening of patients or hospital staff is appropriate depend upon the level of risk of transmission in a health care setting and the precautions that could be taken if the screening program were to be put into operation.

Several studies show that hospital and laboratory settings do not pose significant risk of transfer of the AIDS related virus. In five separate studies, a total of 1,498 health care workers have been tested for HTLV-III antibody. In these studies, 666 (44.5%) had direct parenteral (needle puncture or cut) or mucous membrane exposure to patients with HTLV-III infection. Of the 26 who tested seropositive after the incident, only 3 could not be identified as also within a major risk group.[56] One case from England also describes a nurse who seroconverted following a needlestick accident.[57]

The general risk in the health care setting does not appear to justify a widescale screening program. Even if such a screening program were to be implemented voluntarily the question arises as to the use to be made of the test results. Clearly health care personnel will wish to use strict precautions to avoid contracting HTLV-III from the body fluids of a patient who is seropositive. This includes double bagging specimens, use of rubber gloves if the worker has a cut or open sore, and taking great care in avoiding parenteral exposure. Health care workers should always be cautious in handling of blood, other body fluids and items soiled with blood or other body fluids. It should be noted that these precautions are already recommended in the prevention of transmission of the hepatitis B virus (HBV). The Public Health Service regards HBV as a "worst case scenario" in regard to the transmission of disease in the health care context. The PHS, therefore, advises adoption of hepatitis B precautions throughout health care settings where there is possible exposure to blood or other body fluids.[58] Focusing on the context of risk by adopting general precautions avoids the need for compulsory screening of persons.

a. Invasive procedures

While there is consistent evidence suggesting the low general risk of transmission of HTLV-III in health care settings, there is less clear evidence in relation to particularly invasive or hazardous procedures where there is greater potential for intimate contact with blood and other bodily fluids.

One immediate difficulty in arriving at any special policy approach for invasive or hazardous procedures is defining the activities that qualify. There are potentially numerous candidates for special attention: e.g., surgery, emergency rooms, burn units, endoscopes, obstetrics, and kidney dialysis. In each activity there is a case for suggesting that contact with blood cannot easily be controlled and that the activity, if carried out on a person who harbors the AIDS virus, would be unusually risky.

(i) <u>Hemodialysis</u>

Hepatitis B transmission has been documented between patients in hemodialysis units, where blood contamination of the environment has been extensive or where HBV-positive blood from one patient has been transferred to another through contamination of instruments.[59] PHS guidelines for controlling hepatitis B in hemodialysis units require testing and the separation of those who test positive, either on separate machines or in separate locations.[60]

There have been no studies of HTLV-III transfer in hemodialysis units. All that can be said at this stage is that the environment is conducive to transfer. However, HTLV-III infection is transmitted less readily than HBV. This is because the blood of an AIDS patient has at least one million times fewer infectious viral particles per milliliter than does the blood of a patient with hepatitis B. Accordingly, screening programs would have to be based upon a speculative possibility of risk.

There are a number of potential problems with screening and segregation within dialysis units which must be balanced against the expected advantages. First, as hemodialysis involves the transfusion of blood, it is possible that antibody testing will produce more false positives than in other populations. More people could be incorrectly assumed to be positive than actually were. Second, segregation of hemodialysis patients may result in their sero status being made obvious to family, friends, employers, insurance companies and others, thus breaching doctor/patient confidence. Third, there is the potential that the test results will be used to exclude patients from dialysis or to visit other adverse consequences on them such as inadequate treatment and care on the unit. Patients require dialysis as a life giving scarce resource. Any use of the test to exclude the person from that service on grounds of the antibody test would be unethical. Fourth, absent a legislative ruling, informed consent would be required before the test could be given. If the unit required the test as a condition of admission, this probably would be perceived as a disguised form of compulsion.

We note that, in balancing the justifications for and against screening, the National Association of Patients on Hemodialysis and Transplantation (NAPHT) is opposed to routine screening for HTLV-III.[61] They favor continuation of sterilization, disinfection and sanitation facilities but feel that the minimal level of risk of transfer of HTLV-III does not justify mandatory routine screening and segregation within dialysis units.

10. Screening in Custodial Institutions

Custodial or closed institutions such as prisons, hospitals for the mentally ill or mentally retarded, and juvenile establishments are all targets for screening programs. The rationale given for such programs is the potential for sexual activity and the use of intravenous drugs. One of the most disturbing hazards is forced sexual intercourse which results in contagion to the coerced party.

The strongest case for compulsory screening programs in closed institutions can be made in relation to prisons and it is this area we will focus upon. There is considerable interest and activity around the country in screening and segregation in prison systems.

a. Federal and State proposals for screening of prisoners

The American Civil Liberties Union's National Prison Project has done a state survey which complements our own in this area.[62] Twenty-nine of the 48 states that responded to the ACLU survey (60%) use the ELISA in some fashion, and five more are considering it. Most of the states, however, use the test only for individual diagnostic purposes, with only Nevada currently mass-screening their entire prison population; Nebraska has a proposal to do so. Six states (Indiana, Maine, Louisiana, Kentucky, Minnesota and Nevada) screen all new admissions to prison, with Missouri planning to do so. Two of the states with the largest number of AIDS cases, New York and New Jersey, have a policy of not using the ELISA at all in the state prisons. Our survey did not reveal any additional states with screening programs in prisons.

There is a proposal in the Michigan House of Representatives which would require the Corrections Department to test prisoners prior to being placed in any state correctional facility. If there is a positive test result and if the prisoner is diagnosed as having AIDS, then he or she must be placed in isolation. Similar proposals for screening and segregation of prisoners are pending in Alaska and Alabama.

The American Federation of State, County and Municipal Employees has issued guidelines calling for screening for HTLV-III antibodies of "all prisoners with a history of drug abuse or homosexuality." In addition, the Federation has urged that all inmates be medically examined for AIDS before joining the general prison population. The union advises that prisoners who are antibody positive should be segregated from other inmates "to make sure that the disease does not spread throughout the institution from homosexuality or drug abuse, to reduce the chances of violence from other prisoners, and to reduce the chances of accidental exposure to body fluids."[63]

Segregation on the basis of a confirmed diagnosis of AIDS is the policy of 20 of the 42 states (48%) in the ACLU survey; seven (17%) others are in the process of developing a policy and two (5%) segregate on a case by case basis.

b. <u>Judicial review of prisoner screening, segregation and hospitalization</u>

Two court cases have been brought, one by HTLV-III antibody positive prisoners seeking to question the constitutionality of their segregation, and one by "healthy" prisoners who sought the removal of all persons with AIDS from the prison.

In <u>Cordero v. Coughlin</u>[64] New York prisoners with HTLV-III infection contended that segregation resulted in inadequate social, rehabilitative and recreational activities. The court rejected the Equal Protection claim because a policy of segregation is ordinarily related to the legitimate objective "to protect both victims and other prisoners from the tensions and harm that could result from the fears of other inmates." It did not matter whether the existence of such fears were realistic or not. Were the segregation to deprive the prisoners of adequate food, clothing, shelter, sanitation, medical care and safety, the plaintiffs would have had a valid claim of cruel and unusual punishment under the Eighth Amendment.

In LaRocca v. Dalsheim[65] a New York court heard a claim made by prisoners that correction officials should not form or maintain a central AIDS program at the facility, should not move any inmates or employees in or out of the prison until examinations were given, and should remove all persons with AIDS from the prison for treatment at hospital. The court directed that each inmate be handed a copy of an AIDS brochure prepared by the State Department of Health. It noted that the state was already segregating prisoners known to have AIDS which was a reasonable policy in endeavoring to prevent forceable sexual transmission. However, the court hearing pre-dated the development of HTLV-III antibody testing. The court held that in the absence of a test, an injunction of all traffic in and out of the prison until entrants were screened, could not be granted. The court did not find it necessary to remove patients with AIDS from the facility, since they were already isolated and precautions for hepatitis B were being followed. The court found no evidence that there was a state policy to congregate all prisoners with AIDS in the state at that facility; if such a policy were instituted the Commissioner must give 30 days public notice of such an intention.

Further court cases are pending. In Jackson County, Missouri, a prisoner informed the governor that he had tested positive for HTLV-III antibodies. The prisoner was then placed in isolation and is seeking redress.[66] In New York,[67] and Massachusetts[68] prisoners with AIDS are seeking improved medical treatment. The Alabama Department of Public

Health reported to us that two law suits involving prisoners have been filed in the state. No further information was available on these suits.

There is concern among prison employees about contracting AIDS which can result in refusals to cooperate in supervising prisoners who are HTLV-III antibody positive. In the first arbitration decision[69] on AIDS in the workplace, Arbitrator Thomsa P. Gallagher decided that a prison wrongly dismissed a guard who refused to "pat down" or search prisoners because he feared contracting the virus. The arbitrator found that the prison had failed to give the guard accurate information about the transmission of HTLV-III.

These legislative, correctional, trade union and judicial statements all indicate considerable interest in screening and isolation in prisons. The humane justification in favor of such a policy is the prevention of a healthy person coming into prison, perhaps on a relatively minor charge, and then to seroconvert while in custody. This scenario is distressing enough even when the prisoner unwittingly consents to intercourse or to the use of drugs; it becomes even more repugnant when the cause of infection is a forced homosexual contact in the prison.

c. Reservoir of infection and likelihood of spread in prisons

The ACLU survey noted earlier found that approximately 420 cases of AIDS had been diagnosed in state prisons across the country. More than half of the prisoners with the disease have died; 85% of the cases diagnosed were in New York, New Jersey and Florida. A study by the National Institute of Justice and the American Correctional Association found a total number of 765 prisoners diagnosed with AIDS, of which 72% were in correctional facilities in the mid-Atlantic region (New York, New Jersey and Pennsylvania).[70] Adopting the ACLU figures and the ratio of AIDS to infection used by Curran et al.,[71] there would be between 21,000 and 42,000 prisoners infected with HTLV-III. A high percentage of prisoners have had experience with the use of intravenous drugs and/or homosexual acts before entering prison. In New York State, for example, 13 to 15 percent of prisoners have been convicted of drug-related offenses and 25 percent acknowledge having used illegal drugs. It is certainly possible that the level of infection in prisons is even higher than estimated, and could represent 10% of the national prison population.

The precise level of drug abuse and homosexual activity (including rape) in prisons is not known. Despite the fact that these are proscribed and controlled activities, they do occur. It is reasonable to assume that prison environments contribute to the spread of HTLV-III, although the ACLU study concludes (without actual support of any evidence) that instances of transfer of HTLV-III infection in prison are rare. Currently the New Jersey Public Health Department is considering federally sponsored research designed to quantify the level of HTLV-III infection in prisons.[72] Decisions to install general compulsory screening of prison populations should await the outcome of this and other investigations.

d. The critical consequences of prison screening

There are two apparent public health purposes which correctional officials maintain are served by screening for HTLV-III. In fact screening is not necessary to serve either purpose. The first rationale is that isolating or segregating AIDS patients may prevent immunosuppressed individuals from acquiring infections in the prison environment. This limited objective could be achieved without a mass screening program by hospitalization of AIDS patients where therapeutically indicated on a case by case basis.

The second rationale is that screening will prevent seronegative prisoners from acquiring the infection. This result might be achieved at disproportionate cost, if all seropositive prisoners were segregated. Yet, many state programs screen all new inmates but do not segregate those who test positive unless they have full blown AIDS. It is therefore difficult to find a clear public health benefit which is achieved by current prison screening programs.

A more likely explanation for mass screening programs is that prison populations are relatively easy targets for screening and control measures because of their low political visibility. Screening and segregation would adversely affect many prisoners. The public health risk in prisons is caused by those who engage in forceable or voluntary sexual acts or illegal use of intravenous drugs. These practices are already prohibited activities. Screening and segregating the population does not specifically target the prisoners who are responsible for causing avoidable harm. Some of those who are seropositive and placed in segregated facilities will be responsible for engaging in violence and unlawful acts (thus helping to spread HTLV-III) while most likely will not. Similarly, there will be no selectivity as to who within the "healthy" population has acted improperly or violently. While the real challenge is to discover aggressive wrongdoers and to control their behavior, prison resources will be used to discover who is seropositive and who is not. We suspect that the reason why sero testing is proposed as a method of segregating the population is simply because it is administratively easy to impose antibody screening.

Antibody screening and social isolation would be a reasonable policy in prisons if AIDS were an airborne disease. As the actual method of transfer is through sexual intercourse and IV drug abuse, these are the behaviors which should be focused upon. Forceable sexual contact is a gross invasion of personal rights and requires the strictest preventive measures, whether or not the aggressor is seropositive. The introduction of better lighting, supervision, monitoring and enforcement in prison to prevent such dangerous activity should clearly be the major priority, and the presence of HTLV-III in America's prisons should be a strong reason to re-double efforts in this direction.

One of the basic principles of public health is that the control measure itself should not cause harm to its subjects. One of the conceptual problems of segregation of all seropositive prisoners is that this could result in a further health hazard within the segregated population. There is currently no clear understanding of the natural history of HTLV-III infection; between 6 and 20 percent of those with the infection will contract the full blown disease within a five year period. It is conceivable that repeated exposure to the virus and/or less healthful living conditions could contribute to coming down with the full-blown disease. Given these risks, the segregation of all seropositive prisoners in an environment with the potential of repeated exposure to the virus could well result in significantly increased health hazard for these persons. Furthermore, in such an environment, there would be great difficulty in recruiting staff. Isolation in inadequate facilities and without sufficient opportunity of social integration and use of other prison facilities such as recreational and exercise resources could also lead to serious psychological disturbance.[73]

The decision to screen and segregate prison facilities also sends a significant message to the public, as if the state were developing an "AIDS colony." It could convey a leprosy image that could affect public perceptions of the nature of the disease and how to deal with it. It could also further lower the already damaged reputation of prisoners in the segregated facility long after discharge. Friends and potential employers would likely know or seek information about the prisoner's placement in the segregated facility and infer his disease status from that information.

If prison screening and segregation were adopted as policy in geographic areas at high risk for AIDS substantial parts of the prison population would need to be housed in separate facilities. Due to existing overcrowded conditions, it could require the building of "AIDS prisons."

F. Conclusion

There are currently no preventative or therapeutic interventions for HTLV-III infection. The only compelling public health purpose of widespread, organized testing and screening, therefore, is to inform persons in high risk groups and hazardous environments of their health status and to provide a focus for public education and counseling designed to alter future behavior in those who test positively.

Experience with hepatitis B, which is transmitted in much the same way as HTLV-III, has demonstrated that voluntary compliance with health directives can reduce the spread of the disease. Emerging evidence on AIDS already shows significant alteration of behavior necessary to reduce spread within high risk groups. In the absence of evidence that compulsory measures would result in changed behavior more effectively than voluntary compliance, it is difficult to justify legally the introduction of widespread mandatory testing or screening programs.

References

1. Levine C, Bayer R. Screening blood: Public health and medical uncertainty. AIDS: The Emerging Ethical Dilemmas; Hastings Center Report; 1985:8.

2. Sarngadharan MG, Popovic M, Bruch L, et al. Antibodies reactive with human T-lymphotropic retrovirus (HTLV-III) in the serum of patients with AIDS. Science 1984; 224:506-8.

3. Petricciani JC. Licensed tests for antibody to human T-lymphotropic virus type III: Sensitivity and specificity. Annals Int Med 1985; 103:726-9.

4. Bayer R, Levine C, Murray TH. Guidelines for confidentiality in research on AIDS. IRB: A Review of Human Subjects Research 1984; 6(6):1-7.

5. Institute for the Protection of Human Subjects, 45 C.F.R. 46. Revised as of March 8, 1983. See also "Dear Colleague" letter from Charles R. McCARTHY, ISSUING OPRR REPORTS, NIH, PHS, HHS, "GUIDANCE FOR Institutional Review Boards for AIDS Studies."

6. For a discussion of informed consent see pp. infra.

7. Canterbury v. Spence, 464 F.2d 772 (D.C. Cir.), cert. denied, 409 U.S. 1064 (1972); Cobbs v. Grant, 8 Cal.3d 229, 502 P.2d 1, 104 Cal. Rptr. 506 (1972); Harnish v. Childrens Hospital Medical Center, 387 Mass. 152 (1982).

8. See Clark v. Gerael, 29 Misc.2d 791, 298 N.Y.S.2d 564 (1960).

9. See Alberts v. Devine, 395 Mass. 59 (1985); Humphers v. First Insterstate Bank, 298 Or. 706 (1985); Horne v. Patton, 291 Ala. 701, 708-09 (1974); Simonsen v. Swenson, 104 Neb. 224, 227 (1920: Hague v. Williams, 37 N.J. 328, 336 (1962); MacDonald v. Clinger, 84 A.D.2d 482 (N.Y. 1982); Hammonds v. Aetna Casualty & Sur. Co., 243 F. Supp. 793, 802 (N.D. Ohio 1965). But see, Logan v. District of Columbia, 447 F. Supp. 1328, 1335 (D.D.C. 1978); Collins v. Howard, 156 F. Supp. 322, 324 (S.D. Ga. 1957); Quarles v. Sutherland, 215 Tenn. 651, 657 (1965).

10. Alberts v. Devine, 395 Mass. 59, 69 (1985).

11. People ex rel Director of Public Health v. Calvo, 89 Ill. 2d 130, 432 N.E.2d 233 (1982).

12. In re Baker's Mutual Insurance Company of New York, 301 N.Y. 21, 92 N.E.2d 49 (1950); McGowan v. Metropolitan Life Insurance Company, 141 Misc. Rep. 834, 182 N.E.2d 81 (1932).

13. Tarasoff v. Regents of University of California, 131 Cal Rptr. 14, 551 P.2d 340 (S. Ct. Cal. 1976).

14. McIntosh v. Milano, 168 N.J. Super. 466, 403 A.2d 500 (1979); Lipari v. Sears, Roebuck & Co., 497 F. Supp. 185(1980); Estate of Mathes v. Ireland, 419 N.E.2d 782 (1981); The Bradley Center v. Wessner, 287 S.E. 2d 716 (1982); Davis v. Lhim, 335 N.W. 481 (1983); Chrite v. United States, 564 F. Supp. 341 (1983); Peterson v. State, 671 P.2d 230 (1983); Jablonski v. United States, 712 F.2d 391 (1983); Cairl v. State, 323 N.W.2d 20,25-26 (S. Ct. Minn. 1982); Mutual of Omaha Ins. Co. v. American National Bank, 610 F. Supp. 546 (D.C. Minn. 1985). See Durflinger v. Artiles, 673 P.2d 86 (1983) (Negligent release of dangerous patient).

15. Alberts v. Devine, 395 Mass. 59 (1985); Simonsen v. Swenson, 104 Neb. 224, 177 N.W. 831 (1920).

16. E.g., Brady v. Hopper, 570 F.Supp. 1333 (1983).

17. Cairl v. State, 323 N.W.2d 20,25-26 (1982).

18. Lipari v. Sears, Roebuck & Co., 497 F. Supp. 185 (1980) (in order to establish liability there must be foreseeability to an injured party or a class of persons of which the injured party was a member).

19. E.g., Hasenei v. United States, 541 F. Supp. 999 (1982); Lundgren v. Fultz, 354 N.W.2d 25 (Minn. 1984).

20. As to reporting requirements see pp. 338-341 infra.

21. Skillings v. Allen, 173 N.W. 663,664 (S. Ct. Minn. 1919).

22. Hofmann v. Blackmon, 241 So.2d 752 (1970), cert. den. 245 So.2d 257 (Fla. 1971) (physician owes duty to child in immediate family to inform those charged with her well-being that her father is infected with T.B.); Davis v. Rodman, 227 S.W. 612 (S. Ct. Ark. 1921) (duty of physician to advise family members and others liable to be exposed of patient's typhoid fever); Wojcik v. Aluminum Co. of America, 183 N.Y.S. 2d 351, 18 Misc. 2d 740 (1959) (employee's wife could claim against employer for negligent failure to inform her husband that physical exams had disclosed T.B.); Skillings v. Allen, 173 N.W. 663 (S. Ct. Minn. 1919) (knowing child had scarlet fever, physician negligently advised wife that it was safe to visit the child); Derrick v. Ontario Community Hospital, 47 Cal. App. 3d 145, 120 Cal Rptr. 566 (1975) (doctor has duty to advise patient and her mother that patient has contracted an infectious disease). See McIntosh v. Milano, 168 N.J. Super. 466, 403 A.2d 500,509 (1979) (dictum that doctor has duty to warn third parties against possible exposure to infectious disease).

23. Davis v. Rodman, 221 S.W. 612,614 (1921).

24. Gammill v. United States, 727 F.2d 950 (10th Cir. 1984). Accord, Derrick v. Ontario Community Hospital, 47 Cal. App. 3d 145, 120 Cal. Rptr. 566 (1975) (hospital has no duty to warn members of general public that one of its patients being released is suffering from a contagious disease).

25. Washington Post, Aug. 31, 1985.

26. New York Times, Oct. 3, 1985.

27. New York Times, Feb. 2, 1986.

28. Redfield RR, Wright DC, Tramont EC. The Walter Reed staging clasifications for HTLV-III/LAV infection. N Eng J Med 1986; 314:131-2.

29. Batten v. Lehamn, USDC, DC. No. CA 85-4108, Jan. 18, 1986.

30. AIDS Policy & Law, Feb. 26, 1986.

31. Application of District 27 Community School Board v. Board of Education of the City of New York. Sup. Ct. N.Y. County of Queens. Index No 14940/85. (Feb. 11, 1986).

32. Phipps v. Saddleback Valley Unified School District, 474981.

33. New York Times, Feb. 4, 1986.

34. The Board of Education of the Borough of Washington v. Cooperman. Sup. Ct. N.J., Appel. Div. Docket No. A-605-15T5; Board of Education of the City of Plainfield v. Cooperman (Docket No. A-1378-85T5).

35. H. Con. Res. 224.

36. Fla. H.B. 137, R-115.

37. Friedland GH, Saltzman BR, Rodgers MF, et al. Lack of transmission of HTLV-III/LAV infection to household contacts of patients with AIDS or AIDS-related complex with oral candidiasis. N Eng J Med 1986; 314:344-9.

38. See Sande MA. Transmission of AIDS: The case against casual contagion. N Eng J Med 1986; 314:380-2.

39. CDC. Education and foster care of children infected with HTLV-III/LAV. MMWR 1985; 14:517-21.

40. See, e.g., U.S.C. 1401 et seq. and New York City Executive Law 292.21.

41. New York State Assn. for Retarded Children, Inc. v. Carey, 672 F.2d 644 (2d Cir. 1979).

42. Kampmeiier v. Nyquist, 553 F.2d 296,299 (2d Cir. 1977).

43. Arline v. School Board of Nassau County, 772 F.2d 759 (11th Cir. 1985).

44. CDC. Education and foster care of children infected with HTLV-III/LAV. MMWR 1985; 14:517-21.

45. Index no. 14940/85, Feb. 11, 1986.

46. Id. at p. 49.

47. Phipps v. Saddleback Valley Unified School District, Sup. Ct., Orange County, CA, No. 474981 (Feb. 18, 1986).

48. New York Times, Feb. 14, 1986. See also decision of Kathleen Madinger Angelone, hearing officer (Nov. 25, 1985).

49. Sup. Ct. of N.J., Appel. Div. Docket No. A-1378-85T5.

50. Docket No. A-605-85T5.

51. CDC. Recommendations for preventing transmission of infection with human T-lymphotropic virus type III/lymphadenopathy-associated virus in the workplace. MMWR 1985; 34:683,693-4.

52. CDC. Additional recommendations to reduce sexual and drug abuse-related transmission of HTLV-III/LAV. MMWR 1986; 35:152-155.

53. Information provided directly by Congressman Dannemeyer's office.

54. Zablocki v. Redhail, 434 U.S. 374 (1977).

55. "Dear Colleague" letter from William E. Dannemeyer dated Sept. 24, 1985. In discussion with Mr. Dannemeyer's office we were informed that it is his intention to annex each of his bills where relevant to bills if and when they arise on the floor of the House.

56. CDC. Recommendations for preventing transmission of infection with HTLV-III/LAV in the workplace. MMWR 1985; 34:682,684.

57. Anonymous. Needlestick transmission of HTLV-III from a patient infected in Arica. Lancet 1984; ii:1376-7.

58. CDC, supra, note 56.

59. Ibid., at 683.

60. CDC. Control measures for hepatitis B in dialysis centers. Investigations and Control Series. Nov. 1977.

61. National Association of Patients on Hemodialysis and Transplantation. Consensus guidelines for dialysis patients concerning transfer of HTLV-III. 1986.

62. Vaid, U. NPP gathers the facts on AIDS in Prison. National Prison Project Journal, Winter 1985; 1-6.

63. Guidelines: Procedures for health, prison workers set by AFSCME. AIDS Policy and Law, Feb. 12, 1986; 4-5.

64. Cordero v. Coughlin, 607 F. Supp. 9 (S.D.N.Y. 1984).

65. LaRocca v. Dalsheim, 120 Misc. 2d 697, 467 N.Y.S.2d 302 (Sup. 1983).

66. National Public Radio, January 30, 1986.

67. Vaid, U. NPP gathers the facts on AIDS in prison. National Prison Project Journal, Winter 1985; 1-6.

68. Boston Globe, Aug. 18, 1985.

69. American Federation of State, County and Municipal Employees, Council 6, and the State of Minnesota, Dept. of Corrections. Case No. 85M-XU-600-3183, Dec. 10, 1095.

70. Institute of Justice and the American Correctional Association. AIDS in Correctional Facilities: Issues and Options 1986.

71. Curran JW, Meade Morgan W, Hardy AM, et al. The epidemiology of AIDS: Current status and future prospects. Science 1985; 229:1352-7.

72. Direct personal communication between L. Gostin and Jack Rutledge, Deputy Commissioner for Public Health, New Jersey.

73. Gostin L & Staunton, M. Rights of prisoners: A case for minimum standards. In: McGuire M, Vaag J, & Morgan R. Prisoners and Accountability. London: Tavistock 1985.

CHAPTER SIX

Public Health Legal Control Programs

Introduction

In this chapter we will examine public health control measures that could potentially be applied in the context of HTLV-III infection and provide legal justifications for and against their implementation. We will examine the various methods of disease investigation and data collection such as reporting requirements, surveillance and case registers; the use of voluntary programs of public education and counseling and "conferring a benefit" as positive methods of behavior change; personal control measures including isolation, segregation and quarantine. We will also suggest a sliding scale of less coercive measures including community health orders.

Basic Legal Structures

A. Reporting Requirements

All states require certain specified diseases to be reported to public health departments. Commonly this duty to report is placed on physicians, hospitals, and laboratories. AIDS has been made a notifiable condition throughout the country. The state reporting requirements can be divided into three kinds: reporting only of CDC defined AIDS; specific additional requirements to report positive HTLV-III antibody test results; and additional general provisions which do not specify HTLV-III infection as reportable, but do require the reporting of any "carrier state" relating to listed diseases including AIDS. The impact of the various statutory provisions is that the disease status of AIDS as defined by the Centers for Disease

Control is reportable in virtually every state. A positive HTLV-III antibody test is reportable in a few states, either as an explicit requirement (Colorado, Montana, Arizona, Idaho, South Carolina and Wisconsin), or by implication (Minnesota, Mississippi and Kentucky). Nearly all states were found to require reporting of names and addresses and some a list of sexual contacts. A very few states, as a means of encouraging a higher level of reporting, require identification only by a code (Kentucky) or by initials (Montana).

Individuals infected with HTLV-III have concern that information reported to health departments will become publicly known. Personal decision-making about health care may be affected by the potential invasions of confidentiality inherent in reporting requirements.

Whether such confidentiality concerns are sufficient to implicate a constitutionally protected interest depends on the precise requirements in the statute. As indicated, nearly all states compel the reporting of identifying information including name and address. Identifying data are needed to avoid duplication of reports, a reasonable epidemiologic objective. The Supreme Court in Whalen v. Roe[1] said that if disclosure pursuant to reporting requirements is limited to public health officials who have a need to know the information, and if there are adequate statutory or regulatory procedures to ensure the confidentiality of the register, the privacy interest of the individual is minimal. The court regarded the potential of negligent or intentional disclosure by public health officials, or judicially compelled disclosure of confidential information, as "remote possibilities."

The state has a valid epidemiologic objective in collecting information as to disease status used solely for epidemiologic purposes. A reporting requirement of the carrier state of HTLV-III has superficial advantages. It enables public health officials to keep records of those who are infectious and, therefore, capable of transmitting the AIDS related virus. For every one patient who has CDC-defined AIDS, it is estimated that between 50-100 persons harbor the AIDS-related virus and are assumed to be infectious. Infected individuals are as, and probably more, likely to engage in behavior leading to spread of the virus than those who have full blown AIDS. An asymptomatic carrier is generally physically more able to engage in sexual relations than a person who is sick and actively exhibiting AIDS related symptoms.

There are, however, arguments against requiring the reporting of positive HTLV-III antibody test results. First, from an epidemiological perspective, mandatory reporting of positive test results would not necessarily provide a valid representation of the population at risk. Currently, HTLV-III antibody testing programs cover only limited groups in the population. Sero-testing is essentially a voluntary self-selection process, and the individual who chooses to be tested may not be representative of the infected population.

There would be an additional problem with assuring the consistency of reporting requirements. While in practice states seem to operate on the expectation that a reporting requirement would be triggered only by sequential testing (i.e. a doubly reactive ELISA and a positive Western Blot), this requirement is seldom incorporated into regulations.

Without uniformity of reporting criteria from state to state, the epidemiologic value of the data collection would be severely limited.

If these epidemiologic limitations can be overcome, there may be other, more serious, negative consequences of requiring HTLV-III test result reporting. Mandatory reporting of all positive test results would involve the collection of sensitive, potentially damaging personal information which may not be adequately protected by current public health confidentiality statutes. Even with updated statutes, confidentiality could not be absolutely guaranteed. Creation of a registry for individuals who have received positive test results would entail inherent risks of intentional, negligent, or judicially compelled disclosure. Given the growing problem of AIDS-related discrimination, disclosure of such information could be especially damaging to the individual.

From a public health standpoint, however, the most serious consequence of imposing a statutory requirement for the reporting of positive test results would be its chilling effect on individuals who might otherwise seek testing. Since confidentiality of the information could not be guaranteed, and because of the potential for subsequent coercive use of the information, many individuals may opt out of testing. This disincentive for voluntary testing would lessen the chance for early detection and thus would defeat the purpose of encouraging the individual awareness and appropriate behavior change that is necessary to control the spread of the disease.

Although mandatory reporting of positive antibody test results may not seem at this time to be advisable public policy, it is not clear that such legislation would be constitutionally invalid. The United States Supreme Court in the Whalen case, noted earlier, made it clear that disease reporting requirements did not ordinarily implicate a constitutionally protected interest, and need not necessarily be absolutely essential to further a public health interest. It is probably that, under the reasoning of Whalen, the Court would uphold states' legislative efforts to impose a "carrier" reporting requirement as a part of their infectious disease control strategies. Such legislation, however, would have to be clearly drafted to achieve valid public health objectives; legislation borne of homophobia or grounded in prejudice associated with any of the identified risk groups is unlikely to be upheld.

B. Medical Surveillance Requirements: Contact Tracing

Contact tracing is a method of medical surveillance whereby public health officials seek to identify the susceptible contacts of an index case (i.e. an individual known to be infected) and then, if possible, to treat those persons and prevent future contacts. Such efforts have been a common element of venereal disease control programs, since effective treatment can now usually be provided.

It has been clearly established that the AIDS-related virus is transmitted primarily through sexual intercourse. Male-to-male intercourse was identified as a major risk factor very early in the AIDS epidemic; subsequent studies have documented heterosexual transmission of the virus, primarily through male-to-female intercourse. Despite the evidence of sexual transmission, however, there has been no organized effort to implement an active program of contact tracing in this field.

The potential advantage of contact tracing in AIDS cases would be the opportunity for the identification of individuals who have been exposed to HTLV-III/LAV, and who are thus at risk for developing and/or possibly transmitting the disease. Notification of these individuals could facilitate behavior changes which might prevent future transmission.

There are, however, several disadvantages in programs of voluntary or compulsory contact tracing in AIDS cases. First, in the absence of an effective vaccine or treatment, sexual contacts could not benefit from specific medical intervention. The knowledge of exposure to the virus would impose a heavy psychological burden, because the individual would not know when or if he or she would develop the disease. Second, infected patients have a particularly strong privacy interest in not revealing their sexual contacts to public health officials. That being the case, active programs of contact tracing could dissuade individuals from seeking voluntary testing and treatment. Third, because of the long incubation period of HTLV-III/LAV infection, most patients would probably have transmitted the virus to their sexual partners well before they were identified as being seropostive.

C. Voluntary Means of Behavior Change

Reliance on voluntary means of inducing behavior change to achieve public health objectives is generally preferable to the imposition of compulsory measures. The lease restrictive but effective control measure should be the primary focus of any public health program to control the spread of AIDS. Public education, aimed at inducing individuals to eliminate dangerous conduct, represents the least restrictive public health measure now available. Moreover, comprehensive education and counseling efforts offer the most effective means for reducing the transmission and spread of the disease and counteracting the wave of AIDS hysteria which continues to grow.

Education and counseling efforts should be designed to reach a diverse population. Explicit information about the known mechanisms of transmission and practical steps which may be taken to reduce the chance of transmission must be readily available; "safe sex" practices must be clearly identified and publicized. Information should be presented in a way likely to reach the greatest number of individuals. For high risk populations, STD and drug treatment clinics may provide a particularly useful focus for educational and counseling programs. Cooperative efforts with groups active within the gay community may also facilitate public education efforts.

To counteract myths and fears which underlie discrimination against individuals with AIDS or HTLV-III/LAV infection, general information about the epidemiology of HTLV-III/LAV infection and AIDS should be widely disseminated to the public. Materials should focus on answering the questions most frequently posed by the public. Coordination through a single agency or organization at the state level could assure that information is presented in a cohesive manner, not a piecemeal approach influenced by media pressures.

For certain high risk populatins such as intravenous drug users, education may not offer the most effective means of reducing the transmission of HTLV-III/LAV infection. An alternative, non-coercive measure which could achieve this objective would be the distribution of sterile needles, eliminating to a large extent the need for IV drug users to share contaminated needles. Obviously such a proposal is weighted with political implications, for there will be those who would regard such an effort as an encouragement to illegal drug use. Given the evidence of the growing magnitude of disease transmission within this population, however, the potential benefits of blocking transmission may outweigh arguments against encouraging drug use. If sterile needles are distributed as a part of a wider program of information, counseling, and treatment of drug dependent persons, it is certainly a proposal not to be easily rejected. An alternative proposal would be to authorize pharmacists to dispense needles without a prescription but with a reasonable charge for the needles.

D. Compulsory Public Health Measures

Communicable disease control strategies have long relied on the belief that, in order to avoid the transmission of an infectious agent, it is necessary to isolate infected individuals from the rest of the population. This is a control model ill-suited to controlling a blood borne disease such as AIDS, which is transmissible only via certain behaviors and exposures. Physical isolation of all individuals harboring HTLV-III/LAV infection might reduce transmission, but it would be an impermissibly overbroad, highly intrusive measure. Compulsory segregation measures represent the opposite pole from voluntary programs and incentives designed to induce behavior changes which would reduce the spread of infection. But while properly financed and organized non-coercive programs can be highly effective, there will remain individuals unwilling or unable to alter their behavior. When these individuals pose an imminent health risk to others, public health officials should have access to a range of carefully delineated powers.

In this section, we first examine the most restrictive powers generally provided in public health legislation --isolation and quarantine of individuals. We then discuss the feasibility of authorizing the issuance of a "community health order" which would provide a range of less intrusive measures designed to alter dangerous behavior.

1. General Isolation or Quarantine

Our survey indicates that the power to isolate or quarantine individuals is the most commonly recognized legal control measure found in public health statutes. Many state provide statutory authority for public health officials to isolate an infected individual, typically under venereal disease or sexually transmitted disease (STD) control provisions. No state has, as yet, amended its legislative or regulatory structure to specifically authorize the quarantine of individuals who have been exposed to the HTLV-III/LAV infection, or the isolation of individuals diagnosed with AIDS.

Isolation or quarantine is a deprivation of liberty which may be imposed on an unwilling but competent individual for public health purposes. Historically, application of such measures has been premised upon the individual's disease status; before disease transmission mechanisms were understood, it was believed to be necessary to segregate ill individuals or those exposed to disease in order to protect the healthy. Confinement under isolation and quarantine measures has not generally been subject to the rigorous due process procedures afforded individuals faced with incarceration under criminal statutes. Given the severe impact on liberty and freedom of movement entailed in compulsory isolation or quarantine, such measures today are likely to trigger the strictest level of judicial scrutiny. A general isolation or quarantine provision would be upheld only if a "tight fit" is demonstrated between the provision and the attainment of a compelling public health benefit. Such a close relationship could not be demonstrated for a general quarantine of all individuals who test positive for exposure to HTLV-III/LAV, or for the isolation of all individuals diagnosed as having AIDS. Such measures would be regarded as unconstitutionally overbroad. Given the inability to predict with any reasonable certainty who would communicate the virus, deprivation of liberty of entire population groups would be impossible to justify. Strict judicial scrutiny would demand that no more individuals should have their liberty restricted than is clearly necessary for the preservation of the public health.

There are, moreover, numerous public policy arguments against issuance of general isolation or quarantine orders which flow from the unique combination of scientific findings relating to AIDS and HTLV-III/LAV infection: the sheer number of individuals now presumed capable of transmitting the disease is estimated to be approaching one million and increasing geometrically, making the application of general isolation or quarantine measures wholly impractical and unmanageable; because there is no known finite period of infectiousness, confinement would be without time limit; the long incubation period of the disease means that most AIDS patients would have transmitted the virus to their sexual contacts long before they manifested symptoms, and therefore their confinement would have little public health benefit; there is no prevention or treatment, so those whose liberty was infringed would have no way to restore themselves to a non-infectious condition in order to rejoin the community; and, finally, because the virus is not transmitted through casual contact, any general segregation from society would be unnecessarily restrictive. These factors set AIDS and HTLV-III/LAV infection apart from other communicable diseases which have typically been the focus of compulsory public health control measures.

2. Limited Quarantine or Isolation

"Limited" quarantine or isolation is a compulsory control measure sometimes proposed in connection with AIDS control programs; it is the applicability of the measure and not the restriction on liberty that would be "limited". This type of compulsory measure would be triggered not by the individual's health status, but rather by conduct which is likely to transmit the virus. A limited quarantine or isolation would, in theory, be based upon a determination that the individual in question is capable of transmitting the virus and cannot or will not refrain from engaging in conduct likely to do so. A 1985 amendment to the Connecticut public health statutes, for example, authorizes a local health director to order the confinement of an individual if there are reasonable grounds to believe that the individual is infected with a communicable disease and is unwilling or unable to act in a manner so as not to expose others to the danger of infection. The constitutionality of the statute has not been judicially reviewed.

The most obvious subject of a limited isolation order would be the so-called recalcitrant individual who intentionally and continuously refuses to comply with reasonable public health directions designed to reduce the danger of infection. Arguably, an isolation statute aimed at such individuals might be upheld if its application was limited to situations in which there was clear evidence that the subject of the order was infectious and highly likely to engage in behavior exposing others to infection, and there was no less restrictive means of controlling his or her behavior. If the law were to pass judicial scrutiny, it should allow isolation only of limited duration and subject to periodic review; decisions on placement of the individual should be governed by the individual's need for counseling, care, and treatment. Full due process protections should be afforded any individual sought to be confined under authority of the statute. The key to appropriate application of an isolation order under such a statute would then be the ability to accurately predict and prove the individual's potential for engaging in future dangerous behavior.

Although it has long been a constitutionally accepted feature of civil commitment, the concept of predicting future dangerousness is inherently uncertain. Applying a limited isolation concept in the AIDS context poses the disturbing possibility that determinations of predictability might be influenced by deep-seated societal prejudices regarding the supposed "lifestyle" or character of members of identified high risk populations.

Even if a statute authorizing imposition of some form of behavior-triggered confinement of individuals could withstand legal challenge, there are strong public policy arguments against the use of such a measure as a part of an AIDS control program. First, such a coercive measure could discourage members of risk groups from seeking testing or treatment, or from speaking honestly to counselors concerning their future behavior intentions. Second, it would be difficult if not impossible to frame valid statutory criteria and psychological standards which would predict future dangerousness or define who was "recalcitrant". Adequate proof would be difficult to gather. Would evidence of past dangerous conduct be sufficient or required, or would an individual's stated intent to engage in dangerous conduct suffice as grounds for confinement? Third, isolating individuals to prevent intimate personal behavior raises severe monitoring and enforcement difficulties. How would public health officials discover or prove whether an infected individual was engaging in unsafe sex? Such a statute could be viewed as a license for public health officials and law enforcement officers to intrude into the most private aspects of the lives of individuals in risk groups. Finally, any statute authorizing confinement of individuals with AIDS should probably be enacted as a part of the criminal law. Otherwise, confinement for isolation purposes could potentially be unlimited since there is currently no known effective medical treatment. Under these circumstances, a criminal statute would actually offer more appropriate due process protections for the targeted individual than the application of public health measures of indefinite duration.

5. Community Health Orders

A less restrictive alternative to be considered for responding to the "recalcitrant" or "incorrigible" individual would be to establish, by statute, a carefully delineated range of public health measures or orders which could be used by public health officials. These measures, called here community health orders, could fill the middle ground between voluntary actions on the part of the individual and state imposition of the highly intrusive restrictions of isolation or quarantine. The objective of adopting such measures would be to provide public health officials with greater flexibility while at the same time protecting individuals against the imposition of unwarranted or overbroad personal restrictions.

Issuance of a community health order would be authorized only when there was clear evidence that an individual was infectious and was engaging in conduct posing an imminent threat to the health of others. Although the proposed restrictions would be less intrusive than those imposed under isolation or quarantine, a community health order would nevertheless limit the individual's freedom, and could adversely affect his or her reputation in the community. The order would be a compulsory control measure, and as such would require the observance of strict due process safeguards. The individual should be entitled under the statute to a full judicial hearing and right of appeal, with appointed legal counsel if necessary, before any order could be issued. The enabling statute should also specify the maximum duration of an order, e.g., not to exceed 30 days, with the possibility of renewals upon a showing that the conduct is continuing.

If it were to be legally supportable, tha statute would have to be narrowly drawn, identifying the range of powers available and the conditions for their exercise; an order is not a license for public health officials to impose any type of personal control short of isolation or quarantine. The powers authorized would be limited to those necessary to achieve the objectives of (1) encouraging voluntary compliance through individual counseling and education about the risks of dangerous behavior (e.g. "unsafe" sexual practices or the sharing of needles); (2) providing for medical surveillance of the individual, if required, in a less restrictive environment than available under isolation or quarantine.

Any community health order statute should be designed to allow the individual to continue to live and work in the community. The intrusiveness of the restriction would be geared to the danger presented by the individual's conduct. Community health orders could range from a directive that an individual attend counseling or educational sessions at specified times and places, to a requirement that the individual submit to periodic medical examination and/or treatment for conditions associated with conduct which may transmit HTLV-III/LAV infection. If the individual is engaged in a business or profession where there is a heightened risk of transmission, inspection of the business premises might be ordered to determine whether appropriate risk reduction guidelines are being followed. An order could not go so far as to permit inspection of the individual's home or to authorize continuous monitoring of his or her contacts and activities.

Penalties for violation of community health orders could range from the imposition of small fines for first violations to more severe fines for subsequent violoations. Continued failure to attend counseling or education sessions could also result in a requirement for compulsory attendance at a hospital, clinic or alcohol or drug treatment facility as an outpatient or day patient to enable public health officials to supervise the infected individual.

As with other compulsory measures such as quarantine or isolation, there are public policy arguments which militate against the extensive use of community health orders as a part of AIDS control efforts. It must be realized that targetting the relatively few individuals who act irresponsibly will not effectively control an epidemic which is primarily spread by individuals unaware that they are carriers. Focusing attention on recalcitrant individuals may divert attention from more effective efforts, and may foster a false sense of security within the risk groups. Second, as with a limited quarantine, there would be problems in identifying individuals who are behaving irresponsibly. Third, an infected individual identified as a result of the imposition of a community health order may be subject to discrimination in employment, housing, or access to other services. Fourth, because of fear of discriminaiton or harassment, some individuals will be discouraged from seeking appropriate testing and treatment because of fear of even limited restrictions. Fifth, given the lack of societal support or acceptance for the "lifestyle" of the members of the key risk groups - gay and bisexual men and IV drug users - there is the potential for discriminatory application of community health orders.

6. Criminal Law Deterrence of Behavior Leading to the Transmission of HTLV-III

Public health measures are usually concerned with preventing _future behavior_, and we have discussed a range of options which are, or could be, available to alter behavioral patterns. The criminal law is often thought to be based upon a model of retribution for _past behavior_ and is therefore inappropriate in the public health context. Yet, one of the principal objectives of the criminal law is prevention. By establishing clear penalties, the criminal law seeks to deter individuals from engaging in certain well specified behaviors. The transmission of a potentially lethal infection with forethought or recklessness is just as dangerous as other behaviors that the criminal law already proscribes.

It is not unreasonable for society to establish clear parameters as to the behaviors it will not tolerate. By drawing a bright boundary line around the behaviors that pose serious public health risks, the law gives clear notice of the conduct which will be subject to criminal penalty.

This approach can hardly be considered unfair to those individuals in high risk groups for AIDS because it serves as a measure of protection for those same groups against the spread of infection. Nor can it be considered unfair to the potential subjects of criminal penalties, for it is better to give clear forewarning of unacceptable conduct rather than to confine a person who *might* engage in that behavior in the future.

The civil liberties advantages of the criminal law are well known: it is based upon behavior which is objectively stated in the statute; it requires proof of a specific dangerous act beyond a reasonable doubt; it requires the highest level of procedural due process and appeal; and the period of confinement is usually finite and proportionate to the gravity of the offense. The criminal law offers the "tightest fit" between means and a public health objective. Each person convicted of the offense has demonstrably failed to comply with behavioral standards set by the law; conversely, "prospective" public health control measures almost invariably can have an impact on individuals who will not pose an actual risk to the public health.

There is an attraction based upon clarity, objectivity and sufficient safeguards which makes the criminal law a good candidate for public health enforcement consideration. Our survey found that six of twelve jurisdictions (Texas, New York, California, Pennsylvania, Colorado and Florida) have "public health crimes." These statutes make it unlawful (usually a misdemeanor) for an individual who knows he has an infectious venereal disease to have sexual intercourse with another. Except for the Texas provision, these statutes apply only to venereal diseases and, consequently, do not apply to AIDS.

One policy option would be to draft a public health criminal-law statute of a corrective nature applicable to HTLV-III infection. The minimal elements of the offense would be as follows: actual knowledge by a person that he is infected with HTLV-III; knowledge of the means of transmission; an appreciation of the threat to health or life posed by transmitting the infection; and proof that the person has engaged in behavior likely to transmit the infection with forethought, malice or reckless disregard of the consequences. We have considered whether actual harm should be a necessary element of the offense. This could require, for example, that the victim sero- converted as a result of the proscribed act. The justification favoring such a course would be that a person would not be subject to criminal penalties where no current harm was proved. The reason for omitting such a requirement would be that it would be necessary to wait for long periods of seroconversion to occur before a charge could be brought. This delay would be substantially counterproductive from a public health policy perspective.

We have also considered whether consent should be a defense to the proposed public health offense. We note that consent is often no defense to a crime involving severe physical injury. Yet there are strong advantages of making informed consent a defense. Many couples will make an informed decision to assume the risk of sexual intercourse, particularly if it is practiced as safely as possible. Further, contracting AIDS is not an inevitable outcome of sexual intercourse or a shared needle. Therefore, we feel it would be contrary to public policy to attach criminal sanctions to a consensual act.

A number of prosecutors across the country have filed felony assault charges against defendants thought to have HTLV-III infection who spit at or bite police officers. Among the criminal cases so far are those involving:

(i) a person with AIDS in Flint, Michigan, who was charged with assault and intent to commit murder after he spat on four police officers. People v. Richards, 85-1715 FG.

(ii) a person suspected of having AIDS in El Cajon, California, who pleaded guilty in December, 1985, to a felonious assault charge for biting an officer. People v. Prairie Chicken, CRE-77357.

(iii) a person suspected of being a carrier of HTLV-III who pleaded guilty to a misdemeanor assault charge in the San Francisco Municipal Court after prosecutors abandoned plans to file felony charges over another police biting incident. People v. Julius, 761210.

In all three cases, prosecutors contended felony charges were called for because of the risk of spreading AIDS. An analogy to "offensive weapons" was put forward as a justification. We fail to see the wisdom of a serious criminal charge where the actual capability for doing harm is absent. Biting and spitting may be criminal assaults whether or not the person is infected. We believe that, as the likelihood of transmission of HTLV-III resulting from this conduct is negligible, a person's infectious condition should not be a relevant factor.

We do not place undue reliance on the criminal law as a method of impeding the spread of AIDS, and do not believe its regular use would be beneficial. Rather, recourse to the criminal law could be one option for use in those rare cases where it was possible to prove beyond a reasonable doubt that a person knowingly or recklessly transferred the infection.

E. Control Over the Behavior of Incompetent Persons

Incompetency among patients with HTLV-III infection is an increasingly serious problem. It is estimated that up to 40-50% of AIDS patients may have loss of higher cerebral function. It is now clear that HTLV-III infection is neurotropic as well as lymphotropic.

The psychological impact of HTLV-III infection can be severe. The organic brain syndrome is associated with marked progressive mental deterioration and disintegration in cognition, emotion and behavior. This could include failure to comprehend, disorientation, loss of memory (particularlly recent memory), expressive and/or receptive dysphasia, and organic lability. There may be changes in behavior patterns such as disinhibited sexual activity, aggressiveness and loss of self-care skills.

There are also non-organic causes of psychiatric symptoms, particularly depression and anxiety. Knowledge that a person has a precursor to, or a fully diagnosed, disease which is almost invariably fatal, and where there can be social rejection, discrimination and financial ruination understandably causes distress. Depressive symptomatology can include feelings of sadness, hopelessness, withdrawal, isolation, and lethargy. Anxiety may take the form of tension, tachycardia, agitation, insomnia, anorexia and panic.

Each individual will respond differently to the organic and environmental impact of HTLV-III infection. But the psychosocial parameters of HTLV-III infection, and the legal complications, warrant careful separate study.

In this section we briefly examine the various legal alternatives which are acvailable to restrict the liberty or autonomy of persons with HTLV-III infection whose competency is in question. None of these civil procedures were specifically intended as infection control measures. Nevertheless, incompetency among AIDS patients with neurological damage can result in a danger to self through grave disablement and inability to meet the basic needs of life for food, shelter and clothing; incomptency can also lead to behavior dangerous to others through physically aggressive or irresponsible conduct posing a risk of transmission of a lethal infection. Both grave disablement and danger to others may provide grounds, if other criteria are met, for the exercise of compulsory powers of a civil nature.

1. Civil commitment of the mentally ill

Since involuntary civil commitment of mentally ill people entails a restriction of liberty, civil commitment statutes must be based upon clear, constitutionally adequate, criteria. There are two prevailing legal justifications for the exercise of compulsory powers over the individual--the parens patriae and police powers. The parens patriae power is based upon the philosophy that the state is required to promote the interests and welfare of its wards when they are unable to care for their own needs. The criteria for civil commitment under a parens patriae rationale should provide for a determination of mental illness, rendering the person incompetent to evaluate the necessity for hospitalization. The state must always act in the best interests of its wards.

The police power is based upon the philosophy that the state has a power to protect the public health, safety, welfare and morals. When civil commitment is used to promote a societal interest rather than the interest of the mentally ill person, it constitutes an exercise of the police power. Civil commitment in the exercise of police powers should require a determination that the person is mentally ill and poses a danger to self or others. Since the exercise of civil commitment does not involve the commission of a crime, the state should also demonstrate that the patient is incompetent. The difficulties of predicting future dangerous conduct have been well documented. Several jurisdictions, therefore, have required a showing that the person has engaged in recent overt behavior of a magnitude threatening the safety of the person or others.

The goal of civil commitment under each theory is to improve the mental condition of the individual in order to restore him to a level where he can lead an independent existence without presenting a public danger. Consequently several elements are found in many progressive state and model mental health statutes: severe mental illness, a finding of incompetency to evaluate the necessity of hospitalization, and grave disablement or danger to self or others (the latter often requiring a recent overt act), susceptibility to treatment, and actually providing treatment in a humane environment.

The Supreme Court has yet to construct a careful theory of the criteria which are constitutionally required under the parens patriae or police power rationale. Each of the foregoing criteria is not necessarily constitutionally mandated, yet we regard each as important to ensure the proper use of the mental health services. The mental health system cannot solve all of society's problems including those caused by the transmission of infectious agents. It is only where an AIDS patient is mentally ill and could benefit from mental health services should consideration be given to civil commitment.

The threshhold criterion for commitment is whether the person is suffering from a mental illness of sufficient seriousness that his decision-making regarding hospitalization is called into question. Traditionally the class of psychiatric disorders amounting to severe mental illness were limited to psychotic illness. Nevertheless there is no reason why an organic brain disorder should preclude a person from being designated as severely mentally ill under a state statute so long as his or her mental processes are sufficiently impaired. Accordingly, a person with AIDS dementia whose cognition, perception, emotion or judgment is badly impaired, could be considered severely mentally ill within the meaning of the law. It should be noted that a mild or transitory impact on psychological processes--such as an understandable reaction to the knowledge that a person has AIDS--is insufficient to warrant civil commitment. Further, the AIDS dementia should be observable by gross behavioral abnormality, not merely eccentric behavior.

In Lessard v. Schmidt,[4] the court said that a mentally ill person should be permitted to determine whether to seek hospitalization "unless the state can prove that the person is unable to make a decision about hospitalization because of the nature of his illness." The court in Winters v. Miller[5] was even more explicit in requiring a finding of mental incompetence as a foundation for civil commitment. A person with AIDS dementia may indeed have an organic brain syndrome meeting a statutory standard of severe mental illness. However, it must be shown that the person is unable to comprehend his need for hospitalization. The AIDS dementia must rob the person of the ability to engage in a rational decision-making process regarding his need for treatment. Simple refusal to be admitted to hospital is insufficient. What is required is a lack of comprehension as to the nature and purpose of hospitalization including its benefits and risks.

The state in the exercise of its police power must act for the safety of the individual or the public. It may well be that the person is severely mentally incompetent but if he is causing no harm to himself or others there is no police power rationale for his involuntary confinement. Thus, if AIDS simply renders a person confused and disoriented, perhaps pushy or verbally aggressive, there is no basis for his civil confinement. The danger to others must be of a magnitude and probability which justifies deprivation of liberty. HTLV-III infection may impair the mental processes so greatly that the person loses control over his behavior, and poses a real and immediate risk of physically injuring others. That is a sufficient warrant for commitment even if the risk does not relate to transmission of the infection. The more interesting question is whether the risks of transmitting an infection come within the concept of "danger to others." While mental health laws never specifically contemplated "danger" as including communication of an infectious agent, there is no reason why the term should not have that meaning. Uncontrolled sexual activity in itself is not a ground for confinement. But if a person with HTLV-III infection does not comprehend the danger involved in sexual activity, and if there is a likelihood that he or she will engage in such activity, then the grounds for commitment may be present.

A *parens patriae* rationale for civil commitment is often based upon a finding of grave disablement. The concept of grave disablement means that the person is unable to care for his or her basic needs to support an independent life. Thus, if a person would not take sufficient care to eat, dress warmly, and take care of his health and sanitary needs to an extent that he could not survive independently, the grave disablement criterion could be met. This is the criterion which is probably most relevant to a person with symptoms of dementia. Accordingly, there is no reason why an AIDS demented patient should not come within the grave disablement criterion if his behavioral patterns fulfilled the statutory requirements.

The U.S. Supreme Court in O'Connor v. Donaldson[6] declined an opportunity to decide whether civil commitment constitutionally required a showing that the patient is susceptible to psychiatric treatment, and whether treatment must in fact be provided. The court did hold that if a mentally ill patient posed no danger to himself or others and could live with the help of family or friends in the community, then the state could not custodially confine him without treatment.

It would be a misuse of the mental health services if a patient with AIDS were confined in a mental hospital if his condition were not susceptible to psychiatric treatment. The "treatability" criterion is the most difficult to fulfill for an AIDS demented patient.

HTLV-III infection of the central nervous system probably persists throughout a patient's life. There is no therapeutic intervention that can reverse this progressive deterioration of the brain. Like other forms of dementia, the only available treatment is management of the person in a safe environment, helping to re-orient the person, preventing wandering and other forms of self-injurious behavior, and providing for the person's life needs which the patient might otherwise neglect.

While these essentially nursing services can be provided in a mental hospital, it could be considered an inefficient use of scarce specialist resources if an AIDS patient were admitted. While demented patients are sometimes admitted to psychiatric hospitals, it is more common to admit them to nursing homes. If the patient is not unwilling to be admitted to a nursing home, this could be accomplished without the use of compulsion. Where the patient will not consent to such an admission then a guardianship application may be the appropriate procedure.

In August, 1985, a physician at a large teaching hospital in a major metropolitan area examined a man with Kaposi's sarcoma. The patient left the hospital against medical advice. In mid-September, he was picked up by the police dressed only in a towel, and brought back to the hospital. The hospital made a diagnosis of AIDS dementia. The patient again refused to stay, and left for home with clothes provided by the hospital. The following day he was found at the airport saying that he was an African prince. He was returned to the hospital, which asked for the advice of the Mental Health Commissioner about whether the individual could be admitted compulsorily under the state Mental Health Act. The hospital was faced with a number of difficulties which required resolution: the hospital is a highly specialized facility designed to provide acute care, not long term care for demented patients; there was no chronic care facility (mental hospital or nursing home) prepared to take a difficult demented AIDS patient; the department of mental health had given no guidance on whether the civil commitment statute encompassed patients with an organic brain syndrome who were essentially untreatable and whether civil commitment to a general hospital was permissible.

This patient might have been subject to commitment because of his mental disorder resulting in grave disablement. Nevertheless the case illustrates clearly the need for careful planning of the pattern of services for AIDS demented patients, including needed resources and training of staff. It also points to the legal problems associated with compulsory admission of AIDS patients. In reviewing the range of possible powers, the alternative of guardianship should be carefully considered.

2. Guardianship of mentally ill people

A guardianship application is based upon a parens patriae rationale that the person is incapable of caring for his life needs. A guardian is appointed in order to safeguard the welfare of the ward. Guardianship should involve a judicial finding that the person is incompetent to make decisions regarding particular aspects of his or her personal affairs. An AIDS demented patient who posed a danger or was gravely disabled, and who did not comprehend the need for more intense care, support and supervision, might be a suitable candidate for the making of a guardianship order. The guardian would have powers to make substitute decisions for the ward. A guardian would be authorized by the court to exercise a range of less restrictive powers than would be involveld in compulsory hospitalization. For example, the guardian could ensure that the ward receives close supervision, medical and nursing attention in the community; ensure that the person lives in a specified place; or attends an outpatient clinic for psychiatric treatment or treatment for substance abuse or sexually transmitted disease. These less restrictive, community based powers would enable the guardian to help monitor the ward's behavior in the community. Attention would be paid not only to the best interests of the ward, but the prevention of viral transmission.

Guardians can also exercise more restrictive powers including the power to admit the ward as an informal patient in a mental hospital or to a nursing home or other appropriate care facility.

We emphasize that guardianship applications were not designed as infection control measures. All of the criteria for guardianship (including incompetency and danger or grave disablement) must be met. Further, courts should be expected to closely monitor the carrying out of guardianship duties to ensure that they are always exercised in the best interests of the ward. The guardian has a fiduciary duty to the ward and may not cause him or her any avoidable harm. All decisions must be based upon a humane regard for the ward's interests.

F. Civil Confinement of Drug Dependent Persons

Statutory powers exist in many states, particularly in those with a serious drug abuse problem, allowing civil commitment of seriously dependent persons who cannot control their drug dependency and who, as a result, constitute a danger to themselves or others. The provisions are invoked quite rarely. Most drug dependence treatment is voluntary, except for criminal offenders diverted to treatment programs in lieu of criminal sentence or in place of criminal confinement. In the instances where civil commitment is applied, it is usually reserved for persons who are a danger to themselves because of severe physical and mental deterioration.

The question can be raised as to whether civil commitment can properly be applied to a drug dependent person who has AIDS or is positive for HTLV-III and who persists in exposing other persons to infection primarily through the shared use of contaminated needles. We are inclined to answer that the statutes on civil commitment could be used for such purposes if the provisions can be interpreted to allow such persistent conduct to be included under the statute's requirement of a showing of "danger to others" due to the person's drug dependence. It should be recalled that a similar issue was raised in the earlier pages on civil commitment of the mentally ill when the mentally disturbed infected person was deemed a highly likely public health danger to others.

The argument could be made concerning IV drug users that the needle sharing behavior is not essentially out of the control of the person as may be the case with mentally ill persons unable to control their general conduct. This argument should not be persuasive, however. The needle sharing activity is very intimately connected to the uncontrollable dependence upon the drugs. To treat the person for the dependency would, in itself, be a direct means of preventing the continued use of needles. In fact, the existence of an effective treatment for the drug dependence, at least with many drug users, is a strong reason for making the option of civil commitment available in appropriate cases where a medical judgment is made that there is potential for successful treatment and rehabilitation of the person. The most common application of the "danger to others" provision in drug dependence commitment laws is the potential for violent conduct and theft by the person seeking money to buy drugs for an ever-increasing and costly habit. It does not stretch this concept very much to extend its application to the very serious danger of exposure of other persons to a deadly disease through the use of shared IV needles.

G. Regulation of Public Meeting Places

As intimate sexual behavior is the most frequent method of transmission of HTLV-III LAV, public meeting places which facilitate such behavior have been a favorite target for government regulation. Some bathhouses, clubs, cinemas and bookstores which have developed as meeting places for the gay community may also allow the premises to be used for anonymous sexual encounters, offering individuals the opportunity to meet and the privacy conducive to engage in sexual intimacy. As male-to-male sexual intercourse may be among the highest risk activities in the transmission of HTLV-III LAV infection, appropriate measures aimed at reducing this behavior among risk groups is a justified health policy. That is a position for which we have found consensus in gay rights organizations as well as among public health officials. Two major municipalities--New York City and San Francisco--have carefully considered the public health utility of closure or regulation of public meeting places.

New York

On October 25, 1985, the Public Health Council of the State of New York passed an emergency amendment to the New York Sanitary Code to define anal intercourse and fellatio as "high risk sexual activity." The Council passed a resolution providing that no establishment shall make facilities available where high risk sexual activity takes place. Such facilities "shall constitute a public nuisance dangerous to the public health." The regulation was promulgated as permanent and became effective on December 23, 1985.

City health officials, having documented the presence of "high risk sexual activity" at the Mine Shaft Club and at the New St. Mark's Baths obtained temporary orders closing the premises pursuant to section C16-2.6(a) of the New York City Administrative Code.

Mayor Edward Koch wrote to fourteen establishments where high sexual activity was observed asking them to take voluntary steps to assure the cessation of such behavior, including the closure of cubicles or other enclosed spaces and the establishment of large, and more open rooms. Several establishments agreed to voluntary closure.

San Francisco

On October 9, 1984, the San Francisco Public Health Department ordered the closure of fourteen gay bathhouses and other establishments where unsafe sexual activity had been observed by department investigators. The establishments refused to comply with the order and the department sought to enjoin the businesses from operating. Judge Roy L. Wonder of the Superior Court allowed the businesses to operate subject to certain restrictions.[7] The businesses were ordered to hire employees to observe client activity every ten minutes and eject patrons observed engaging in "unsafe" sex as defined by the San Francisco AIDS Foundation; private cubicles and rooms had to be removed; and public education efforts had to be commenced.

Constitutional review of decisions to close public meeting places effectively hinges on whether the closures would burden constitutionally protected interests in privacy and association. Homosexual intimacy deserves the same protection as heterosexual intimacy. Both are private actions between individuals with a reasonable expectation that the state will not intrude in the relationship. Any association between consenting adults in a private place merits constitutional protection. As one court stated, "It is not the marriage laws which make intimate and highly personal the sexual behavior of human beings. It is, instead, the nature of sexuality itself as something intensely private to the individual that calls for constitutional protection."[8]

Yet, the U.S. Supreme Court has not extended its jurisprudence to find a constitutionally protected privacy interest inherent in sexual behavior in public meeting places. The U.S. Supreme Court, in <u>Bowers v. Hardwick</u>, has recently explicitly rejected the argument that homosexual behavior <u>per se</u> is a fundamental right;[9] a sexual act in a quasi public venue certainly would not attract constitutional protection. The Court has carved out a sphere of constitutional protection for decision-making closely intertwined with private <u>heterosexual</u> activity. The judicial trend is to link privacy rights to intimate decisions relating to marriage, family and birth. While the Court has ventured to protect the privacy of intimate decision-making outside of the narrow boundaries of marriage, it has not strayed far from decisions relating to birth and children. Given the decision in <u>Bowers v. Hardwick</u>, it will be difficult to place homosexual activity within the scope of the Court's extant privacy jurisprudence.

Even if some narrow right to privacy were acknowledged by the Supreme Court in the future, it would be unlikely to extend the privacy right to places to which the public has access such as commercial clubs and bathhouses. Here there is no reasonable expectation of privacy. The state has no constitutional mandate to countenance the operation of premises existing for the express purpose of sex between members of the public where that activity poses a demonstrable risk to health. It is true that some proportion of the unsafe sexual activity which takes place in bathhouses would simply shift to private forums over which the state has no direct control. But that does not obviate the duty of the state to proscribe or regulate unsafe sexual activity in establishments it licenses or otherwise controls.

An additional troubling constitutional difficulty for public health regulators is the First Amendment right of association. Implicit in the right to free expression is the right to join with others as a form of collective expression. Where a significant aspect of the business to be regulated is the exchange of beliefs and ideas such as a book store or cinema, or the cameraderie of associating with peers, such as a bathhouse, the court would be likely to require the state to achieve its public health objective, if possible, by minimizing the burden on collective expression. Regulations which closely regulate sexual activity, for example, would be less intrusive than closure. Where the nature of the establishment is predominantly either for entertainment or gratification the courts may have less inclination to defend them as fundamental rights. Further, a tangential impact upon association or expression is insufficient to obstruct the exercise of the state's police power to protect the public health and safety. The precise determination for a court is whether the prohibition on behavior endangering the public health unnecessarily limits the individual or collective expression of ideas. To the extent that the overriding purpose of a bathhouse might be to facilitate anonymous sexual contacts, it would lack the characteristics which would protect associational rights on the premises.

Sexual intercourse with anonymous multiple partners is a prime risk factor in the spread of HTLV-III, and selective measures to eliminate this conduct are clearly justified. The more difficult question is whether closure of selected meeting places is the most effective means of reducing irresponsible sexual activity, or whether it is potentially counterproductive in terms of disease prevention. The major concern of health authorities is unsafe human behavior, not where it takes place. It is possible that reducing the opportunities for meeting anonymous partners will reduce the number of sexual experiences for some proportion of individuals who frequent bathhouses. For others, closure of a single type of public facility is unlikely to result in significant change of personal behavior patterns in other localities. Further, closure of selected homosexual meeting places raises the legitimate question of whether similarly situated heterosexual establishments should also be closed.

It would be irresponsible if public health departments were knowingly to countenance <u>unsafe</u> activity in premises over which it has control, even if some percentage of that activity would occur in more private forums. In such circumstances there are only two policy options. Closure of bathhouses would be a certain, <u>albeit</u> sweeping, method of ensuring the cessation of unsafe sexual activities in those locations.

An alternative approach is to develop an enforceable policy closely regulating or proscribing sexual activity in such places. It would be exceedingly difficult to enforce a selective ban distinguishing between "safe" and "unsafe" sex; indeed the sheer intrusiveness of measures to enforce such a selective ban would be problematic. Regulatory measures controlling sexual activities could include requirements for adequate lighting in all areas, removal of partitions and doors, and regular on-site inspections by the health department. The advantage of the latter policy is that meeting places could be used as a focus for public education, including distribution of health literature, information on referrals for assessment, counseling and other services. If the sole purpose for establishments were to provide anonymous, multiple sexual opportunities for patrons, then proscription of such activities would effectively amount to a closure order. Establishments operating to provide an environment for community expression and non-sexual associational purposes would not be subject to regulation. This would accomplish the compelling public health purpose without restricting the opportunities for the gay community to meet in social venues.

References

1. 429 U.S. 589 (1977).

2. Boston Globe, Sept. 25, 1985, p.9.

3. Greene v. Edwards, 265 S.E.2d (W.Va. 1980).

4. 349 F. Supp. 1078 (E.D. Wisc. 1972) (three judge court), *vacated and remanded on other grounds*, 94 S.Ct. 713 (1974).

5. 446 F.2d 65 (2d Cir.) *cert. denied*, 404 U.S. 985 (1971).

6. 422 U.S. 463 (1975).

7. California ex rel. Agnost v. Owen, No. 830,321 slip op. (Cal. Super. Ct., Nov. 30, 1984).

8. Lovisi v. Slayton 363 F. Supp. 620, 625 (E.D. Va. 1973), *rev'd*, 539 F.2d 349 (4th Cir. 1976).

9. Bowers v. Hardwick, 54 U.S.L.W. 4919 (June 24, 1986).

Summary and Policy Options

Methods

We surveyed public health statutes and regulations for the control of infectious disease in twelve jurisdictions selected to provide a representative overview of the existing public health powers. This review was not limited to AIDS-related activity, but covered the entire public health statutory and regulatory framework. We also surveyed all fifty states and the District of Columbia. This survey concentrated on legislation, regulations and proposals specifically relating to AIDS or HTLV-III/LAV infection.

Scientific Foundations

We made a brief statement of the current medical, scientific and epidemiologic evidence relating to AIDS. Legal and regulatory controls **should be founded upon** an accurate assessment of scientific evidence.

Legal and Constitutional Foundations

Early Public Health Cases

The early public health cases were highly deferential to public health officials. But they also set a few clear boundaries on the exercise of public health powers which would be the minimum the courts could be expected to apply today:

(a) True purpose - The courts would look beyond the nominal statutory intent to discover the true legislative purpose. The courts would not be bound by mere forms or pretenses under the guise of public health powers. If control measures exercised for the ostensible purpose of controlling AIDS were shown to be guided by prejudice or homophobia, the courts would not uphold the statute.

(b) Public Health necessity - The constitutional foundation for the exercise of public health powers is "public necessity." A scientific foundation must be established for the exercise of any power. Thus, a demonstratable need for public health measures based upon scientific and epidemiologic evidence must be established; and the person against whom control measures are exercised must actually have been exposed to the infectious agent.

(c) Safe environment - A person subject to control measures cannot be placed in an unsafe or unhealthy environment. The state should afford the finest possible care and conditions for those whose individual rights may be restricted for the collective good.

(d) Substantial relationship between the control measure and a valid public objective - The U.S. Supreme Court in Jacobson v. Massachusetts set the standard that the state must refrain from acting in an "arbitrary, unreasonable manner" or "going so far beyond what was reasonably required for the safety of the public."

Modern Constitutional Requirements

Most public health cases were decided before the 1960s when the U.S. Supreme Court began to develop stricter standards for constitutional review. They are, therefore, unreliable precedent. The U.S. Supreme Court's "minimum rationality" review requires some reasonable relationship between the state action and the achievement of a valid public health objective. It is not far different than the Jacobson doctrine and is highly permissive. Any statutory or regulatory measure which genuinely seeks to reduce the spread of AIDS and which does not interfere with certain fundamental rights, is likely to be upheld. Current requirements in most states to report CDC defined AIDS, for example, would clearly be rationally related to a valid epidemiologic objective.

The courts use a higher level of constitutional review where state action interferes with fundamental liberties. These include the right to travel, to marry and to certain privacy interests such as the freedom to choose whether to bear children. The heightened scrutiny which flows from the infringement of a fundamental right requires that the state action be suitably tailored to serve a compelling public purpose. Thus, there must be a "tight fit" between means and ends. A public health power cannot be over-inclusive by infringing the rights of more people than strictly necessary to accomplish the objective. The means used must also be the least restrictive necessary to achieve the compelling public purpose.

Testing and Screening

Operational Definitions of "Testing" and "Screening"

"Testing" is used to refer to the application of diagnostic ELISA and supplemental procedures to individuals. "Screening" is used to refer to the systematic application of the ELISA and supplemental procedures to specific populations.

Screening in the Aggregate

Screening which is applied in the aggregate, without any impact on any identified individual, can be of great public health benefit. Screening of blood, tissues, organs and semen donors helps avoid contamination of products received by third parties. Screening within an approved research protocol also does not adversely affect identified individuals. Research is an indispensible strategy for controlling AIDS. Examination of the legal and ethical requirements of research is outside the scope of this report.

Informing persons of the results of HTLV-III antibody tests

A policy question of some importance is whether to inform persons that they are seropositive. The option of informing such people has strong support in ethical medical practice and in general legal requirements. Information may also help precipitate change of behavior to avoid infecting others. Thus, a compelling case can be made to require informing persons of positive test results.

Some patients may choose not to know the outcome of test results. Supporters of this view suggest that this choice must be one for the patient alone, particularly as there is no certainty about the meaning of positive test results. The right of a patient to choose must be balanced against the duty of the patient to avoid transmitting the infection.

Proposed Criteria for Population Screening

We propose a set of guidelines for helping to determine the validity of population screening programs: the selected population should have a reservoir of infection; the environment or setting within which the population operates must pose a significant risk of communication of the infection; knowledge of the results of testing must enable authorities to take efficient precautions to reduce the spread of the infection which could not otherwise be taken without that knowledge; and the critical consequences of the screening must not be disproportionate to the benefits achieved.

General Legal and Policy Implications of Screening

Justification for legally authorized selective screening must be based upon the undisputed achievement of protection of the public health which clearly outweighs the invasion of individual privacy and loss of occupation or profession which could result to individuals in these groups. Generally speaking, the presumed benefits of screening are either that the results will lead to voluntary changes in behavior, or that the results will support the use of some effective compulsory control measure.

The U.S. Public Health Service has encouraged voluntary screening in all high risk groups. Such a policy can only be effective if there are sufficient resources and planning relating to the availability of accurate, speedy and confidential testing and counselling and education services.

Confidentiality

The confidentiality of test information is of importance to the individual. Disclosure can lead to social opprobrium and to loss of employment, housing and insurance. Indeed, the cooperation of patients with important public health objectives and programs such as STD and drug treatment clinics depends upon their expectation of privacy. Specific statutory provisions ensuring the confidentiality of the information would instill greater confidence in relation to voluntary testing programs. The law often places a premium on the presentation of full information to a court of law. But statutes could provide that confidentiality considerations override the interest in full information in the legal process. Specific subpoena and testimony exemptions could be added to confidentiality statutes to reflect the importance of keeping test information private.

Military

The only population, apart from blood donors, which has already been subject to systematic compulsory anti-HTLV-III screening is the U.S. military. Justifications in favor of such a program are their susceptibility to contracting illnesses from live vaccines or travel abroad; the need to protect against transmission of HTLV-III around foreign bases; and, most importantly, the increased risk of transmission arising from blood spillage and transfusion during combat. However, screening and exclusion or discharge of sero positive military personnel sets a sweeping precedent with doubtful application to the civilian sector.

Exclusion from Schools

Exclusion of children from school who have AIDS or HTLV-III infection has unsuccessfully been sought in court actions in New York City and California, and cases are pending in New Jersey and Indiana. Exclusion of school children is legally supportable only if there is evidence that the virus is reasonably likely to be transmitted in the school environment. The trial court in District 27 Community School Board v. Board of Education of the City of New York held that an automatic exclusion policy would be arbitrary and capricious, violating both equal protection of the laws and section 504 of the federal Rehabilitation Act.

Screening in STD and Drug Treatment Centers

Attendance at STD or drug treatment centers is usually voluntary and beneficial to patients who receive treatment. Sero testing could be offered voluntarily to patients, together with educational counselling services. This is the course suggested by the Public Health Service. Any move towards compulsory testing would discourage use of the centers which perform a vital public health function.

Pre-marital

Compulsory screening has been proposed in various state legislatures. Pre-marital testing would offer the advantage of informing both partners of the risk of HTLV-III/LAV infection. A further advantage would be the collection of extensive data on the spread of the virus. There is likely to be a low incidence of HTLV-III infection among marriage license applicants, however. Compulsory testing would affect all applicants even though a very small proportion is likely to be infected. Further, knowledge of a positive test result will not prevent the spread of infection which may have occurred through pre-marital relations.

Substantial constitutional obstacles would have to be overcome in order to introduce a complete bar to marriage of seropositive applicants. A less restrictive alternative would be voluntary testing; seropositivity need not be an absolute bar to issuance of a marriage license.

Pre-natal

CDC currently advises pre-natal testing on a voluntary basis for women in high risk groups.

Health Care Patients and Staff

Hemodialysis units are used as a "worst case" scenario. Blood contamination of the environment is often extensive, and there is a potential for transfer of infection. Screening would enable staff to identify those who are seropositive in order to take precautions such as segregation of individuals who are infected. Testing and separate facilities are already accepted practices in relation to hepatitis B.

The analogy to hepatitis B, however, is not wholly appropriate as the efficiency of transmission of HTLV-III is much lower than HBV. Further, screening and separation of HTLV-III positive patients may result in their sero status being made obvious to family, employers, and friends.

Prisons

The ELISA is presently used in state prison systems more than in any other context. The justification for population screening and segregation is the prevention of transmission as a result of forcible sexual contact and needle sharing involving infected prisoners. Decisions to screen and segregate prisoners have been upheld by the courts.

In states with a high prevalence of HTLV-III infection, segregation of seropositive prisoners could involve separate facilities. This could pose a potential health hazard for those in the segregated facility. An attractive alternative to screening and segregation is to invest renewed resources to help prevent forced sexual contact and shared needles in the prison.

Personal Control Measures

National Review

Our national review of public health statutes has shown that they often cannot deal sensitively and flexibly with the wide range of diseases that modern public health departments must be prepared to control. Many are severely outdated, having been fashioned largely on an ad hoc basis, with new statutory or administrative layers being added from time to time as a new health crisis arose. Several deficiencies in public health law were identified: an artificial boundary between venereal and other communicable diseases; inadequate confidentiality protection; inflexible powers without a graded series of less restrictive alternatives; and inadequate procedural safeguards.

A further study as to the future of public health legislation with guidelines and a model statute would be a valuable contribution to the development of well balanced and effective regulatory systems.

Reporting Requirements

Virtually all states require reporting of cases and "suspected cases" of CDC defined AIDS. This is necessary for epidemiologic purposes--for disease trends and estimates of infection trends.

A few states - notably Colorado - are moving towards a requirement to report seropositivity. The case in favor is that there is growing concern that current statutes are not providing accurate data as to current prevalence of infection; there is a time lag between onset of the infection and manifestation of the disease. Accordingly, data on the prevalence of the disease may only be informing public health officials of infection trends as they existed several years ago. It is also argued that early identification of seropositive persons is necessary for behavior change or for more aggressive programs of contact tracing and/or personal control measures.

There is, however, substantial mistrust among risk groups to the introduction of mandatory reporting of seropositivity. Any precipitous move in that direction - particularly if coupled with aggressive sexual contact tracing - could drive vulnerable groups underground and undermine the good cooperation thus far given to public health officials.

Reporting requirements of the disease state or of seropositivity would be likely to be supported constitutionally provided there were a genuine epidemiologic purpose. The state should have adequate practices and procedures in place to protect the confidentiality of the information.

Quarantine and Isolation

General quarantine or isolation based upon seropositivity or disease status would be met with strong legal challenge, and would trigger the Supreme Court's strictest review. Applicability to all infected or diseased persons would be over-inclusive and likely to be invalidated by the court. There are also numerous policy objections to a general quarantine: the unmanagably large number of people who are infected; the long incubation period; the absence of a vaccine or treatment; and the long period of infectiousness making for a potentially unlimited period of confinement.

Limited Quarantine and Isolation

Some states, such as Connecticut, allow for a quarantine based upon a documentable risk of future dangerous behavior. A major legal and policy question is whether it is justifiable to confine an infected person who is thought likely to engage in sexual intercourse without informing his sexual partner. Health officials have a duty to protect against transmission of a potentially lethal communicable disease. Whenever possible, voluntary, or less restrictive, compulsory measures should be utilized. Yet, there are strong pressures to exercise some power of restriction of liberty in the face of clear evidence that the person is engaging in conduct seriously detrimental to the public health. Clearly, strong procedural due process protections must be in place before such measures would be invoked.

If the state had strong grounds, established in a procedural due process hearing, to show that the person posed a serious public health danger, than it is likely that a narrowly drawn limited quarantine or isolation statute would be upheld by the courts.

The contrary arguments, particularly against routine use of limited quarantine or isolation, are equally as persuasive: coercive measures could discourage members of risk groups from seeking testing or treatment; there is extreme difficulty in reliably predicting future dangerous behavior; there is no systematic way of identifying those who are, and are not, dangerous; and the monitoring and enforcement provisions associated with limited quarantine could be unacceptably intrusive.

Procedural Due Process

The courts would be likely to require procedural due process safeguards in the exercise of a compulsory public health power. The West Virginia Supreme Court held that the procedural safeguards in cases of civil commitment of the mentally ill are applicable to cases of involuntary confinement of infectious persons. This includes written notice, counsel, presentation of evidence and cross examination, a clear and convincing standard of proof and a verbatim transcript for appeal.

Less Restrictive Alternatives

State public health statutes seldom contain a graded series of less restrictive measures. In most states, the options for public health officials are limited to voluntary programs or severe restrictions on personal liberty.

A comprehensive public health program should be able to utilize a variety of less restrictive powers, more varied in scope than are currently contained in most public health statutes. The use of less restrictive powers could allow affected persons to continue association with family, community and work environments.

Community Health Orders

One way to achieve this goal is the creation of a community health order. This order could issue from the public health department following a full due process hearing. It could require the person to attend at reasonable places and times for the purpose of education, counselling, testing and medical examination or treatment; to report changes of address; or to receive visits from the health department at a person's place of business or profession. Methods of enforcement could range from a small fine to some restrictions on liberty of movement including compulsory attendance at a hospital, clinic, or at an alcohol or drug treatment facility on an outpatient or day-patient basis.

Criminal Law Deterrence

There is legal precedent for the use of a public health statute of a corrective nature. The criminal law is not used simply as a punishment, but also to deter future dangerous behavior. The elements of such an offense are knowledge of the infection and means of transmission, and behavior likely to transfer the infection with intentional or reckless disregard of the consequences. We discourage routine recourse to the criminal law in the AIDS context, and note that there are strong grounds for making informed consent a defense to the crime.

Control of Incompetent Persons

Incompetency of patients with HTLV-III/LAV infection is an increasingly serious problem which can result in dangerous behavior to self or others. Several legal interventions are discussed including civil commitment of the mentally ill and confinement of drug dependent persons. In both cases, commitment statutes may be applicable. The major question, however, is the appropriateness of using mental health or drug treatment resources to prevent transfer of an infectious agent. It is suggested that if the person is susceptible to treatment for mental illness or drug dependence, and if the placement is beneficial and appropriate, the use of the statutes would not be unlawful.

Sources of Law

Concentration in this report is given to statutory and regulatory controls in the public health field. This has proved to be a fruitful exercise, particularly by pointing the way to much needed future work on existing statutes and regulations which are ill-suited to addressing modern public health problems. Our national survey, however, revealed little new statutory or regulatory provisions relevant to AIDS. One reason for this is that most "law" in the area of AIDS control has come in the form of guidelines. We have examined U.S. Public Health Service guidelines relating to numerous aspects of controlling the spread of AIDS. The existence of these guidelines has meant that there has been far less pressure to adopt statutes or regulations.

We found that many states have specifically "adopted" U.S. Public Health Service guidelines. Other states have adopted their own guidelines which may have only subtle differences in emphasis from Public Health Service guidelines.

Considering the dominance of Public Health Service guidelines in controlling the spread of AIDS, it is important to ask what the legal effect of the guidelines are. Guidelines issued by the U.S. Public Health Service or one of its agencies differ in important respects from regulations. Regulations at the federal level must be within the enabling framework of a statute passed by Congress. The regulatory agency must act within the scope of the statute, and must follow clear procedures, including notice, publication and consultation, before issuing final guidelines. This is the route, for example, that the Federal Food and Drug Administration has taken in issuing proposed rules on mandatory screening for HTLV-III in blood and blood products. The rules, when finally promulgated, will be binding and require testing, labelling, and specific recordkeeping. The proposed rules are published and disseminated widely to enable interested parties to comment and influence the regulatory process. In some states, such as Massachusetts, the law requires a public hearing prior to adoption of regulations.

Guidelines issued by the Public Health Service are not legally binding, but they do influence professional practice. More importantly, they might well be taken into account by the courts of law in molding a standard of care for health care facilities and professionals. Failure to comply with a recognized standard of care can result in a finding of negligence and liability for damages.

Accordingly, health care facilities, professional groups, and the organizations who represent them, have a genuine interest in guidelines. Members of vulnerable risk groups and the organizations who represent them also have a strong interest as guidelines directly affect their care, privacy, and rights.

Public Health Service guidelines have characteristically been restrained and limited to areas of clear consensus in the scientific field. The speedy issuance of sensible guidelines has been a notable and remarkable achievement. The adoption of federal guidelines has been a critical factor in impeding the spread of HTLV-III/LAV infection, and, more importantly, in maintaining calm and perspective. In the absence of the guidelines, more precipitous, possibly prejudicial, public health action might have been taken in the states and localities.